THE ANARCHIST TURN

The Anarchist Turn

Edited by
Jacob Blumenfeld,
Chiara Bottici
and Simon Critchley

PlutoPress
www.plutobooks.com

First published 2013 by Pluto Press
345 Archway Road, London N6 5AA

www.plutobooks.com

Distributed in the United States of America exclusively by
Palgrave Macmillan, a division of St. Martin's Press LLC,
175 Fifth Avenue, New York, NY 10010

British Library Cataloguing in Publication Data
A catalogue record for this book is available from the British Library

ISBN   978 0 7453 3343 4   Hardback
ISBN   978 0 7453 3342 7   Paperback
ISBN   978 1 8496 4854 7   PDF eBook
ISBN   978 1 8496 4856 1   Kindle eBook
ISBN   978 1 8496 4855 4   EPUB eBook

Library of Congress Cataloging in Publication Data applied for

This book is printed on paper suitable for recycling and made from fully managed and
sustained forest sources. Logging, pulping and manufacturing processes are expected to
conform to the environmental standards of the country of origin.

10 9 8 7 6 5 4 3 2 1

Designed and produced for Pluto Press by Curran Publishing Services, Norwich.
Simultaneously printed digitally by CPI Antony Rowe, Chippenham, UK and
Edwards Bros in the United States of America

CONTENTS

Introduction   1
Simon Critchley

Part I Subverting boundaries   7

1 Black and red: the freedom of equals   9
Chiara Bottici

2 The politics of commensality   35
Banu Bargu

3 Friendship as resistance   59
Todd May

4 An-archy between metapolitics and politics   80
Miguel Abensour

Part II Paint it pink: anarchism and feminism   99

5 Undoing patriarchy, subverting politics: anarchism
as a practice of care   101
Mitchell Cowen Verter

6 Of what is anarcha-feminism the name?   111
Cinzia Arruzza

7 Black, red, pink and green: breaking boundaries,
building bridges   125
Laura Corradi

Part III Geographies of anarchy   143

8 The anarchist geography of no-place   145
Stephen Duncombe

9 The fighting ground   158
Alberto Toscano

10 Reiner Schürmann's faultline topology and the
anthropocene 172
Stephanie Wakefield

Part IV The anarchist moment **185**

11 The anarchist moment 187
Andrej Grubačić

12 Palestine, state politics and the anarchist impasse 203
Judith Butler

13 Spread anarchy, live communism 224
The accused of Tarnac

14 Postface: Occupation and revolution 235
Jacob Blumenfeld

Index 247
Notes on contributors 261

INTRODUCTION

Simon Critchley

The contributions that make up this book are derived from papers presented at a conference called 'The Anarchist Turn', which took place at the New School for Social Research in New York on May 5–6, 2011. The three editors of this book – myself, Jacob Blumenfeld and Chiara Bottici – were also the conference organizers. I have left this Introduction in almost exactly the form in which it was initially composed because the multiplicity of events that we could summarize with the word OCCUPY that erupted in the autumn of 2011 would have required separate and sustained analysis and revision. Let's just say that some of the hope that Jacob, Chiara and the other contributors to 'The Anarchist Turn' expressed in their talks, which the reader will find in the chapters of this book, found unanticipated and glorious expression in events later in the year. And that was only the beginning.

I would like to begin with a text co-written by the three people who collaborated on the organization of 'The Anarchist Turn'. Collaboration, or working together, is the key here. It is the very ethos of the anarchism that we intend to both discuss and try to enact with this conference. The three of us have worked together closely over the past year in order to make something happen that might simply be interesting, maybe even worthwhile. But we do not know what is going to happen. This could be rubbish. This could be a disaster. We hope not, but you never know.

> For a long time, the word 'anarchist' has been used as an insult. This is because, at least since Hobbes and maybe for a lot longer, the concept of anarchy has been extended from its etymological meaning (absence of centralized government) to that of pure disorder – the idea being that, without a sovereign, with a sovereign state, the life of individuals can only be miserable, brutish and short. This shift in the meaning of anarchy was certainly useful in the ideological discourse of justification of

1

modern sovereign states, but it does not provide an understanding of what anarchy might be, particularly when those states have either died, or shriveled, or transformed, or become an imperium that desperately tries to shore up its authority through a politics of the external and internal enemy.

However, in the last decade, maybe longer, this caricature of anarchy and anarchism has begun to crack. What we a little too easily call 'globalization' and the social movements it spawned seem to have proven what anarchists have long been advocating: an anarchical order is not just desirable, but also feasible, practicable and enactable. This has led to a revitalized interest in the subterranean anarchist tradition and the understanding of anarchy as collective self-organization without centralized authority. But the ban on 'anarchism' has not yet been lifted.

(Blumenfeld, Bottici and Critchley, 2011)

The aim of this conference is to help lift that ban and argue for an 'anarchist turn' in politics and in our thinking of the political. We want to discuss anarchism with specific reference to political philosophy in its many historical and geographical variants, but also in relation to other disciplines, like politics, anthropology (where anarchism has had a long influence), economics, history, sociology, and of course geography (why are so many anarchists geographers, cartographers or explorers, like Kropotkin? We need new maps). Our approach is, first, transdisciplinary; second, it also wants to put theory and praxis into some sort of communication, and that is why we have the work of academics here alongside activists, and many of the academics are activists. By bringing together academics and activists – activists in some case past and in other cases very present – this conference will assess the nature and effectiveness of anarchist politics in our times.

Of all the political visions of another social order or another way of conceiving and practising social relations, anarchism has proved the most condemned, and yet the most resilient. Outlawed, repudiated, ridiculed by liberals, by neoliberals, but most of all, of course, by Marxists (from the expulsion of the anarchists from the meeting of the International in the Hague in 1872 onwards), the anarchist idea simply will not die.

There are multiple motivations behind this conference, including the facts that anarchism is still scoffed at and laughed at by political philosophers, that it still has a minor academic presence in relation to liberalism or Marxism or Frankfurt School critical theory (which have always done such good academic business), that it consists of many thinkers – like Stirner, Proudhon, Bakunin, Kropotkin, Malatesta – who are not read as widely as they should be. I could go on.

But there are other motivations. We might recall that this is the 'Arendt–Schürmann Conference in Political Philosophy' at the New School for Social Research. For obvious and perhaps understandable reasons, people tend to prioritize the work of Hannah Arendt over Reiner Schürmann. Now, although Arendt was no particular friend of anarchism, her work might be harnessed for a thinking-through of the politics of the street, as Judith Butler recently attempted (2011). But it is perhaps the political dimension of Schürmann's work that should be emphasized here, in particular *Le principe d'anarchie: Heidegger et la question de l'agir* (1982), a nicely oxymoronic title that was mysteriously rendered into English as *Heidegger on Being and Acting: From principles to anarchy* (1987). This was a hugely important book when I was a graduate student in France in the 1980s. My teacher, Dominique Janicaud, was a close friend of Reiner's, and it was through him that I first read Schürmann. Indeed, as readers of Miguel Abensour's decisively important book, *La democratie contre l'etat* (1997), which has finally been published as *Democracy Against the State* (2011), will know, Abensour tries to bring together Arendtian and Schurmannian themes in a defence of what the very young Marx called 'true democracy' in 1843. True democracy, or what Abensour also calls 'insurgent democracy', reactivates the anarchic impulse and might allow us to imagine a deconstitution of the political field based on the primacy of an *arche* (a first principle, a supreme power, an act of sovereignty or dominion), and the cultivation of what we might call an anarchic meta-politics.

There is also a very local and nicely ironic motivation for this conference. A little – in fact very little – over two years ago, in April 2009, 65 Fifth Avenue, the former home of the New School for Social Research, was occupied for a second time, by a small number of students who were protesting peacefully for improved study conditions and for accountability and transparency from the school administration – wild anarchist claims, as you can tell. Someone, some say the former president of the New School (although he denied it), dialled operation COBRA and hundreds of police descended on the building with dogs, hostage negotiators, the whole paranoid security apparatus of the Homeland. Students were chased down the street, and force was used against them; many were arrested. Then, of course, lies were told about what had happened. A long, rancorous situation ensued. For those of us who came to work at the New School for Social Research because of its radical traditions of intellectual freedom, activism, disobedience and protest – and the New School is an institution born out of protest at a war and established as a place of refuge for those threatened by war – this was a deeply troubling and painful period. I remember being in 65 Fifth Avenue during the first occupation in December 2008 and being given some photocopied texts by *Tiqqun* to read, which came out last year in *Introduction to Civil War* (2010). They had just been translated as part of the occupation itself. I am really happy that some of the accused of Tarnac are here with us today.

Chiara, Jacob and I spent a lot of time thinking about whom we might invite to contribute, and we were delighted and flattered that so many people accepted our invitation. In addition to the people I have already mentioned, we are immensely grateful for the presence of Laura Corradi, Andrej Grubačić, Alberto Toscano, Ben Morea and Cindy Milstein. I would also like to thank Jacob and Chiara themselves, Todd May, Cinzia Arruzza, Banu Bargu, Stephen Duncombe, Stephanie Wakefield, Mitchell Verter and Judith Butler.

Anarchism is not so much a grand unified theory of revolution based on a socio-economic metaphysics and a philosophy of history, as a moral conviction, an ethical disposition that finds expression in practice and as practice. Anarchism is a different way of conceiving and enacting social relations between people, where they are not defined by the authority of the state, the law and the police, but by free agreement between them. Its aspiration was perhaps best described by the English poet Shelley in 'Prometheus unbound':

Sceptreless, free, uncircumscribed, but man
Equal, unclassed, tribeless and nationless
Exempt from awe, worship, degree, the king
Over himself; just, gentle, wise ...
(Shelley, 1820–2010, pp. 3.4.194–7)

Because of my distaste for the macho mannerism and fake virility of contemporary neo-Leninism – I name no names – I personally favour the rather quiet and indeed crappy, small-scale and rather English version of anarchism that you find in writers like Colin Ward and George Woodcock, where anarchism begins with planting vegetables and designing playgrounds for kids. Arguably, this tradition goes back to 1381, the Peasants' Revolt and the Lollards. The only extant fragment from John Ball, preserved and probably embellished by chroniclers, is worth recalling here:

> Things cannot go well in England, nor ever will, until all goods are held in common, and until there will be neither serfs nor gentlemen, and we shall be equal. For what reason have they, whom we call lords, got the best of us? How did they deserve it? Why do they keep us in bondage? If we all descended from one father and one mother, Adam and Eve, how can they assert or prove that they are more masters than ourselves? Except perhaps that they make us work and produce for them to spend!
>
> (Ball, as cited in Froissart, 1968, pp. 212–13)

Things did not go well in England, sadly.

I have been combing through my books for an articulation, if not a definition, of anarchism with which we might begin. The best example I know is from Errico Malatesta, from his wonderful pamphlet *Anarchy* from 1891. He writes:

> Abolition of government does not and cannot signify destruction of the social bond. Quite the opposite: the cooperation which today is forced and which is today directly beneficial to a few, will be free, voluntary and direct, working to the advantage of all and will be all the more intense and effective for that.
>
> ... Out of the free collaboration of everyone, thanks to the spontaneous combination of men in accordance with their needs and sympathies, from the bottom up, from the simple to the complex, starting from the most immediate interests and working towards the most general, there will arise a social organization, the goal of which will be the greatest well-being and fullest freedom of all .... Such a society of free human beings, such a society of friends, is Anarchy.
>
> (Malatesta, 1891)

We hope something of that friendship, something of that social bond, will be in evidence in the next couple of days.

Simon Critchley
May 5, 2011

ACKNQWLEDGMENTS

We would like to thank the Department of Philosophy of the New School for Social Research for hosting the conference from which this book derives within its series of political philosophy symposia dedicated to Hannah Arendt and Rainer Schürmann.

For their editorial assistance in the preparation of this book, we are grateful to Elizabeth Suergiu and Jacob Parkinson.

REFERENCES

Abensour, Miguel (1997) *La democratie contre l'etat*. Paris: PUF.

Abensour, Miguel (2011) *Democracy Against the State*. Cambridge: Polity.

Blumenfeld, J., Bottici, C. and Critchley, S. (2011) Original announcement for The Anarchist Turn conference at the New School.

Butler, Judith. (2011). 'Hannah Arendt and the politics of the street', delivered at Fourth Annual PSWIP Colloquium at the New School. www.newschoolphilosophy.com/audio/tnw/JB-04-14-11.mp3 (accessed September 4, 2012).

Froissart, Jean. (1968) 'The Peasant Revolt in England', in *Chronicles*, trans. G. Brereton. London: Penguin.

Malatesta, Errico. (1891) 'Anarchy'. www.marxists.org/archive/malatesta/1891/xx/anarchy.htm (accessed September 4, 2012).

Schürmann, Reiner. (1982) *Le principe d'anarchie. Heidegger et la question de l'agir*. Paris: Seuil.

Schürmann, Reiner. (1987) *Heidegger on Being and Acting: From principles to anarchy*. Bloomington, Ind.: Indiana University Press).

Shelley, Percy B. (2010) *Prometheus Unbound*. Whitefish, MT: Kessinger.

Tiqqun (2010) *Introduction to Civil War*. Los Angeles, Calif.: Semiotext(e).

PART I

SUBVERTING BOUNDARIES

PART I

1

BLACK AND RED:
THE FREEDOM OF EQUALS

Chiara Bottici

> Today the immense development of production, the growth of those requirements which can only be satisfied by the participation of large numbers of people in all countries, the means of communication, with travel becoming a commonplace, science, literature, businesses and even wars, all have drawn mankind into an ever tighter single body whose constituent parts, united among themselves, can only find fulfilment and freedom to develop through the wellbeing of the other constituent parts as well as of the whole.
>
> (Malatesta, *Anarchy*)

> Omnia sunt communia.
>
> (Luther Blissett, *Q*)

In 1967, Italian anarchist Belgrado Pedrini wrote a poem entitled 'The Galleon'. The image is that of a miserable galleon, in which everybody works as a slave, deprived of freedom. Days and nights pass but nothing changes, until someone starts to incite their fellow slaves to revolt by pointing out that they have nothing to lose and all to gain from the rebellion. As the poem reads:

Siamo la ciurma anemica	We are the anaemic crew
d'una galera infame	of an infamous galley
su cui ratta la morte	which quick death
miete per lenta fame.	cuts down slowly as we grow hungry.
Mai orizzonti limpidi	Never do clear horizons

9

schiude la nostra aurora
e sulla tolda squallida
urla la scolta ognora.

I nostri dì si involano
fra fetide carene,
siam magri smunti schiavi
stretti in ferro catene.

Sorge sul mar la luna
ruotan le stelle in cielo
ma sulle nostre luci
steso è un funereo velo.

Torme di schiavi adusti
chini a gemer sul remo
spezziam queste catene
o chini a remar morremo!

Cos'è gementi schiavi
questo remar remare?
Meglio morir tra i flutti
sul biancheggiar del mare.

Remiam finché la nave
si schianti sui frangenti,
alte le rossonere
fra il sibilar dei venti!

E sia pietosa coltrice
l'onda spumosa e ria
ma sorga un dì sui martiri
il sol dell'anarchia.

Su schiavi all'armi,
   all'armi!
L'onda gorgoglia e sale
tuoni baleni e fulmini
sul galeon fatale.

Su schiavi all'armi,
   all'armi!

open up our dawn
and on the squalid deck
cries the guard all day long.

Our days pass as we sail
in fetid-bottomed boats,
we are thin and pale slaves
bound together by iron chains.

The moon rises above the sea
stars revolve in the sky at night
but, for us, a funeral veil
lies draped over our lights.

Swarms of scorched slaves
bent to groan over the oar,
let us break these chains
or we will die bent to row!

Tell me, groaning slaves,
why do we row just to row?
Better to die among the waves
on a sea of whitening foam.

Let us row until the ship
dashes upon the reef,
raise the black and red
upon the whistling breeze!

And let the frothy wave
be a pitiful place to lay
but let the sun of anarchy
rise o'er the martyrs one day.

   Rise, slaves, to arms, to arms!

O, gurgling waves and brine
thunder and lightening clash
above the fateful galleon.

   Rise, slaves, to arms, to arms!

Pugnam col braccio forte!   Let us strike with all our strength
Giuriam giuriam giustizia! Justice, we swear, justice!
O libertà o morte!   Give us liberty or give us death!
                    (Pedrini, 2001a, p. 69; translation mine)

The image of the galleon conveys a crucial political message. If you are on the side of the oppressed, you do not have anything to lose from the revolt. On the contrary, you have all to gain, as slaves are the overwhelming majority that makes the galleon work. This is because on a galleon, we are so dependent on one another that it becomes impossible to be free alone. Even if you are the master, you will constantly be threatened by the slavery of others. There is no intermediate: we are either all free or all slaves.

Pedrini's biography is similar to that of many anarchists who lived through the troubled years of the Italian fascist regime.[1] Chased for his antifascism, he was finally imprisoned for the death of a fascist policeman in a clash between a group of anarchists and the fascist secret police (Pedrini, 2001b). A few years later, he was liberated by the partisans and fought with the Resistance against fascists and the Nazi's army for a couple of years. After the end of the war in 1945, the newly constituted Italian Republic recognized the importance of his fight against fascism, but then put him back in jail. He remained there for 30 years, notwithstanding the numerous international campaigns for his liberation. Why?

For the Italian state, Pedrini was a criminal, a normal murderer. The fact that he had killed the policeman because he was a fascist and was just about to shoot Pedrini and his comrades did not matter. His crime: being an anarchist. Like many of his anarchist comrades he had to be banned. The fact that the minister of justice was then the communist Palmiro Togliatti did not help: quite the opposite. In those days, the hostility between communists and anarchists was perhaps even stronger than that between communists and fascists.

Yet, precisely in Pedrini's galleon, in his invitation to raise the black and red flag, we find the symbol of a peculiar view of freedom which, so I will argue, represents the platform for the convergence of anarchism and Marxism. Pedrini's metaphor tells us two important things: first, that we are all in the same boat, and second, that the freedom of every individual strictly depends on that of all others. You cannot be free alone, because freedom can only be realized as freedom of equals. With this expression, I do not mean that we have to be free *and* equals, but that we cannot be free unless we are all equally so.

The aim of this chapter is to argue that there is a significant convergence between Marxism and anarchism in that they both conceive of freedom in this way. After first exploring the meaning of this conception of freedom, and second, distinguishing it from that of autonomy, I shall, third, argue that today's social, economic and political conditions render this view particularly timely, and fourth, call for an overcoming of the historical divisions between anarchism and Marxism. The ban on the black and red that led Pedrini to prison is still there, but time has come to lift it.

THE FREEDOM OF EQUALS

At the beginning was freedom. It is commonplace to say that freedom is the crucial issue for anarchism, so much so that some have claimed that this word summarizes the sense of the entire anarchic doctrine and credo. There are good reasons to argue that freedom is also the crucial concern for Marx, who from his very early writings is concerned with the conditions for human emancipation. Indeed, the entire path of his thought could be described as a reflection on the conditions for freedom, understood first as a more general human emancipation, and later on, as freedom from exploitation in light of his theory of surplus value.[2] In this section, I illustrate this view of freedom and distinguish it from that of freedom as autonomy, and in the following one, I will show that Marxism and anarchism can provide each other with the antidote to their possible degeneration.

But why freedom at the beginning, and moreover what freedom? Max Stirner has a very helpful way to phrase the answer. In *The Ego and its Own*, he observes that most theories of society pursue the issue of 'What is the essence of man? What is its nature?' (1990), and as such, they either expressly begin with such a question or take it as their implicit starting point. However, Stirner observes, the question is not *what* is the human being, but rather *who*: and the answer is that 'I', in my uniqueness, am the human being (1990). In other words, we should not start with an abstract theory about a presumed essence or (which is equivalent) the nature of the human being, but with the simple fact that 'I' am, here and now, in my uniqueness. Otherwise said, there is no other possible beginning because, as an answer to the 'who?' question, 'I've set my cause on nothing' (*Ich hab' mein' Sach' auf nichts gestellt*) (Stirner, 1990, pp. 41, 351).

It may appear paradoxical to start with a quotation from Stirner, an author who has been very much criticized within both Marxism and anarchism for his strong individualism. But it is nevertheless a helpful starting point to think about the centrality of freedom: freedom is at the beginning, because at the beginning there is the 'who?' question, and thus every being endowed with the capacity to say 'I am'. The ego is at the beginning as activity, as the capacity to move and speak, and here lies the root of its capacity to be free. And yet, if this interpretation is correct, and the being who says 'I am' cannot but be a being endowed with language, then it follows that Stirner's deduction of a radical individualism, which depicts a continual war between the individual and society, is potentially contradictory. To put it in a nutshell, the individual cannot be at 'total war' with society as Stirner claims, because the individual is to a large extent its own product.

The ability to speak, and thus language, presupposes a plurality of 'egos' because language can never be learned without a plurality of beings. An entirely asocial being, such as the one that Stirner depicts, would be a speech-less being. So if Stirner is right in identifying this primordial activity of consciousness as the starting point for thinking about freedom, he is nevertheless wrong in deducing from it such a radical egoism. His individualism, which he presents as a rigorous logical deduction, may then well be the historically identifiable egoism of the then emerging European bourgeoisie, as Marx and Engels suggested (1976: I, III, 'Saint Max'). To use another Marxian expression, we can say that the very idea of an individual separated from all other individuals is a 'Robinsonade' (Marx, 1978c, p. 221), the fantastic representation of an isolated individual lost on a desert island, which is nothing but the imaginary representation of the concrete economic development of a specific epoch.

But such an isolated and unrelated individual cannot exist, because the human being does not become social at a discrete point in time and for the sake of particular purposes, but is so from the very beginning. We do not create society, but are rather created by it. In one of his lectures on anarchy, Bakunin illustrates this point through the following example: take an infant endowed with the most brilliant faculties (Bakunin, 1996, p. 28). If thrown in a desert at a very young age, such a being will perish (as it is very likely) or else survive but become a brute, deprived of speech, and all the other traits that we usually associate with humanity. Together with speech, the infant will also be lacking in the development of proper thinking, because there cannot be any thought without words. Sure, people can also reflect through images, but in order to *articulate* a complex thought they need words, words that can only be learnt by interacting with other human beings.

As we shall see, this view lies at the heart of Bakunin's idea that you can be free only if everybody else is free (Bakunin, 1996, 2000). Otherwise stated, freedom can only be a freedom of equals. If this view appears paradoxical, this is so because we have so internalized the ideological construction of human beings as independent individuals that we have difficulties representing freedom as a relation, rather than as a property with which separate individuals are endowed. Let me illustrate this view in more detail.

According to Bakunin, since human beings are so dependent on one another, you cannot be free in isolation, but only through the web of reciprocal interdependence. Although quite refined in its developments, it is not a view very far from common sense. Freedom, in Bakunin's view, consists 'in the right to obey nobody other than myself and to determine my acts in conformity with my convictions, mediated through the equally free consciousness of everybody' (1996, p. 81). Freedom is therefore the capacity to do what I want, to act in conformity with my convictions, but – and here it comes the refinement – in order to know what my own convictions are I need the mediation of the 'equally free consciousness of everybody.' This is a view of freedom that clearly resonates with Hegelian themes.[3] However, as it will be clear later on, it is a view that Bakunin will bring well beyond Hegel (and the Hegelians) by extending it to the whole humanity – beyond any border, be it social, political or even historical.

On the other hand, we can clearly see how such a view differs from the mainstream liberal view of freedom as self-determination. While Marx observes that the image of the isolated individual is not at the beginning, but rather at the end of history (1978c, p. 222), Bakunin, in a passage that echoes contemporary theorists of the technologies of the self such as Foucault,[4] observes that it is not individuals who create society, but the society that, so to speak, 'individualises itself in every individual' (Bakunin, 2000, p. 85). Bakunin is well aware that freedom as self-determination is empty, if there is no such thing as a 'self' that can choose autonomously. The crucial point is not simply doing what I want, but to be sure that what I believe to be the fruit of my free choice actually is. If I am led by the circumstances of my life to believe that my servitude is immutable or even desirable, there is no way I can be free. It is the dilemma of voluntary servitude, and therefore of the techniques through which compliant subjects are created, that has been at the centre of anarchist thinking for a long time.[5]

In Bakunin's view, human beings are determined by both material and representational social factors. When still in the womb of their mother, every human being is already determined by a high number of geographical, climatic and economic factors which constitute the material nature of their social condition (Bakunin, 2000: 86). In addition to such a series of material factors, which Marx investigated in far greater detail, Bakunin also mentions a series of beliefs, ideas and representations that are equally crucial. Again, in an extremely timely passage, Bakunin observes that every generation finds as already made a whole world of ideas, images and sentiments that it inherits from previous epochs (2000, p. 87). These do not present themselves to the newborn as a system of ideas, since children would not be able to apprehend it in this form. Rather, such a world of ideas imposes itself as a world of 'personified facts', made concrete in the persons and things that surround them, as a world that speaks to their senses through whatever they see and hear since their very early days (Bakunin, 2000, p. 87).[6]

Put in more contemporary words, the individual becomes such only through a process of socialization that begins immediately, at least with their very first encounters with language and the presence of other human beings. As psychoanalysis has shown, it is through such a process that the individual is led to internalize and assimilate the imaginary significations of that particular society they live in (Castoriadis, 1987). To put it in Castoriadis's words, individuals are at the same time instituting and instituted by society: society does not exist without the individuals that constantly create and re-create it, but, at the same time, individuals exist only as a product of society itself (1987).

But if individuals are at the same time instituting and instituted; if, to use Bakunin's phrase, individuals are nothing but the society that individualizes itself in them, they cannot be free unless everybody else is free. Hence also the importance of the notion of recognition in Bakunin: 'For the individual to be free means to be recognized, considered and treated as such by another individual, and by all the individuals that surround him' (Bakunin, 2000, p. 92, my trans.). In order to recognize freedom you need the mediation of the imaginary significations of society. Freedom implies recognition, to be recognized and to recognize the other as free.[7] Masters who do not recognize the freedom of their slaves are – for this very reason – themselves not free. In this way, they contribute to perpetuating the image of slavery in the society of which they are part, and this very slavery will come back to them, in one form or another. As Malatesta puts it, by quoting Bakunin:

> No man can achieve his own emancipation without at the same time working for the emancipation of all men around him. My freedom is the freedom of all since I am not truly free in thought and in fact, except when my freedom and my rights are confirmed and approved in the freedom and rights of all men who are my equals. It matters to me very much what other men are, because however independent I may appear to be or think I am, because of my social position, were I Pope, Tzar, Emperor or even Prime Minister, I remain always the product of what the humblest among them are: if they are ignorant, poor, slaves, my existence is determined by their slavery. I, an enlightened or intelligent man am, for instance – in the event – rendered stupid by their stupidity; as a courageous man I am enslaved by their slavery; as a rich man I tremble before their poverty; as a privileged person I blanch at their justice. I who want to be free cannot be because all the men around me do not yet want to be free, and consequently they become tools of oppression against me.
>
> (Malatesta, 2001, p. 23)

It is a very radical idea of freedom, but one that, if read in light of more recent developments, is today more timely than ever before.

BACK TO FREEDOM, BEYOND AUTONOMY

In sum, freedom is inevitably a freedom of equals, because I cannot be free if everybody else around me is not free, or, which is the same, if I do not have both the material and the cognitive means to realize my freedom. We are imbued with the customs, ideas and images that dominate our society. Human beings are not independent selves that, like billiard balls, collide with each other on green baize. They are bodies that are instituting and instituted by the society in which they live. There are two main consequences that follow from such a view. Let me briefly illustrate them.

The first is that, however abstract this view may appear, it can only be realized in a very concrete way. It is not by chance that Bakunin calls it a 'materialist conception of freedom' (2000, p. 91; translation mine) and opposes it to the idealistic one. If freedom is to be realized not just by a separate self (which does not exist) but also through society, it follows that an entire reorganization of society is necessary for its realization. For Bakunin, this implies a restructuring of society from below, according to the principle of free association and federation (see for instance 2000, p. 96). But why is it so? Free federalism follows from a view of freedom articulated in three moments. The first, Bakunin says, is the positive and social moment, and consists in the development of all human faculties and potentialities through education and material well-being – all things that can only be acquired through the psychical and intellectual work of the whole society (2000, p. 82). It is a view very close to Marx's positive conception of freedom, according to which freedom does not consist in the negative capacity to avoid this or that, but in the positive power to develop our potentialities.[8]

The second moment for the realization of free federalism is instead more negative: Bakunin calls it 'the moment of the revolt' (2000, p. 82; trans. mine). It is the revolt against every authority, human or divine. First and foremost it is a revolt against God, because, in Bakunin's words, 'as long as we have a master in the sky, we will not be free on earth' (2000, p. 82). At times Bakunin seems to have a very traditional idea of God, but I think we can extend his thought to all forms of transcendent authority. If we believe that we owe a divine authority unconditional obedience, we are necessarily slaves to it, as well as to its intermediaries, such as ministers, prophets or messiahs (2000, p. 82). This is the reason why Bakunin strongly criticized nationalism as a new form of 'political theology': by presenting the 'nation' as a transcendent being, to which unconditional obedience is due just because it is our supposed 'fatherland', nationalists such as Giuseppe Mazzini have replaced a god in the sky with another one on earth (Bakunin, 1974). We begin here to see why Bakunin's notion of freedom, despite its Hegelian origins, goes well beyond Hegel: far from celebrating the nation state as the culminating point of ethical life, Bakunin calls for its elimination as a new form of political theology.

The revolt against god and transcendent authority must indeed be combined with the revolt against specifically human authority. Here Bakunin introduces a fine distinction between the legal and formal authority of the state and what he calls the 'tyranny of the society' (1974). The revolt against the first is easier because the enemy can effortlessly be identified, but the revolt against the second is much more complicated because, to a large extent, we are its products.

Society, as we have seen, exercises its tyranny through customs, traditions, sentiments, prejudices, images and habits, on both our material and intellectual life. Part of its influence is natural, and we cannot escape it (Bakunin, 2000, p. 84); however, part of it is not. Bakunin seems to believe that education and scientific knowledge is sufficient to this end, but I believe that we have more grounds today to be sceptical about it. Knowledge is not enough. Knowledge does not liberate from power, because it is itself power. The production of scientific knowledge is no exception to the tyranny of society, because, as Michel Foucault has shown us, it may even be the chief means for the domestication of revolt and the creation of compliant subjects.[9] Natural and social sciences, such as chemistry, demography and sociology, have all proved to be potential means to discipline and domesticate human beings rather than to liberate them.

Where to start from, then? Where to get liberation from the subtle tyranny that society exercises through its customs, traditions and sentiments? Here, I believe, enters the more radical interpretation of federalism. The old anarchist motto 'multiply your associations and be free' can indeed be seen as a multiplication of both the political and also the social and imaginary ties people are subjected to. By entering into contacts with different social imaginaries and expanding our knowledge to different regimes of truth, it is possible to find a moment of friction where the tyranny of society breaks down. As I will try to show, it is here that, particularly today, the possibility of freedom lies.

Before I do so, let me briefly illustrate the second main consequence of this conception of freedom as freedom of equals. Recovering this view today is an implicit invitation to go beyond freedom understood as autonomy. There are many possible definitions of autonomy, but the most important (because it is the most influential) is that which goes back to its etymology: autonomy literally means 'autos'-'nomos', to give the law to oneself. From this original meaning and through the influence of philosophers like Rousseau and Kant, the term came to mean self-determination more generally, as if every determination would be a subjection to the law (which, I believe, is far from being the case). I cannot discuss here the details of the historical path of the concept of autonomy, but let me just briefly mention the deep influence that it has exercised on liberal and democratic thought until very recently.[10]

Of course, the concept of autonomy has not been immune from criticism. The most obvious is that it presupposes a 'self' that actually gives a law to itself. As we have already suggested, this assumption is far from being unquestioned. Furthermore, the idea of a separate self is an assumption that inevitably leads to what we may call a 'limitative view of freedom'. If we believe that human beings are self-enclosed selves, endowed with autonomy, the problem necessarily becomes that of restricting such autonomy, in order to make space for the autonomy of the others. Like the billiard balls colliding on green baize, the freedoms of individuals are deemed to conflict with one another, and the problem inevitably becomes that of limiting them. On the contrary, if we assume that we are the product of the society we live in, a completely different perspective emerges: the problem is no longer how to *limit* freedom, but rather how to *enhance* it. In other words, the imperative is no longer 'limit freedom, so that everybody can enjoy it', but rather 'create it, because it might not be there yet'.

Different interventions have addressed the problem of autonomy and have certainly brought the discussion much further than where modern liberal thinking had left it.[11] Yet, as I shall now try to argue, focusing on autonomy is misleading. Autonomy may also be an important condition for freedom, but it is only one part of it. You cannot be free without being autonomous, but being autonomous does not automatically mean being free. This particularly emerges if we consider that the contrary of 'autonomy' is 'heteronomy', a condition where people are given the law by somebody else, whereas the opposite of freedom is 'domination', something that can occur in ways other than simply being given the law by somebody else. The tyranny of society can take place in many different ways, which go well beyond law-giving, and include even self-oppression and voluntary servitude. In sum, freedom and autonomy are conceptually speaking only partially overlapping.

To sum up, to be autonomous does not yet mean to be free. But it is not just a terminological issue. It is a question of conceptual clarity that has crucial consequences on the practice of freedom. For instance, many autonomist movements gave rise to utopian communities, based on the principle of autonomy understood as the main road for the realization of freedom. Let us admit for the moment that we could still realize completely autonomous communities in our globalizing world. The question is: are the people living in such communities really free? My impression is that they are (possibly) autonomous in the sense of being (materially) independent from the outside, but by no means free and perhaps not even self-determined. If you live in a self-imposed ghetto, separated from the rest of the world, you are not free, because you cannot live where you want, but you are not even self-determined because your choice to live in that particular community is imposed by some external factors.

To conclude on this point, the critics of the concept of freedom, such as Goodman, who argue that freedom is a cumbersome metaphysical concept (2009, p. 331), are perhaps right. Autonomy is much thinner and therefore at least apparently easier to realize. However, they are also wrong because they do not realize that it is a burden that we have to take on if we want to avoid the self-imposed ghetto of autonomy.

BLACK AND RED: RECIPROCAL ANTIDOTES

In the previous sections I have tried to illustrate why Marxism and anarchism converge in the idea that freedom can only be a freedom of equals. What I want to do now is to argue that a marriage between Marxism and anarchism is particularly beneficial in that they can find in each other a reciprocal antidote to their possible degenerations.

First, anarchism finds in Marxism a good antidote to prevent a possible individualist twist in its absolutization of freedom. It is a fact that the radical praise of freedom that characterizes anarchism in its historical manifestations has been interpreted in both directions, the individualist and the social. According to the former, freedom is mainly the freedom of the individual, whereas according to the latter, which we have analysed here under the name of Bakunin, freedom can only be attained collectively.[12] The point is not only that, historically speaking, an individualist interpretation of anarchism has proved to be possible. Much more radically, individualism is a temptation that is always present within anarchism. We began this chapter with Stirner's advocacy of a radical egoism, but many other examples can be added. We just have to think of anarcho-capitalism, which, particularly in the United States, combines the emphasis on freedom with the advocacy of an unrestricted development of capitalism.[13] You could simply dismiss these positions as fallacious 'Robinsonades', but the point remains that they are still very influential because they align with the prevailing individualist assumptions that underpin our societies.

In light of the difficulties encountered in promoting the realization of the freedom of equals on a large scale, anarchists may easily fall into the individualist temptation and limit their fight to the realization of spaces of autonomy in small self-enclosed communities. This, I believe, is the risk that many autonomist movements have in the past fallen into, without realizing that the creation of autonomous communities may well turn into a form of individualism on a large scale. The creation of such self-enclosed spaces is usually justified on the basis of the argument that they prefigure what a free society might look like, but they risk prefiguring nothing but what the society actually is: individuals, singular or collective, pursuing their own interests in isolation.

For this possible degeneration, Marxism contains a powerful antidote. Marx's critique of the Robinsonades can be extended to all levels to concretely support the idea that either we are all free or all equally slaves. The reason why Marxism is better equipped than traditional anarchism to make this point (as we have seen, Bakunin equally supported the idea of freedom as freedom of equals) is that it focused more systematically on the economic conditions for the realization of such a freedom. Few intellectuals have embarked on such an extensive analysis of the concrete economic conditions for the realization of freedom as Marx did. As such, his critique of utopian socialism (and more generally the idea that to describe an ideal state of things will automatically engender change simply because of its intrinsic intellectual value) is a powerful reminder of the dangers of any abstract metaphysics of freedom. By envisaging utopian communities on the sole basis of the fanatical belief in the miraculous effects of their theory, people risk ending up in a reactionary position, unable to keep pace with the current state of the world.[14]

I cannot enter here into a detailed reading of Marx's analysis of capitalism and modernity. There are parts of it that are outdated, in particular as a result of the novelties brought about by post-Fordism and flexible capitalism.[15] Let me simply point out here what I believe are the most timely parts of Marx's work. In the first place, there is the analysis of capitalism's capacity to overcome all sorts of political barriers. We live in an epoch where there is so much talk about globalization and the crisis of the nation states in relation to the capacity of the economy to go beyond national boundaries, but this is something that nobody predicted more acutely and more precisely than Marx. In many places in his work, he talks about capitalism's capacity to go beyond national boundaries. Consider for instance the following passage from the *Manifesto of the Communist Party*, which he wrote with Engels:

> The bourgeoisie has through its exploitation of the world market given a cosmopolitan character to production and consumption in every country. [...] In the place of old wants, satisfied by the productions of the country, we find new wants, requiring for their satisfaction the products of distant lands and climes. In

place of the old local and national seclusion and self-sufficiency, we have intercourse in every direction, universal interdependence of nations. And as in material, so also in intellectual production. The intellectual creations of individual nations become common property. National one-sidedness and narrow-mindedness become more and more impossible, and from the numerous national and local literatures, there arises a world literature.

(Marx and Engels, 1978, pp. 477–8)

In a time when there is so much talk about the novelty of globalization which, so many argue, calls for a new form of cosmopolitanism, it is worth returning to this passage. Here Marx and Engels clearly point to the 'cosmopolitan character' of capitalistic production and consumption, to the fact that with the heavy artillery of the 'cheap prices of its commodities' capitalism will batter down all Chinese walls (1978, p. 8), so that in place of the old local and national self-sufficiency, we have 'intercourse in every direction' at both the material and cognitive level (1978, p. 477). We cannot but be struck by the timeliness of these remarks. It has become something like a commonplace to say that we live in a globalizing world, where material and cultural boundaries are being challenged from different sides. Only the historical amnesia of a generation of scholars who, after 1989, have too quickly become militantly 'ex-Marxist', can explain how it is possible to talk so much about globalization without mentioning the author who most emphatically and accurately predicted it more than a century ago.

Marx's economic analysis gave further underpinning to the concept of freedom of equals that we have highlighted above with his path-breaking analysis of commodity fetishism (Marx, 1980, pp. 103–15). If Bakunin is right in saying that freedom has to be a freedom of equals because from the beginning we are subjected to the tyranny of society which imposes its material and representational significations on our minds and bodies, then it is precisely from the possible commodification of such significations that we have to start. Perhaps, only the visionary and Situationist Guy Debord has sufficiently underlined this point (1994) with his idea of a society of spectacle. Whereas Marx begins *Capital* by arguing that the world has become an immense collection of commodities, Debord rephrases this claiming by saying that 'In societies dominated by modern conditions of production, life is presented as an immense accumulation of *spectacles*'(Debord, 1994, first thesis). We live in a society of spectacle that rests upon the commodification of the social imaginary within which all are socialized. The global social imaginary we live in is imbued with commodity fetishism to the point that even our bodies are constituted by it.

However, it is not only anarchism that needs Marxism, if a freedom of equals is to be realized. Anarchism plays an equally crucial role because it contains the antidote for a possible statist and authoritarian degeneration of Marxism. It is a fact that Marx remained vague about the path to realize freedom. If it is clear that, according to him, the freedom of equals can only be obtained through a radical revolution that subverts the capitalist system of production, the ways to bring about such a revolution remain open to dispute, and change considerably through his various works. Whereas Marx is ambiguous on this point and in some places does not hesitate to speak of a 'dictatorship of the proletariat' as a necessary transition period from a capitalist to a communist society,[16] Bakunin is crystal clear: if freedom is the end, freedom must also be the means to realize that end. As Bakunin and Malatesta after him put it, to endanger freedom with the pretext of protecting it, be it through the dictatorship of the proletariat or an avant-garde party that should authoritatively lead the masses to the revolution, is a dangerous non-sense which cannot but ultimately destroy freedom itself (see for instance Bakunin, 2000, p. 98 and Malatesta, 2001, p. 52).

Incidentally, this is a clarity that was to lead to Bakunin's expulsion from the International Workingmen's Association dominated by Marx and the German social democrats. If Marx was ambiguous in his writings, he was much less so in calling for Bakunin's ban on the basis of his unorthodox view.[17] However, the experience of the Soviet Union showed that Bakunin was right when he criticized the idea of a dictatorship of the proletariat, along with any other authoritarian attempt to realize the freedom of equals. There is not just one absolute truth about the road to revolution, and thus no avant-garde party, however well versed in theory it might be, can ever explain to the masses how they should liberate themselves (Bakunin, 1872). If you restrict freedom, albeit temporarily, with the pretext of preparing its realization, you cannot but end up destroying it. As a consequence, any workers' state, be it a dictatorship of the proletariat or not, cannot but reproduce the same logic of every state, where a minority of bureaucrats rule over the majority of people: that is, authoritarianism (Bakunin, 1872).

To conclude this point, anarchism not only provides the antidote to the statist degeneration of Marxism. It can more generally prevent the authoritarian trap into which any attempt to realize the freedom of equals can fall. This is an antidote that communists of all sorts need, since, as Proudhon pointed out very clearly, communism can well be realized through the principle of authority itself (2001, pp. 125–33).[18] Anarchism, on the contrary, cannot. To put it bluntly, Marxists have proved to be able to become Stalinists, whereas a Stalinist anarchist is a contradiction in terms.

ONE WORLD, ONE FREEDOM

The connubial between Marxism and anarchism that we have outlined above is not simply a demand of theoretical reason. It is not a marriage that *ought* to take place if the freedom of equals is to be realized. It is something that is inherent to the changes we are witnessing and that, for the sake of brevity, we can summarize under the name of globalization. Put in a nutshell, there is only one freedom because the world has become one. Globalization does not just mean that there are processes that objectively unify the globe, but also, and foremost, that we have come to recognize this fact. In a minimal sense, this has always been the case, because we have always inhabited one and the same planet. What is different today is that we have to recognize this, because there is no longer the possibility of adopting an exit strategy.

Let me briefly illustrate what I mean by this. Globalization is often presented as a set of processes which shift the spatial form of human organization and activity to transcontinental and inter-regional patterns of activity, interactions and exercises of power.[19] Globalization, in its numerous aspects – economic, technological, political and cultural – has created a situation such that events, decisions and activities in one part of the world can have significant consequences for individuals and communities on the other side of the globe. The concept of globalization points, thus, to the stretching and deepening of social relations and institutions across space and time.

Fluxes from the local to the global and vice versa have unified the planet. Together with economic globalization already diagnosed by Marx and Engels comes political globalization: they are inseparable from many points of view. A promoter of economic and financial globalization, the nation state seems to be one of its most illustrious victims. Sure, sovereign states are far from vanishing, but they are becoming something else, challenged as they are by a dispersion of sovereignty both above and below them.

Perhaps where the crisis of the system of nation states is most evident is in the domain of security. It is in this field, where the modern state, at least since Thomas Hobbes, has traditionally, although surreptitiously, drawn the strongest justification for its existence, that we can best measure the degree of its crisis. Human beings, so the modern argument went, are led to cede their unconditional freedom to the sovereign power in order to enhance their individual security.[20] Even admitting that this was once the case (and I would deny that it was), it no longer holds true. The state is today patently incapable of guaranteeing the security of its citizens, not only from attacks with nuclear, bacteriological or other non-conventional weapons, but also, and perhaps most importantly, from ecological and other kinds of human-made global challenges. No single state could ever arrest an epidemiological attack or even simply contrast global warming effects. Hence, sovereignty is dispersed through what some have called a 'multilayered global governance'[21] and what Negri and Hardt named instead 'empire'.[22]

All this points to the fact that, whether we want it or not, an anarchist turn has already begun. This dispersion of state sovereignty both below and above nation states closely resembles what anarchists called for centuries 'federalism'. Indeed, if it is true that there is a sort of historical amnesia among political scientists about Marx's prediction of globalization, there is an even more striking form of amnesia over the contribution of classical anarchists in depicting what a post-sovereignty world might look like. Titles such as *The Anarchical Society* (by Hedley Bull, 1995), *The End of Sovereignty* (by Falk and Camilleri, 1992), or even *The Global Covenant* (by David Held, 2004) could well have been envisaged by classical anarchists.[23] But they are all books by political thinkers trying to make sense of what is happening in the world, and with very little awareness of how helpful classical anarchism could be in this enterprise.

Conversely, there are many passages in classical anarchist thinkers, such as the one quoted at the start of this chapter, that could have been written by one of the contemporary theorists of globalization. Malatesta's idea that the development of production, the increase of needs that can only be satisfied through the concourse of everybody, the new means of communication, the habit of travelling, science, literature, wars themselves, are tightening humanity into a single body, whose parts can only find their freedom in the health of the other parts and of the whole itself, can be taken to be a description for what globalization amounts to (2001, p. 24). Yet, it was Malatesta's definition of anarchy. This shows how strong the ban on anarchism still is: anarchy is already there, but it cannot yet be named.

This is however only one side of the story. If it is true that an anarchist turn has already begun, we must immediately add that it is far from going in the right direction. Globalization does not only mean a horizontal extension of the chains of interdependence. It also implies an intensification of vertical ones. Power is not only dispersed below and above the nation states, it has also penetrated within the deepest mechanisms of life: in a word, it has become bio-power. The biopolitical transformation that Hardt and Negri integrated in to their concept of empire (2000) was first diagnosed by Michel Foucault, who traced it back to the intimate constitution of modernity. Foucault's major intuition is the idea that, while in the first part of modernity, the sovereign power was mainly a power to inflict death, in late modernity it becomes a power that is aimed at inciting, promoting, articulating, in a word disciplining life itself. The two poles of such a bio-power are the body of the individual and the body of the population, whereas the means through which it is exercised are various disciplines such as medicine, biology, statistics, demography and the science of police.[24] But today biopolitical transformations seem to go beyond Foucault's classical analysis: they now invest not only modes of governance, but also economic production, in that it is the whole of our subjectivity that is invested in post-Fordist capitalism (Bazzicalupo, 2006).

Today's governance is global both in its spatial dimension and in its inner nature. People felt the need for a new word ('governance' or 'governamentality' instead of 'government') because the thing itself has changed. No longer the centralized, vertical power of the modern nation state, governance denotes a reticular and decentralized form of power which is enriched by the pervasiveness provided by new biopolitical technologies. It is a transformation that can offer possibilities for liberation, but also open the path to the most horrible servitude. Power can today more than ever control the deepest mechanism(s) of life,[25] as well as the way in which we think about it.

Today's governance is global because it governs our bodies as much as it disciplines our minds. The stretching and deepening of the social chains of interdependence also means the stretching and deepening of the imaginary chains that potentially connect the entire globe. We think globally, because the globe has become the horizon of our perception of the world, but also because our social imaginaries are increasingly intermingled. This is what Debord tried to convey with his idea of a society of spectacle. In the epoch of the global communication networks, his prophecy about the transformation of the world into an immense collection of spectacles seems to have become true (Debord, 1994, thesis 1). The spectacle is not only a set of images, but also, and foremost, a social relationship between people mediated through images (1994, thesis 4). This means that the way in which we relate to others is mediated by the images we have internalized from the social imaginary.

Just consider what politics has become and what it used to be. The activity we usually denote with this term is inconceivable without the continual flux of images that enter our screens every day. The competition among images, like that among every other commodity, is so steep that the golden rule of the audience imposes itself: only those images that capture people's attention become part of the spectacle. Hence, the increasing spectacularization of politics. What used to be an activity done by real people has become to a large extent a pure spectacle. Images are no longer what mediate our doing politics, but what risks doing politics in our stead. In other words, politics has become 'imaginal politics'.[26]

In one thing, however, Debord was wrong. Like Marx before him, he thought it was possible to counterpoise to the spectacle the reality of things (see, for instance, 1994, thesis 7). In the epoch of virtual reality, images have instead become ongoing processes so that there is no longer the possibility to distinguish between original and fake. In other words, the society of spectacle has become global, in the double sense that it has stretched its boundaries to embrace the entire globe, but also that it has invaded all ambits of life so that we can no longer say where the spectacle ends and real life begins.

In this scenario, Bakunin's idea that you cannot be free unless everybody else around you is free is timelier than ever. If our being increasingly depends on what other people think and imagine we are, then it is clear that freedom can only be realized as freedom of equals. There is no intermediate possibility: we are either all slaves or all free.

The new global movements that have emerged worldwide in the last 20 years have shown this very clearly. Note that I use the term 'new-global' and not 'no-global'. The reasons why the media worldwide has called a movement that is the result of and even advocates globalization 'no-global' is because they looked at it from the point of view of neoliberal ideology itself. The idea behind this is that neoliberalism is one and the same thing as globalization, so that whoever criticizes neoliberalism with its dogma that 'there are no alternatives' is immediately stigmatized as a critic of globalization itself. With their direct actions on the occasion of G8 and other summits, the new global movements may not have changed the course of those specific political meetings, but they have certainly changed the spectacle that was staged by them.

The organization and the actions of the new global movements perfectly respond to the challenges of our epoch. This is not only because many of their militants creatively combine elements of Marxism and anarchism, the two traditions of thought from which we derived the idea of freedom as freedom of equals. This is because as Graeber put it, 'anarchism is at the heart of the movement, its soul; the source of most of what's new and hopeful about it' (2002, p. 62). By this I do not mean that its activists openly recognize themselves as 'anarchist' – which is far from being the case, as many have noted (Juris, 2009). I mean that the intimate logic of their functioning is anarchical in its essence because it responds to the principle of free federation and association.

As is well known, the new global movements lack any central authority, a single charismatic leader or even a fully fledged programme decided once and for all. Yet this does not mean that activists do not know what they want, as observers locked into traditional terms of hierarchical politics may think. It means that this is a movement that grew up according to a logic of networking which strictly follows the emerging needs and affinities of the people. Its organization is non-hierarchical, its coordination decentralized, its decision making shaped by a new attempt to reinvent new forms of direct democracy (and thus favouring strategies for consensus finding rather than simple majority rule). In brief, it works according to what anarchists have for a long time called free federalism.

Some people thought that the new global movements died soon after 9/11. But this is in my view far from being the case. The reactionary turn that followed 9/11 made those movements dormant, but their legacy continued to work more or less underground over the next ten years. And the news arriving these days from the so-called 'Arab spring' is telling us that the time may have come for them to wake up again. The spontaneous rebellions currently going on in the Middle East show indeed exactly the same logic that we have seen at work in the new global movements of the first years of the twenty-first century. It is perhaps too early to say where this will lead, whether the revolutions will lead to permanent changes in the deep structure of those societies, or whether new dictators will take the place of old ones. But one thing is sure: these revolutions have changed the spectacle of politics, they have disclosed new spaces for collective political action, dismantling regimes ossified by decades of authoritarianism, and they have done so through the same modality that we have seen at work for some time in other regions of the world, from Seattle to Genoa: horizontal networks that have no single, central leader, or vertical forms of organization, and are thus, strictly speaking, 'an'-'archical'.

CONCLUSIONS

Globalization has become reflexive. People act in the world and think about their actions with the entire globe as their horizon of experience. Activists networking from one side of the globe to the other, migrants crossing (legally or illegally) borders, and even political institutions above and below the nation states, they all proclaim one and the same thing: networks are better than hierarchies. Otherwise said, globalization has demonstrated what modern political thought has always been reluctant to recognize: an anarchic order is not only possible, but also desirable.

As we have seen, this is only one side of the story. If it is true that an anarchist turn has already begun, it is still far from going in the right direction. A freedom of equals has more chances today than ever, but it is still far from being realized. Capitalism's omnivorous capacity to overcome every challenge by incorporating its inner logic is the main threat. When the social movements of the 1960s criticized Fordist capitalism for its totalitarian logic that aimed at producing one-dimensional men, capitalism replied by becoming fluid, multidimensional, horizontal. In other words, it incorporated the logic of its opponents. This has been capitalism's strategy to survive, but this time it may prove to be lethal for it, because it has created new and unprecedented possibilities for radical political action.

In conclusion, let me recall Pedrini's poem with which we began. It is not by chance that this poem has recently become a very popular song within the new global movement in Italy and elsewhere. The reason why people find it inspiring these days is that it perfectly expresses the view of freedom outlined before: one is the world, one must be freedom, because we are all in the same boat. In a world in which the fate of a few islands depends on the behaviour of industries on the other side of the globe, in which a nuclear explosion in Japan can have effects worldwide, in which the planet has become a global society of spectacle, we cannot be autonomous without being free, or, equivalently, we cannot be free on our own.

It is a very radical view of freedom, but one that is timelier today than ever before. History itself has reversed the liberal motto 'your freedom ends where that of the others begins' into a black and red one: 'your freedom can only begin with that of everybody else'.

NOTES

1   If not in the fact that he was my great-uncle. Although I cannot (yet) speak about his life and writings, it is important for me to say that the following, more or less abstract, philosophical disscussion is my own way for speaking about him.

2   On *The Economic and Political Manuscript of 1844* and *On the Jewish Question* (1978a, 1978b), whereas the second is the view that emerges from his mature writings, at least since *Capital* (Marx, 1980). For a general analysis of the problem of freedom in Marx, see Petrucciani (1996).

3   In particular, it is a view that resonates with the influence of the left young Hegelians that Bakunin met in Berlin.

4   See, for instance, Foucault (1988). On the convergence between post-structuralism and anarchism, see May (1994).

5   On voluntary servitude, a classical reference point is de la Boetie (2005).

6   I have tried to develop a very similar idea through the concept of political myth (Bottici, 2007).

7   The concept of recognition has recently been at the centre of a very lively debate. See for instance Honneth (1995) and Fraser and Honneth (2003). Bakunin, like Honneth, also probably derives the concept of recognition from Hegel.

8   See for instance *The Holy Family*, where Marx says that man is not free for the negative force to avoid this or that, but for the positive power to develop his own individuality (Marx and Engels, 1975, p. 131).

9   To begin with, see Foucault (1980).

10 On the origins of the concept and its historical roots in modern moral philosophy, see Schneewind (1998).

11 I am thinking here for instance of certain unorthodox form of Marxism (Castoriadis, 1987) or the Italian Workerist movement (Lotringer and Marazzi, 2007, p. 8).

12 In contrast to other scholars who used the term collectivist (Miller, 2001), I prefer to call it 'social' because as such it includes both anarcho-communism, along the lines of Kropotkin, and the collectivist variant, which, following Bakunin, leaves some space for the individual enjoyment of property.

13 See for instance, www.anti-state.com/ and http://www.strike-the-root.com/ (accessed September 1, 2009).

14 On this point, see in particular the critique to utopian socialists and communists in the *Manifesto* (Marx and Engels, 1978, pp. 491–9).

15 For a short but acute presentation of those novelties, see Marazzi (1999).

16 In the *Critique of the Gotha Program*, we read for instance: 'Between capitalist and communist society there lies the period of the revolutionary transformation of the one into the other. Corresponding to this is also a political transition period in which the state can be nothing but the revolutionary dictatorship of the proletariat' (Marx, 1978d, p. 538). The only other place where it appears is a letter to Weydemeyer of 1852.

17 It is clear from Bakunin's letter of protest (1972) that this was the main point of the controversy. On the controversy, see Paul (1980, pp. 300–29).

18 In Proudhon's view, there are four main types of government, which correspond to the two main principles of authority and freedom; regimes of authority are both the government of all by one (monarchy) and the government of all by all (what he calls panarchy or communism), while regimes of freedom are both the government of all by everybody (democracy) and the government of everyone by everyone, which is the anarchy or self-rule (Proudhon, 2001, pp. 125–33). Proudhon's federalism can indeed be interpreted as a combination of the last two forms of government, what he calls respectively democracy and anarchy. And the same holds for Bakunin's free federation, mentioned above.

19 See Held et al. (1999).

20 I cannot enter here into the details of the critique of the prevalence of the problem of security in the justifications for the existence of the modern state. Let me briefly recall the paradox of such a justification, which, as Agamben has recently pointed out, consists in the fact that the subjects confers to the modern sovereign state the right to kill them in order to receive the guarantee of their life (1998).

21 See Held et al. (1999).

22 See in particular Hardt and Negri (2000). In contrast with classical usage, with the term 'empire' Hardt and Negri mean a system of authority which has no definitive centre, and as such their notion of empire comes very close to the idea of a multilayered global governance (Bottici, 2006).

23 On this point see for instance Pritchard (2010), who provocatively raises the question of whether David Held is an anarchist. Indeed that many of the trends in contemporary discourses about globalization, global federation and federalism closely remind us of classical anarchist topics.

24 To begin with, see Part V of the first volume of the *History of Sexuality* (Foucault, 1980–90).

25 To make an example, if an eighteenth-century writer when discussing the natural limits to political power could still observe that 'a Parliament can do everything but make a woman a man, and a man a woman' (Dicey, 1959, p. 43), this no longer holds because even the change of sex of an individual can be regulated by state law.

26 I have further developed the notion of 'imaginal politics' as well as the

way in which this connects with post- Fordist capitalist developments in Bottici (2013).

REFERENCES

Agamben, G. (1998) *Homo sacer: Sovereign power and bare life*. Stanford: Stanford University Press.

Bakunin, M. (1872) Letter to La Liberte', www.marxists.org/reference/archive/bakunin/works/1872/la-liberte.htm (accessed September 3, 2012).

Bakunin, M. (1972) *Stato e anarchia*. Milan: Feltrinelli.

Bakunin, M. (1974) 'The political theology of Mazzini', in *Selected Writings*, pp. 214–31. New York: Grove.

Bakunin, M. (1996) *Tre conferenze sull'anarchia*. Rome: Manifestolibri.

Bakunin, M. (2000) *La libertà degli uguali*, ed. G. N. Berti Milan: Eleuthera.

Bazzicalupo, L. (2006) *Il governo delle vite. Biopolitica e bioeconomia*. Bari: Laterza.

Bottici, C. (2006) 'War and conflict in a globalising world: governance or empire?' *Romanian Journal of Political Science*, 6(1), pp. 3–23.

Bottici, C. (2007) *A Philosophy of Political Myth*. Cambridge: Cambridge University Press.

Bottici, C. (2013) *Imaginal Politics*. New York: Columbia University Press, forthcoming.

Bull, H. (1995) *The Anarchical Society: A study of order in world politics*. London: Macmillan.

Camilleri, J. A. and Falk, J. (1992) *The End of Sovereignty: The politics of a shrinking and fragmented world*. Aldershot: Edward Elgar.

Castoriadis, C. (1987) *The Imaginary Institution of Society*. Cambridge: Polity Press.

Debord, G. (1994) *The Society of Spectacle*. New York: Zone.

De la Boetie, E. (2005) 'On voluntary servitude', pp. 329–31 in R. Graham (ed.), *Anarchism: A documentary history of libertarian ideas*, Vol. II. Montreal: Black and Rose.

Dicey, A. V. (1959) *Introduction to the Study of the Law of the Constitution*. London: ECS Wade Macmillan.

Fraser, N. and Honneth, A. (2003) *Redistribution or Recognition? A political-philosophical exchange*. London: Verso.

Foucault, M. (1980) *Power-Knowledge*. New York: Harvester.

Foucault, M. (1980-90) *The History of Sexuality*. New York: Vintage.

Foucault, M. (1988) *Technologies of the Self: A seminar with Michel Foucault*, ed. L. H. Martin, H. Gutman and P. Hutton. Amherst, Mass.: University of Massachusetts Press.

Goodman, P. (2009) 'Freedom and autonomy', pp. 329–31 in R. Graham (ed.), *Anarchism: A documentary history of libertarian ideas*, Vol. II. Montreal: Black and Rose.

Graeber, D. (2002) 'The new anarchists', *New Left Review*, 13, Jan–Feb, pp. 61–73.

Hardt, M. and Negri, A. (2000) *Empire*. Cambridge, Mass.: Harvard University Press.

Held, D. (2004) *Global Covenant: The social democratic alternative to the Washington Consensus*. Cambridge: Polity Press.

Held, D., McGrew A., Goldblatt, D. and Perraton, J. (1999) *Global Transformations*. Cambridge: Polity Press.

Honneth, A. (1995) *The Struggle for Recognition: The moral grammar of social conflict*. Cambridge: Polity Press.

Juris, J. S. (2009) 'Anarchism, or the cultural logic of networking', in *Contemporary Anarchist Studies. An introductory anthology of anarchy in the academy*. London: Routledge.

Lotringer, S. and Marazzi, C. (2007) *Autonomia. Post-political Politics*. Los Angeles: Semiotext(e)).

Malatesta, E. (2001) *L'anarchia*. Rome, Datanews (Eng. trans, *Anarchy*, on: http://theanarchistlibrary.org/HTML/Errico_Malatesta__Anarchy.html (accessed September 3, 2012).

Marazzi, C. (1999) *Il posto dei calzini. La svolta linguistica dell'economia ed i suoi effetti sulla politica*. Turin: Bollati Boringhieri. (Eng. trans. forthcoming from Semiotext).

Marx, K. (1978a) 'The economic and philosophical manuscripts of 1844', pp. 66–125 in R. C. Tucker (ed.), *Marx–Engels Reader*. New York: Norton.

Marx, K. (1978b) 'On the Jewish question', pp. 26–52 in R.C. Tucker (ed.), *Marx-Engels Reader*. New York: Norton.

Marx, K. (1978c) '*Grundrisse*', pp. 221–468 in R.C. Tucker (ed.), *Marx-Engels Reader*. New York: Norton.

Marx, K. (1978d) 'Critique of the Gotha Program', pp. 525–41 in R. C. Tucker (ed.), *Marx-Engels Reader*. New York: Norton.

Marx, K. (1980) *Il capital*. Rome: Editori Riuniti.

Marx, K and Engels, F. (1975) *The Holy Family, or Critique of Critical Criticism. Against Bruno Bauer and company*, pp. 1–540 in *Karl Marx and Frederick Engels Collected Works*, Vol. 5. London: Lawrence & Wishart.

Marx, K and Engels, F. (1976) *The German Ideology*, pp. 1–211 in *Karl Marx and Frederick Engels Collected Works*, Vol. 4. London: Lawrence and Wishart.

Marx, K and Engels, F. (1978) 'Manifesto of the Communist Party', pp. 469–500 in R. C. Tucker (ed.), *Marx–Engels Reader*,. New York: Norton.

May, T. (1994) *The Political Philosophy of Poststructuralist Anarchism*. University Park, Pa.: Pennsylvania State University Press.

Miller, D. (2001) 'Anarchy', in S. M. Lipset (ed.), *Political Philosophy: Theories thinkers concepts*. Washington DC: CQ Press.

Paul, T. (1980) *Karl Marx and the Anarchists*. London: Kegan Paul.

Pedrini, B. (2001a) *Versi liberi e ribelli*. Carrara: Edizioni Anarchiche Baffardello.

Pedrini, B. (2001b) *Noi fummo i ribelli, noi fummo i predoni: Schegge autobiografiche di uomini contro*. Carrara: Edizioni Anarchiche Baffardello.

Prichard, A. (2010) 'David Held is an anarchist. Discuss', in *Millennium*, 39(2), pp. 439–59.

Proudhon, P. J. (2001) *Critica della proprietà e dello stato*. Milano: Eleuthera.

Schneewind, J. B. (1998) *The Invention of Autonomy*. Cambridge: Cambridge University Press.

Stirner, M. (1990) *L'unico e la sua proprietà*. Milan: Mursia.

2

THE POLITICS OF COMMENSALITY

Banu Bargu

> The moment has come to found the REPUBLIC OF EQUALS, this great home open to all men. The day of general restitution has arrived. Groaning families, come sit at the common table set by nature for all its children.
>
> (Babeuf, 1796)

In *The Human Condition* (1998), Hannah Arendt discusses how society has encroached upon the public sphere, how the social realm has spilled over into and thereby largely extinguished the flame of the political. Arendt laments the loss of the possibility of action, and especially action in concert, which defines the autonomy of the political sphere, because of the rise of mass society. She makes the claim that the conquest of the public realm (and she does use this military metaphor), rather than bringing more equality to more members of a polity, in fact eliminates individuality, restricts the 'fierce agonism' of citizens striving for distinction, engulfs freedom and greatly circumscribes the possibilities of spontaneity, outstanding achievement and new beginnings. Instead of action, it promotes conformist behaviour; instead of equality, it promotes sameness; instead of government, it promotes administration; in short, instead of politics, it promotes statistics. The routines and ordinary concerns of everyday life displace the quest for human excellence, a quest characteristic of a politics defined by extraordinary deeds and words by which individuals seek recognition and immortality among their peers. The political realm in Arendt's conception is free, not only from the necessity that defines our material conditions of existence and entraps us in our own bodies, but also from the inequality and domination that arises from the rulership appropriate to the relations among unequals in our private lives.

To illuminate her conception of the political, Arendt pens a striking metaphor: 'To live together in the world means essentially that a world of things is between those who have it in common, as a table is located between those who sit around it; the world, like every in-between, relates and separates men at the same time' (Arendt, 1998, p. 52). This powerful and inspiring image of the political, however, is revealed to be much more problematic once we take a closer look at its foundational assumptions and implications. The most damaging aspect of this conception is the strict and antagonistic separation that Arendt posits between the social and the political. As a result, Arendt finds the encroachment of the social into this blissful world analogous to the sudden disappearance of the table (1998, p. 53). A communal life where individuals are connected by bonds of fraternity or charity, bonds which do not distinguish individuals as individuated and autonomous moral subjects (the case, for example, in Christian conceptions of community) resembles a group of individuals sitting around a table, only without one.

In this chapter, I look not at the disappearance of the table as the metaphor for the loss of a 'common world of freedom,' but at the act of eating at the same table – commensality – as the metaphor of building (or rebuilding, reclaiming) a common world of equals. Commensality is a form of commoning, both a long-standing practice of communal life and an everyday possibility to reclaim the commons. It substantiates a positive horizon of emancipation at the quotidian, micro-political level, with indigenous forms of sociality which are productive of the relations of friendship and solidarity, which are in turn constitutive of egalitarian and democratic subjectivities. Reclaiming commensality should therefore be an important component of contemporary anarcho-communist politics.

Interestingly, however, commensality, which has been an important theme in ancient and medieval political thought, has largely disappeared from the realm of philosophy with the advent of modernity. Even in utopian, communist and anarchist tracts dating after the sixteenth century, commensality no longer figures as a central component of the alternative organization of social life. In fact, it is hardly ever discussed. How may we account for this disappearance? I propose to evaluate this development in connection with the disappearance of the commons, the process of land enclosures and 'so-called primitive accumulation' at the dawn of capitalism, on the one hand, and the broad societal transformations that rendered dominant a juridical conception of the political (attached, inextricably, to the modern state) at the expense of the progressive constriction of the social sphere, on the other.

Commensality, then, is both a metaphor for reversing the Arendtian interpretation of the crisis of modernity, which she locates in the taking over of the political by the social (or what contemporary theorists call the emergence of biopolitics), and an ordinary social practice whose radical potentiality can move us toward the realization of such a reversal. From the perspective offered by traditions of mutuality, the crisis of modernity lies less in the invasion of the political by the social than in the flattening out of the social by the hegemonic construction of the autonomy of the political and the progressive destruction of the social by the incursion of a capitalist market whose primary form of competitive and individualist action has been detrimental to communal practices and relations. I therefore suggest that commensality provides us with a rich resource that puts into question any account of the political (like Arendt's) that neglects its own social conditions of possibility, sustenance and reproduction and points us toward an alternative where the 'common weal' is really held, produced and consumed in common.

ARENDT'S TABLE

The table is both a material and a symbolic space. For Arendt, the table is the product of human effort; it signifies the creation of an enduring artefact that constitutes the basis of an autonomous and lasting common world (of those around the table, of citizens), a world that both houses the relations between individuals and their actions and enables the experience of freedom within it.[1] This is a space in which the relative permanence of our common world enables us to be seen and heard by others, transcend our transience as individuals and overcome our mortality. In this world, what connects us and brings us together also keeps us apart: it prevents the subsumption of individuals into an undifferentiated, unified mass without individuality. It also precludes the transposition of our inequality as persons and hierarchical social relations into the formalism of the political sphere where relations should instead be characterized by freedom among equals.

However, as a result of the historic attempt to address human poverty and misery politically, social conditions and relations are politicized and the political is colonized and instrumentalized by the social sphere. Arendt dates this development to the dawn of modernity, the rise of mass democracy, and revolutionary politics (particularly in the French idiom). With these developments, the purpose of political life (*bios politicos*) becomes the management of individuals as biological, animal beings. Freedom is reduced to the means of needs, the political sphere becomes heteronymous and we lose what affords us the experience of realizing our humanity fully, all paving a road that may eventually lead to 'totalitarianism'. The table vanishes.

With disappearance of the table, it is as if the enduring foundations of our common world collapse and we are suddenly displayed to one another in our embodied selves, in a metaphorical nakedness and intimacy, as it were, that should have remained private and secret (Arendt, 1998, p. 70). Such intimacy is not only intolerable, for Arendt, especially because we have not chosen to appear and be exposed in that way, it is also a threat to politics as such. Without the metaphorical table, several overlapping yet distinct separations, foundational for Arendtian politics and pertinent to her critique of the rise of mass society, collapse. One is the analytical separation between the aspects of life that human beings share with other living beings and aspects that belong only to human beings: *zoë* and *bios*, the animal (or what has also been called the *species* or the *bestial*) and the properly human. Second is the corresponding spatial/spherical distinction between the private and the public (Arendt, 1998, pp. 61–5). Third, and a corollary of the second, is the behavioural distinction defined by the nature of relations and activities appropriate for each distinctive sphere. Whereas the public sphere is for speech and action, the private sphere is where the maintenance and (material and biological) reproduction of life dictate urgent, cyclical and necessary activities (all of which Arendt designates with her concept of labour).[2] When life in the bestial sense, the animal element of humanity, becomes a common, political concern, the hierarchical, dependent, often violent and therefore nonpolitical, relations of coexistence within the private sphere infiltrate the equal relations in the public sphere. The rift that Arendt has introduced between biological life and human life, labour and action, is thereby crossed.[3]

At the same time, consequent to the disintegration of these foundational distinctions, our normative hierarchies are also reversed. With the politicization of the daily concerns and bread-and-butter issues of the masses, all human activities are progressively reduced to a common denominator, labour. In other words, every activity gains value insofar as it is a means of procuring the necessities of life and providing for their abundance. What was once an arrangement dictated by our needs now becomes a pervasive attitude, a way of life, a mentality, one in which we can no longer hold and esteem as separate, even analytically, what is properly human from what is not. What was once the animality of man now becomes the expression of our humanity. With modernity, it seems that we have forgotten how to live humanly because of our preoccupation with living.

Many scholars have already critiqued Arendt's model of politics, which she takes up as an ideal and idealized form of human life, providing at once a blueprint for contemporary discourses on biopolitics and a normative scale to assess their value in relation to politics proper.[4] Commentators have rightly pointed out Arendt's denigration of activities that she considers nonpolitical in contrast to her glorification of the political sphere.[5] They have drawn our attention to an anti-democratic, even anti-political tendency in her thought, which, particularly in *The Human Condition*, tends to dissociate the authentically political from the participation of citizens, cooperation and shared experience (especially when these involve social issues), and instead conceptualizes it mainly on the basis of the agonistic competition of a select few (Wolin, 1983, pp. 3–19).[6] In this light, Arendt's thought appears largely elitist and critical of the democratic potential of mass society.[7] Her occasional endorsements of the council system, emerging spontaneously as part of a revolutionary insurgency where direct participation of self-selected citizens ensures a richer, though still restricted, public sphere (Sitton, 1987), and her praise for 'action in concert' do not obliterate but complicate the elitist tendency in her thought, which always remains suspicious of the masses and their desire to bring their suffering and dispossession within the milieu of politics.

Arendt's insistence on breaking up the continuum of human relations that blend social, political, economic and biological aspects into one another results in the reification of the separation between freedom and necessity, a separation that can only be sustained by the exclusion, if not the enslavement, of some for the leisure of others.[8] Such realities, which Arendt also acknowledges, put into sharpened relief her otherwise highly romanticized reading of the politics of the ancients as free of relations of arbitrariness and command, as devoid of class conflict and pressures for inclusion.[9] Arendt's conception of the political, with a nostalgic yearning[10] for a time in which heroism and lofty principles animated an aestheticized public space, and inspired by the model of high culture (Canovan, 1994), appears as a serious obstacle for incorporating her legacy within an emancipatory politics. The very popularity of this proliferating trend in contemporary political thought should be cause for some caution.

In what follows, I propose to deepen the critique of Arendt by maintaining that the separation between what Arendt calls the social and the political is not sustainable, and before that we would have much to gain by reckoning with the emancipatory possibilities inherent in the world of necessity as a means to expand the sphere of freedom. Through the study of commensality, I want to emphasize the potentiality of social experience to transgress a strict dichotomization of the public and the private, to generate ties of friendship and solidarity that are indispensable for the constitution of citizens with an egalitarian orientation, a common ethic and critical consciousness. The cultivation of such subjectivities and the ties that bind them is the condition of possibility of a democratic politics, and such cultivation is necessary for the deepening of egalitarian participation in the direction of an anarcho-communist politics. It is time we give up the nostalgia for a politics that never existed, except perhaps in Pericles' *Funeral Oration*, and focus on how the spheres of life that Arendt considers nonpolitical, or not worthy of politics, can become the embryonic forms out of which a critical and autonomous political culture can develop – autonomous, that is, from officially existing politics, which nowhere approaches a sphere of freedom that either Arendt or today's left would cherish in common. Such an un-Arendtian theoretical move is a necessary transgression, I think, dictated by the timely demands of the 'anarchist turn'.

I would like to begin the task of revisiting the social sphere by turning the tables, as it were. I suggest interpreting Arendt's table not as a metaphor for the necessary autonomy of the political, whose precondition is the nonpolitical relations of labour and work that go into the making of the table, but as the commonality created through experience – the act of coming together to share a meal. The common table, instead of disappearing, emerges each time anew from the very practice of coming together to break bread, and it becomes common not because it is between those who sit around it, but because each of us contribute to setting it up and bring food that we have worked to make. It is common because it allows us to share. The common table is a result, an effect, a manifestation of the communal effort that goes into its making and the community that is thus made. Each common table is transient: rather than enduring, it symbolizes the temporary material rendition of the dream of an 'abundant table' – after all, abundance rather than permanence, according to Arendt, is 'the age-old dream of the poor and destitute' (1998, pp. 65, 114–15).[11] The abundance is not merely the material wealth that is on the table, but the immaterial wealth of those gathering around it. As such, the common table allows us an opportunity to think about Arendt's fear of the table's disappearance, as a result of what she calls an erosion, intrusion or growing lack, in reverse: as a potlatch, a proliferation, a pluralization and diversification – a common *wealth*. Just like Mauss (2000) and Bataille (1991) found in the institution of the gift and the potlatch an important alternative to the utilitarian rationality that underpins capitalism, could we not find in commensality both the confirmation of the politically generative potential of sociality and the building block of an emancipatory politics?

Even if we bracket the process leading up to setting the table, the very practice of table fellowship has multiple effects, such as ensuring social cohesion and forging collective bonds, creating conversations of common concern and engendering the possibility of politicizing areas and issues that are deemed nonpolitical from a formal, juridical perspective of politics, and its attendant conception of freedom and equality, built on the neutralization of existing social distinctions.[12] In this view, commensality becomes the metaphor of building the desirable relations and subjectivities necessary for a common world of equals, one that is an active critique of Arendt's worry regarding the destruction of the autonomy of the political via the rise of mass society. Commensality, then, is both a metaphor for the emancipatory potential of biopolitics and a literal rendition of one form of social practice, lodged firmly in biological needs (labour) but not reducible to them, that moves us toward the realization of that potential.

COMMENSAL PRACTICES

Commensality is the everyday, ordinary, recurrent act of eating together, of sharing food, at the same table (*mensa*).[13] Viewed as a domestic practice to serve daily needs of bodily sustenance largely confined to the household, commensality presents no serious challenge to Arendtian distinctions. It is a recurrent, repetitive activity oriented toward everyday consumption and the satisfaction of biological needs. However, this picture tends to change once commensality is understood in a more expansive way, both because the production of food requires the cooperation of others and because food is a mediator of social relations.

Commensality indicates intimacy between those who share a meal

It evokes a common substance among those who eat together. It is a sign of kinship, amity, good will, companionship and conciliation. The bonds that are affirmed by sharing food are attachments that usually presuppose existing filiations (such as family attachments). However, an important aspect of commensality is that it does not simply indicate existing intimacy, it also actively creates it, acting as a practical foundation for the forging of new bonds and filiations. Etymology suggests that some of the most common words indicating togetherness derive from sharing a meal. Some examples are 'companion', 'company' and 'to accompany'. The French word for a pal or friend (*copain*) comes from sharing bread (*pain*). The Roman word for a dinner party, *convivium*, literally meant living together (Gowers, 1993).

In addition to signifying togetherness, commensality also helps forge the identity of the commensal community not only by bringing people together, but also through what is eaten (and sanctioned as edible). Even though there is a great diversity of foodways, historically, geographically and culturally, meat commands a universal value and effectivity in conducting social identity in commensal occasions (Bloch, 1999, pp. 135–6). This, of course, is intimately related to the sacrificial aspect of commensality, one that commands a long history. Anthropological studies document that the consumption of meat is usually the final part of sacrificial ceremonies after the ritual killing of the sacrificial animal. Sacrificial ceremonies consummate in a communal feast, which brings together (or perhaps *brings into being?*) the whole community around the sacrifice and ensures their participation. It is interesting to note that the etymology of the word 'to participate' points us to having one's share in a sacrificial meal (*pars capere*). Furthermore, 'prince' derives from *princeps*, or the one who gets the first/main share of the sacrificial meal (*primus capere*) (Sheid, 1984, 1985; Fischler, 2011). Most organized religions, especially Abrahamic ones, have their specific commensal practices (though some have become more symbolic than others) that act as markers of identity.

However, commensality does not simply construct bonds on the basis of the common food that is consumed. What enables commensality to go beyond consumption and to produce the table as a new space of social interaction is the shared experience it makes possible. The very act of consuming food together is generative of a new, specific form of commonality. The specificity of this shared experience is that what is consumed is in fact internalized and thus is intimately and immediately incorporated into the body. Since the internalization of food implies the transfer of the predominant qualities of the food to the body, eating in common (sometimes from the same cooking pot or the same plate, at least from the same table) creates a sense of approximation between those in each other's company while sharing the same food (Fischler, 2011, p. 533). Maurice Bloch argues:

> Since the sharing of food expresses, and is also believed to cause, the bodily unification of the persons who eat together, it represents something similar to ideas about the unity between parents and children that is understood to result from the processes of procreation, or to the bodily unification that may be imagined to result from sexual intercourse.
>
> (Bloch, 1999, p. 137)

Through shared experience, commensality creates closeness and mutual confidence. It brings together individuals around a common table and enables the forging of bonds on an egalitarian, horizontal basis. It also constitutes an invitation of a common conversation, one in which participation can follow the horizontal relationships of sharing. It is an experience of socialization that promotes solidarity, care, friendship and cooperation, rather than antagonism, enmity and competition. The common table is a site where social relations, ideas and projects are negotiated. It designates a space in which political discourse and action can germinate and proliferate (Dietler and Hayden, 2001). Commensality transforms bodily consumption into social, communicative, cultural and political production.

The social space of the common table, created by and in turn creating a close intimacy between the individuals who inhabit it, depicts a situation in which Arendt's distinctions between work, labour and action, collapse into one another. Different forms of human activity, however analytically distinct Arendt may hold them to be, entwine and blend into one another at a common table, stretching across the private into the public (Hirschman, 1996).[14] The work of our hands in producing food, preparing a meal, and setting the table, just like the labour of eating and drinking, may feel futile and recurrent, but both are essential for the creation, slow and arduous to be sure, of an enduring community of individuals who are free and equal and tied to one another with bonds of solidarity, care and friendship.[15] Commensality thus presents a threat to the 'impure purity' (Matheron, 2008) of Arendtian politics precisely because of its expansive, generative and potentially subversive effects.

Although there is a growing body of scholarship on commensality, mostly within the fields of history, archaeology, anthropology and sociology, it tends to focus on commensality in relation to its prominent functions for the affirmation of group identity, the maintenance of social hierarchies (of class, status, gender, age and ethnicity) and other internal divisions (of religious and political groups), and its establishment of group cohesion and unity in relation to others (Grignon, 2001). In this view, commensality functions less to bring together than to keep apart: it strengthens already existing social groups and their identities against those that are excluded from the table. For example, in Greek and Roman antiquity, this is manifest in the association of commensality with the aristocracy and warrior groups; in the Middle Ages with monks and priests, on the one hand, and guilds, on the other, underscoring its role as an exclusive marker of group identity (Murray, 1995; Hodkinson, 1997; Rosser, 1994). Similarly, studies of commensality in the processes of state formation and imperial expansion also resonate with the same perspective, though they allow more space for process, which makes the community-building function more visible in the emergence and negotiation of new identities (Bray, 2003).

However, in contrast to the emphasis of existing scholarship on commensality as a practice that principally functions to maintain the social order, by mechanisms of exclusion and the reproduction of internal hierarchies, there is an inverse interpretation of commensal practices in which they are seen to foster popular participation, build networks of solidarity and eliminate hierarchical ordering, thereby taking upon a critical, and at times even a subversive, attitude toward the social order at large.[16] Interestingly, it is this latter perspective that characterizes the commensality emphasized in ancient to early modern political philosophy, where common messes are one of the most important components of social life in utopian and proto-communist tracts. In this context, commensal practices express the desire for a communal unity that transcends particular groups and help bring it into existence. Furthermore, these practices are generally correlated with an emphasis on the abolition of property relations and the collective (though not always democratic) administration of life, overcoming the public/private distinction.

The most prominent example of such an interpretation of commensality can be found in Plato's *Republic*. When Plato describes the life he envisions for the city's guardians in the ideal constitution, he emphasizes certain features pertaining to the organization of everyday life, such as the abolition of private property, marriage and the family, on the one hand, and equal education and activities for men and women, on the other (Plato, 2004). Among these features also figures the idea that the meals will be eaten in common at mess-tables (2004, para. 416e). These elements serve, according to Plato, the cultivation of community: 'sharing pleasure and pain bind [the city] together – when, as far as possible, all the citizens feel more or less the same joy or pain at the same gains or losses' (Plato 2004, para. 462b). The harmonious maintenance of the city requires its unity, and the latter depends on the unity of the ruling class (since the other inhabitants seem merely to provide the conditions of possibility of the communal existence of the guardians). If this goal involves the inculcation of discipline through the authoritative micro-regulation of the lives of the guardians (even including the regulation of their mating practices), its main vector passes through the elimination of 'mine and thine'. While the most striking and scandalous measure Plato proposes, in addition to the elimination of private property, is the holding of children and women in common, the everyday basis of this communal orientation, which attempts to equate the common good and personal interest, resides in the sharing of food around a common table.

In Plato, we find that the two different functions of commensality coexist. On the one hand, common messes become the marker of the exclusive identity of the guardians, underscoring the boundary of the ruling group. On the other hand, commensality is the very experience through which the ties of friendship among the guardians, their common project, and their selfless identification with the city are built and maintained. The latter aspect of commensality, as part of a collectivist vision in which horizontal ties of friendship and solidarity are critical for the maintenance of the community, is echoed in philosophy and theology until the early sixteenth century (references can be found in Aristotle, Diodorus of Sicily, Philo of Alexandria, Seneca, and the Gospels, among others) when it finds its most famous iteration in Thomas More's *Utopia* (2003).

On the island of Utopia, everything is under public ownership and no one fears starvation; everyone knows how to cultivate the land and takes up a trade; idleness is not encouraged, but the working day is shortened; more time is devoted to leisure and learning; and everyone wears the same dress, lives in similar dwellings, and dines together. The communal dining halls and the cooking and eating equipment, just like the chains of the slaves who do the dirty work there, are made of precious metals, in order to 'bring these metals into contempt' (More, 2003, p. 67). More provides precise and elaborate details regarding the common meals: how the women should do the cooking taking turns, how seating should be arranged at the mess-tables (for example, political representatives of each household and priests occupying an honorific table, men and women sitting across one another), how the elders should be served first and most, how the rest of the food should be divided in equal portions, and how the topic of conversation should begin with literature and then move into politics and the discussion of 'serious problems' (More, 2003, pp. 61–5). As in Plato, here too we find that commensality is an important factor in ensuring communal solidarity and equality, regulating conduct, inculcating norms and values and, overall, fostering a sense of belonging and participation in a just society. Unlike Plato, where commensality is exclusive to the ruling group, More includes all residents of Utopia in the common dining experience (though it could be argued that More's commensality is still restricted to the inhabitants of an island). Overall, however, the common point of emphasis for both philosophers, and the capacity of commensality that I would like to recover from their interpretations, is the function of commensality to build a common life of egalitarian participation on an everyday basis, with subversive political implications for any social order based on hierarchy, inequality and exclusion.

COMMONING

While the theme of commensality is a recurrent point of reference in ancient and medieval philosophy and in theology, it largely disappears from the theoretical realm after the sixteenth century. It plays little role in the treatises of utopian socialists.[17] It is not a significant component of Marxist or anarchist thinking, with Kropotkin as perhaps the sole exception.[18] Why did philosophers give up on commensality?

Karl Kautsky's interpretation of Thomas More's *Utopia* is revealing in this respect (while also representative of the dominant approach to this issue in the orthodox socialist tradition). On the one hand, Kautsky views More as having made a 'bold intellectual leap; at a time when the capitalist mode of production was in its infancy' (1979), and thus having laid the blueprint of modern socialism. Inspired by Plato and the contemporary conditions of his own time, which led to the misery of the working classes, More proposes an alternative world where the land and its products would be held in common. On the other hand, Kautsky contends, because the industry of More's island was based on handicrafts and peasant agriculture, 'More was obliged to lay all the greater stress upon the social character of meals and pleasures' (1979).

In contrast to the idyllic pre-industrial world of *Utopia*, modern capitalism is characterized by large-scale industrial machinery and organization, which requires large-scale cooperation. That is why, Kautsky explains, '[s]ociality in this sphere is a point of secondary importance for modern Socialism, but a vital condition for More's Socialism. In this respect, More has closer affinity with the so-called socialistic phenomena of Antiquity, above all, with Platonic Communism, than with present-day Socialism' (1979).[19] Accordingly, because the social nature of mass industrial production, enabled by the complex division of labour and the introduction of machinery, brings large groups of workers together and provides other mechanisms of sociality, modern socialism no longer requires (or requires as much) those everyday experiences of socialization outside of the workplace for building solidarity and political identification.

Even if, as Kautsky suggests, the new experience of sociality made possible by the collective nature of the industrial production process partially accounts for the eventual neglect of commensality in revolutionary thought, this explanation is not wholly satisfactory, if only for a rather simplistic determinism that runs from the social organization of economic production to the realm of politics and philosophy. Kautsky explains the difference between More's communal project and modern socialism by drawing a thick line of demarcation between different modes of production and arguing that they determine corresponding forms of social relations and mechanisms of socialization, as well as, by implication, attendant philosophical visions. Regardless of the determinism of his perspective, Kautsky not only optimistically overestimates the capacity of the productive process to generate shared political identities, but also underestimates the continuing importance of other forms of sociality.

In addressing the paradoxical disavowal of commensality within modern philosophy, especially in its radical variants, we could also follow a slightly different track, linking this absence with the disappearance of the commons, the process of land enclosures that came to mark the birth of capitalism. However, the disappearance of the commons, while materially linked with enclosures of communal land, should not simply be construed as the changing ownership of natural resources or the limitation of access to common pastures.

Rather, the full meaning of the term 'commons' suggests the activity of *commoning*, the social practices of producing and consuming in common, and the customary and communal relations of fellowship and mutual aid that go into the making of these practices (Linebaugh, 2008, pp. 279). The destruction of the commons, then, is the totality of complex processes associated with the enclosure of common lands that go hand in hand with the erosion of related social practices, the dissolution of ties of community, and the substitution of abstract and atomized individuality as the predominant form of subjectivity for modern politics. The disappearance of commoning, both materially and politically, also parallels the fading away of the utopian imagination for which these practices of commoning constitute a major source of inspiration.

From the perspective of the tradition of the commons, we can identify commensality to be one of the most ordinary, practical forms of commoning. Sharing a table is an extension of working the land and distributing its products in common and a transparent expression of the prevailing political culture and ethics of the masses living by commoning in daily life. Commensality expands from the sphere of the household into the public sphere, from the social into the political, from individual consumption toward communal nourishment, and it connects these spheres with the commonality of productive, consumptive and social practices concretized in the shared experience of table fellowship. Viewed in this light, history shows us that the processes of land enclosures and the marginalization of the cultures of commoning deeply resonate with the emergence of the abstract, unitary, solitary, self-interested and rational subjectivity of modern politics, as well as with the disappearance of the commensal emphasis in political philosophy during the early development of capitalism.

An important landmark that becomes symptomatic of how disparate processes at the dawn of 'so-called primitive accumulation' (Marx, 1976, p. 873)[20] came to pave the way for the dual disappearances of commoning in theory and in practice is the Magna Carta, the famous charter signed between English barons and King John at Runnymede in 1215. Peter Linebaugh discusses how there were not one but two charters in the Magna Carta: the Charter of Liberties (also known as the Great Charter) and the Charter of the Forest (Linebaugh, 2008, p. 38). The first charter acknowledged the basic liberties of freemen in England, including habeas corpus, trial by jury and inheritance (for widows); it stipulated the prohibition of torture, freedom of travel for merchants, uniform weights and measures, and the end to unrightful seizures of livestock. The second charter involved the restoration of rights to the forest, protecting customary access to pastures, stones, wood, fuel, estovers, honey, nuts, mushrooms, herbs and berries. In other words, the second charter defended the commons, the rights of material subsistence of the people, by enabling free access to all those areas that were deemed forests (and these involved not only the woods, but also large pastures).

Linebaugh skilfully traces how, in the subsequent centuries, the Magna Carta is exalted as a seminal constitutional document, protecting basic rights and liberties, while at the same time it is emptied of its radical material content by the severing of the Charter of Liberties from the Charter of the Forest. For English revolutionaries, such as John Milton, John Lilburne and other Levellers, Gerrard Winstanley and the Diggers, the Magna Carta is a continuous reference point in their appeals to popular sovereignty and justice. It is used against the Crown by American colonies, and it functions as the rallying point for the abolition of slavery and other struggles of emancipation. But the Charter of the Forest is eventually dropped, forgotten or ignored. Linebaugh argues:

> Enclosures were not the only force in the creation of the land market but they destroyed the spiritual claim on the soil and prepared for the proletarianization of the common people, subjecting them to multifaceted labour discipline: the elimination of cakes and ale, the elimination of sports, the shunning of dance, the abolition of festivals, and the strict discipline over the male and female bodies.
> (Linebaugh, 2008, pp. 51–2)

When the Ten Hours Act was passed, Marx wrote in *Capital* that '[i]n place of the pompous catalogue of the "inalienable rights of man" comes the modest Magna Carta of a legally limited working day' (quoted in Linebaugh, 2008, p. 140). From the expropriation of forests in the Rhineland and the abolition of common rights to the struggles around the length of the working day, Marx saw a direct, if implicit, thread.

However, by Marx's time, the disjuncture between basic liberties and common rights, exemplified by the reduction of the Magna Carta to a single charter, was fixed in the theoretical imagination, perhaps even taken for granted (one exception, again, is Kropotkin, who believed that peasant resistance to the enclosures is key to any revolutionary effort). Still, for the most part, the Charter of the Forest enters the modern revolutionary imaginary insofar as it is a negative demand for the elimination of private ownership. In the hesitation to provide a positive programme of social relations, characteristic of most revolutionary discourse and radical philosophy, we can find the greatest evidence of the hegemonic power of the destruction of commoning.

For the tradition of commoning, then, the narrative of modernity is also one of crisis, but of a different nature than Arendt puts forth. Instead of the rise of the social and its invasion of the political, there is a progressive constriction of the social, by the juridical conception of the political based on rights and liberties, on the one hand, and by the commercial relations of private exchange in the market, on the other. These dual forces of the laws of the state and the laws of the market suffocate the shared lifeworlds of ordinary people, atomize individuals and 'set them free' from the land and its products that are shared in common; in short, they dwarf the legacy of commoning by granting a lopsided recognition of political rights (and the right of 'equal' exchange of labour and capital in the market) without the attendant rights to the forest. If the dream of an 'abundant table' thus becomes the 'dream of the poor and the destitute', as Arendt saw it, there is good reason: not only the forests, land and common tables, but also the social experience and collective dignity of the people have been forcibly taken away. The assault on the social is therefore a double dispossession, both material and political. As Linebaugh has expressed it so aptly, in the competition between two great systems of values or norms, namely, *commonwealth* and *commodity*, we know all too well which one has won (so far) (2008, p. 57).

If today we are to speak of an emancipatory, revolutionary politics, particularly in face of the new enclosures – the recent and recurrent attempts at expropriating the remaining planetary commons as part of the process of capitalist accumulation, and the increasing attacks on the 'communal control of the means of subsistence' (Midnight Notes Collective, 2001) – even a minimalist programme cannot afford to neglect the commons: subsistence and mutual aid, justice and fellowship are elements that we must seek in order to nourish, both literally and metaphorically, the new community. Today more than ever, we need to steer our theoretical and practical revolutionary efforts in the direction of commoning.[21] Linebaugh argues, and I agree, that 'communism consists of the generalization of [commoning] practices' (2010, p. 7). Elaborating the relationship between commons and communism, he posits the following:

In the 1840s, then, 'communism' was the new name to express the revolutionary aspirations of proletarians. It pointed to the future, as in 'historic tasks'. In contrast, the 'commons' belonged to the past, perhaps to the feudal era, when it was the last-ditch defence against extinction. Now in the 21st century the semantics of the two terms seems to be reversed with communism belonging to the past of Stalinism, industrialization of agriculture, and militarism, while the commons belongs to an international debate about the planetary future of land, water, and subsistence for all.

(Linebaugh, 2010, p. 15)

The revolutionary desires of the masses, expressed in commoning as a new political horizon, must include the nondeferrable transformation of individual subjectivities in the direction of egalitarian values, mutuality, friendship and care. If this transformation proceeds through the self-transformation of proletarians into *commoners*, it must be built upon the substantive transformation of everyday life in order to create lifeworlds in common. Commensality can figure in this project as a form of resistance against capitalism, atomization and the continuous autonomization of political relations from social rights. It can function as a bulwark against the individualization dictated in private and public life alike by (re)building relations of mutual affection, respect and support, strengthening communal ties and creating a critical consciousness of commoning as a practice and an ethic. If commensality is understood as a form of commoning, it can be viewed as a practice that allows us to take charge and organize our own lives according to principles that do not conform either to the production and reproduction of commodities or to an aestheticized, idealized public sphere that complements the commodity form. Commensality, therefore, should be claimed as one of the important building blocks of the programme of commoning.

OUR COMMON TABLE

Maurice Bloch argues, 'In all societies, sharing food is a way of establishing closeness, while, conversely, the refusal to share is one of the clearest marks of distance and enmity' (1999, p. 133). Eating and drinking together constitute the embodiment of closeness and friendship. Commensality fosters a sense of care for the other while it eliminates a sense of possessiveness and self-interested behaviour; it de-individualizes. It cultivates communicative and deliberative skills while also teaching fundamental civic values. It constructs a common ethic. It moulds subjectivities by counteracting hierarchy, lessening social distance and building solidarity out of the joint experience of sharing food.

Commensality builds amicable relations across gender, sexual, ethnic, religious and racial lines. It forges bonds that do not require either the sharing of the same identity or the lodging of identity on some fixed, innate foundation. Instead, it strengthens processes of identification on an everyday, practical, experiential basis that addresses both a basic biological and social need. It generates communal belonging without necessarily transforming that belonging into a rigid, ossified and exclusionary identity. The centring of processes of identification upon the basis of horizontal, common experience can therefore provide an important resource for opposing existing hierarchies and inequalities. Commensality also gives rise to opportunities of remembering, (re)learning and developing our skills in managing and keeping the commons. The practical, habitual, ideational and affective bonds formed by commensality, and the ethical principles of behaviour that emerge from the common table, may function as the necessary, ordinary basis for the constitution of communities on principles of justice.

Rethinking and reclaiming commensal practices may, therefore, prove to be fertile ground for the development of a new political imaginary for contemporary anarcho-communism. That they have not been fully appreciated in recent scholarship and largely forgotten in philosophy should not deter us from insisting on building our commensal practices as part of a political project of commoning. Of course, the practice of commensality is far from sufficient to achieve a new 'common condition' that effectively responds to the Arendtian 'human condition', but it is a step in that direction. It stands not only as an active critique of the fear of the social, but also acts as a social wellspring out of which new webs of human relationships can be weaved, relationships which do not reify different parts of our lives as private and public, as social and political, as mere animal life and human life. It suggests that the world of necessity can generate new spaces with emancipatory political potential, spaces in which freedom can be experienced in common.

Therefore, by insisting on commensality as an integral part of commoning, we are merely reclaiming the creative capacity that we engender in our everyday lives for politics and allowing ourselves the experience of the common. From the recurrent, monotonous, vanishing activity of nourishment, we feed no longer capital and law but our own solidarity. The utopian dream of a 'land flowing with milk and honey' that we harbour while sharing our meagre bread at the common table may yet be illusory, but it is much better, in any case, than eating alone.

ACKNOWLEDGEMENTS

This paper was presented as part of the 2011 Hannah Arendt-Reiner Schürmann Philosophy Symposium: The Anarchist Turn, at the New School for Social Research, New York City, May 5–6, 2011, and at the international conference on Re-thinking Marx: Philosophy, Critique, Practice, at Humboldt University, Berlin, May 20–22, 2011. I would like to thank Chiara Bottici, Simon Critchley, Jacob Blumenfeld, Daniel Loick and Rahel Jaeggi for their kind invitations. Many thanks to Pavlina Majarosova and Peter Galambos for their research assistance. I am grateful to Cinzia Arruzza, Jay Bernstein, Simon Critchley, Lisabeth During, Ross Poole and Massimiliano Tomba for thought-provoking questions and suggestions.

NOTES

1. Arendt (1998) calls all of those activities, which require skills, specialization and cooperation, and which create (or rather, fabricate) enduring objects for use, work. Work provides the artefacts upon which our common world of freedom is built, but itself is most at home in the market where products are exchanged, rather than in the public space or the household.

2. Labour, Arendt argues, is merely repetitive and does not create or produce anything enduring; the products of labour vanish with or soon after the act of labouring itself. It adds little or nothing to the value of materials that it works upon; the activities of the household are merely for consumption. Modelled after labour as in giving birth, it is painful and self-referential; even though it creates life, it 'remains imprisoned within its own metabolism' (Arendt, 1998, p. 115). Although there may be a 'certain happiness in painful exhaustion and pleasurable regeneration', namely the happiness of being alive, this is not ultimately a specifically human form of happiness but is shared with other living beings.

3. According to Vatter, Arendt reconciles life with politics through her concept of natality (2006, pp. 137–59).

4. Foucault, Agamben and Esposito bear prominent traces of Arendt's reading of the emergence of the social and its effects on the political. Even when they disagree, they are still in a sense responding to Arendt's arguments in *The Human Condition* (1998) and *The Origins*

of Totalitarianism (1968). See Foucault (2003), Agamben (1998) and Esposito (2008).

5   Canovan (1978), for example, indicts Arendt with 'demonstrating a haughty and distant contempt for the vulgarity of the modern world.' See also Kateb (1977).

6   For a more positive assessment of Arendt's political thought as carrying two contradictory tendencies, pulling her both toward elitism and democratic politics at the same time, see Canovan (1977). Levin gives the most positive assessment, arguing that *animal laborans* is not a sociological category corresponding to the labouring masses, but an analytical one describing a way of life, an attitude. See Levin (1979). For Canovan's response, see Canovan (1980).

7   For a sustained criticism of Arendt's elitism, see Brunkhorst (2000) and Pitkin (1981). For a more sympathetic view on the democratic credentials of Arendt's thought, see Isaac (1994), Habermas (1977) and Olson (1997).

8   In an alternative reading of *The Human Condition*, in comparison with the changes made by Arendt in the later German edition, Tsao (2002) emphasizes a greater critical distance in Arendt's relation with the ancient Greeks.

9   Rancière (1999) has persuasively critiqued Arendt's conception of the political from the alternative perspective of a politics that centres on contesting political exclusions.

10 In contrast to the interpretation that privileges the nostalgic tendency, Benhabib (1996) in her reconstructive effort emphasizes Arendt's 'reluctant modernism'.

11 See also Arendt (1990).

12 Here, I follow Marx's critique of the bourgeois democratic state. See Marx (1978).

13 Sobal and Nelson (2003) adopt the broad definition of eating with others.

14 Hirschman's contention takes inspiration from Simmel (1997), who was one of the first sociologists to point to how the common meal transforms self-interested behaviour of individuals into a communal experience with common purpose.

15 Anthropological evidence suggests that in societies where there is no strong state in the modern sense, commensality also constitutes a central practice that establishes a sense of continuity between the living and the dead, creates communal cohesion, and organizes a customary ethical code. Kazuhiko Yamamoto argues that in such societies, 'the ancestor-god, disguised as a stranger, sometimes visits the living to make communion with them. The living must offer shelter and hospitality to the guest-god. In return for the hospitality the guest-god gives the blessing to the hosts, whose magical power ensures the happiness and good health of the living' (1999, p. 223). The violation of commensality has enormous consequences, such as long-lasting blood-feuds, until the

breach of the social order is restored by the spilling of blood (usually the sacrificial killing of the frugal host), whereby the living appease the dead they have offended by the denial of commensality.

16 See, for example, the interpretation of the sharing of sacrificial meat in ancient Greece in Loraux (1981, pp. 614–22). This passage also gives a comprehensive account of the evolution of public meals from an exclusionary role toward a more democratic one.

17 Fourier (1972), for example, while allowing some commensal occasions for the whole phalanx, endorses separation of men, women and children, in both dining space and the types of food for most meals. Especially for the main meal, he argues for free and voluntary groupings, formed according to 'the wishes of attraction', with particular interest in intrigues and cabals.

18 Kropotkin (2006) presents an extensive discussion of commensal practices in the early clan and village community phases of social development across many different groups, as examples of mutual aid that militate against the Darwinian 'struggle for existence.' He reads the development of capitalism and the centralized modern state as the history of the decline of mutual aid institutions. Despite the continuous intrusions upon communal life, he finds that old-seated communal traditions, including common meals, still survive.

19 Also, Kautsky avers that for More, common meals were a 'partial means of emancipating woman from household labors' (partial because he mainly left intact both the patriarchal family and the economic and sexual relations of domination therein) in addition to a means of creating social cohesion. In contrast, the argument goes, modern socialism seeks the full liberation of women from household labour. See Kautsky (1979).

20 As Marx puts it: 'The so-called primitive accumulation, therefore, is nothing else than the historical process of divorcing the producer from the means of production. It appears as primitive, because it forms the prehistoric stage of capital and of the mode of production corresponding with it' (1976, p. 873).

21 For a critical literary analysis of the role enclosures have played in constituting modern spatiality and subjectivity, while representing imperial identity and anxieties (cultural, symbolic, and ontological) about the commons, see Marzec (2002, pp. 130–56).

REFERENCES

Agamben, G. (1998) *Homo Sacer: Sovereign power and bare life,* trans. D. Heller-Roazen. Stanford, Calif.: Stanford University Press.

Arendt, H. (1968) *The Origins of Totalitarianism,* rev. edn. San Diego, Calif.: Harcourt.

Arendt, H. (1990) *On Revolution.* London: Penguin.

Arendt, H. (1998) *The Human Condition*, 2nd edn. Chicago, Ill. and London: University of Chicago Press.

Babeuf, G. (1796) 'Manifesto of the equals', in *The Conspiracy of Equals*, trans. Mitchell Abidor, available at: http://www.marxists.org/

Bataille, G. (1991) *The Accursed Share*, Vol. 1. New York: Zone.

Benhabib, S. (1996) *The Reluctant Modernism of Hannah Arendt*. London and Beverly Hills, Calif.: Sage.

Bloch, M. (1999) 'Commensality and poisoning', *Social Research*, 6(61).

Bray, T. (ed.) (2003) *Archaeology and Politics of Food and Feasting in Early States and Empires*. New York: Kluwer Academic/Plenum.

Brunkhorst, H. (2000) 'Equality and elitism in Arendt', in D. Villa (ed.), *The Cambridge Companion to Hannah Arendt*. New York: Cambridge University Press.

Canovan, M. (1978) 'The contradictions of Hannah Arendt's political thought', *Political Theory*, 6(1).

Canovan, M. (1980) 'On Levin's "Animal Laborans and Homo Politicus in Hannah Arendt"', *Political Theory*, 8(3).

Canovan, M. (1994) 'Politics as culture: Hannah Arendt and the public realm', in L. Hinchman and S. K. Hinchman (eds), *Hannah Arendt: Critical essays*. Albany, N.Y.: State University of New York Press.

Dietler, M. and Hayden, B. (eds) (2001) *Feasts: Archaeological and ethnographic perspectives on food, politics, and power*. Washington DC: Smithsonian Institution Press.

Esposito, R. (2008) *Bíos: Biopolitics and philosophy*, trans. T. Campbell. Minneapolis, Minn. and London: University of Minnesota Press.

Fischler, C. (2011) 'Commensality, society and culture', *Social Science Information*, 50(3–4).

Foucault, M. (2003) *Society Must be Defended: Lectures at the Collège de France 1975–1976*, trans. D. Macey. New York: Picador.

Fourier, C. (1972) *The Utopian Vision of Charles Fourier: Selected texts on work, love, and passionate attraction*, ed. J. Beecher and R. Bienvenu. Boston, Mass.: Beacon Press.

Gowers, E. (1993) *The Loaded Table: Representations of food in Roman literature*. Oxford: Clarendon Press.

Grignon, C. (2001) 'Commensality and social morphology: an essay on typology', in P. Scholliers (ed.), *Food, Drink, and Identity: Cooking, eating and drinking in Europe since the Middle Ages*. Oxford and New York: Berg.

Habermas, J. (1977) 'Hannah Arendt's communications concept of power', *Social Research*, 4(4).

Hirschman, A. (1996) 'Melding the public and private spheres: taking commensality seriously', *Critical Review*, 10(4).

Hodkinson, S. (1997) 'The development of Spartan society and institutions in the archaic period', in L. Mitchel and P. J. Rhodes (eds), *The Development of the Polis in Archaic Greece*. London and New York: Routledge.

Isaac, J. (1994) 'Oases in the desert: Hannah Arendt on democratic politics', *American Political Science Review,* 88(1).

Kateb, G. (1977) 'Freedom and worldliness in the thought of Hannah Arendt', *Political Theory,* 5(2).

Kautsky, K. (1979) *Thomas More and his Utopia,* trans. H. Stenning. London: Lawrence & Wishart. www.marxists.org/archive/kautsky/1888/more/index.htm (accessed September 3, 2012).

Kropotkin, P. (2006) *Mutual Aid: A factor of evolution.* Mineola, N.Y.: Dover.

Levin, M. (1979) 'On animal laborans and homo politicus in Hannah Arendt: a note', *Political Theory,* 7(4).

Linebaugh, P. (2008) *The Magna Carta Manifesto: Liberties and commons for all.* Los Angeles, Calif. and London: University of California Press.

Linebaugh, P. (2010) 'Meandering on the semantical-historical paths of communism and commons', *The Commoner,* December. Available at www.commoner.org.uk.

Loraux, N. (1981) 'La Cité comme cuisine et comme partage', *Annales-ESC,* 36(4).

Marx, K. (1976) *Capital: A critique of political economy,* Vol. 1, trans. B. Fowkes. London: Penguin.

Marx, K. (1978) 'On the Jewish question', in R. Tucker (ed.), *The Marx–Engels Reader.* New York: W. W. Norton.

Marzec, R. (2002) 'Enclosures, colonization, and the Robinson Crusoe syndrome: a genealogy of land in a global context', *Boundary 2,* 29(2).

Matheron, F. (2008) 'Louis Althusser, or the impure purity of the concept', in J. Bidet and S. Kouvelakis (eds), *Critical Companion to Contemporary Marxism.* Leiden and Boston, Mass.: Brill.

Mauss, M. (2000) *The Gift: Forms and functions of exchange in archaic societies.* New York and London: W. W. Norton.

Midnight Notes Collective (2001), 'The new enclosures', *The Commoner,* 2(4). Available at: www.thecommoner.org.

More, T. (2003) *Utopia,* ed. P. Turner. London: Penguin.

Murray, O. (1995) 'Forms of sociality', in J. P. Vernant (ed.), *The Greeks,* trans. C. Lambert and T. L. Fagan. Chicago, Ill. and London: University of Chicago Press.

Olson, J. (1997) 'The revolutionary spirit: Hannah Arendt and the anarchists of the Spanish civil war', *Polity,* 29(4).

Plato. (2004) *Republic,* trans. C. D. C. Reeve. Indianapolis, Ind.: Hackett.

Pitkin, H. (1981) 'Justice: On relating public and private', *Political Theory,* 9(3).

Rancière, J. (1999) *Disagreement: Politics and philosophy.* Minneapolis, Minn.: University of Minnesota Press.

Rosser, G. (1994) 'Going to the fraternity feast: commensality and social relations in late medieval England', *Journal of British Studies,* 33(4), special issue: Vill, Guild, and Gentry: Forces of community in later Medieval England.

Scheid, J. (1984) 'La spartizione a Roma', *Studi Storici*, 25(4).

Scheid, J. (1985) 'Sacrifice et banquet à Rome: quelques problèmes, Mélanges de l'Ecole française de Rome', *Antiquité*, 97(1).

Schmitt Pantel, P. (1992) *La Cité au banquet: histoire des repas publics dans les cités grecques*. Rome: Collection École Français de Rome.

Simmel, G. (1997) 'The sociology of the meal', in D. Frisby and M. Featherstone (eds), *Simmel on Culture: Selected writings*. London: Sage.

Sitton, J. (1987) 'Hannah Arendt's argument for council democracy', *Polity*, 20(1).

Sobal J. and Nelson, M. (2003) 'Commensal eating patterns: a community study', *Appetite*, 41(2).

Tsao, R. (2002) 'Arendt against Athens: rereading the human condition', *Political Theory*, 30(1).

Vatter, M. (2006) 'Natality and biopolitics in Hannah Arendt', *Revista de Ciencia Política*, 26(2).

Wolin, S. (1983) 'Hannah Arendt: democracy and the political', *Salmagundi*, 60.

Yamamoto, K. (1999) 'The origin of ethics and social order in a society without state power', *Collegium Antropologicum*, 23(1).

3

FRIENDSHIP AS RESISTANCE

Todd May

There is in philosophy a long but thin history of reflection on friendship. For some of the ancients, like Aristotle, friendship is tied to politics. With more modern writers like Montaigne, Kant and Emerson, however, friendship becomes caught in the web of the public/private distinction. Where politics lies on the public side, friendship is a private relationship. Between the two is a divide that cannot be crossed theoretically or, presumably, interpersonally.

Recently, there have been several writings that seek to bring friendship back into dialogue with politics. In philosophy, one of the most well known of these is Jacques Derrida's *Politics of Friendship* (1997). In sociology, the question of individual isolation and connection in its relationship with public space has been pressing, particularly since the 1995 publication of Robert Putnam's *Bowling Alone* (2000). Few of these recent writings, however, have raised the issue of the relationship between friendship and political resistance. It was suggested in a late interview with Michel Foucault entitled 'Friendship as a way of life' (1989). There, Foucault contrasted a more reassuring view of homosexuality as a purely sexual affair with another view, one that is more troubling for contemporary social arrangements. He noted that the more reassuring view 'annuls everything that can be uncomfortable in affection, tenderness, friendship, fidelity, camaraderie and companionship, things which our rather sanitized society can't allow a place for without fearing the formation of new alliances and the tying together of unforeseen lines of force' (1989, p. 205). Foucault suggests here that homosexual relationships, in part because they can involve affections that are not able to be monitored or channelled by the policing of contemporary social relationships, are threatening to the social order.

Foucault's suggestion is one that deserves to be pursued, even more so, as I will argue, in a period of neoliberalism. However, its pursuit is not limited to homosexual friendship. So, while Foucault's suggestion about friendship as resistance is one theoretical source of this chapter, another theoretical source lies in the thought of Jacques Rancière. Although a longer explanation of the role of this source will emerge later in the discussion, let me gloss it quickly at the outset. For Rancière, a true democratic politics is one that emerges from the presupposition of the equality of anyone and everyone. Such a presupposition runs counter to prevailing social arrangements, indeed to almost any social arrangements in human history. Rancière does not detail the internal character or texture of such democratic movements, except to note that they are based on a certain trust. He writes, 'The test of democracy must ever be in democracy's own image: versatile, sporadic – and founded on trust' (1995, p. 61).

The final motivation for this chapter comes from my classes in philosophy, and specifically my classes in Marxist and anarchist theory. Often, my students find the arguments of these philosophers at least interesting and sometimes compelling. But they offer a common complaint: Marxism and anarchism are unrealistic. People would never cooperate in the way these views require of them. Marxism and anarchism are, in the end, naïve. In response, I have often resorted to the example of friendship. I tell them that we think of ourselves and our friends as more or less equals, we would never seriously consider exploiting our friends, and we do not generally see our friendships – at least the best among them – as subject to the economy of credit and debt. Moreover, our friendships are among the most meaningful aspects of our lives. Why, then, I ask them, is it thought that we cannot take the form of the most significant of our relationships and extend them into the political and economic arenas?

These three sources converge on the idea that friendship, at least some types of friendship, might have a political impact. It is that idea I want to develop here. Before embarking on it, though, let me say a little bit about what I do not want to do. I do not want to claim that all friendships are politically resistant. I would prefer that people not say to themselves at the end of this chapter: 'I can be a revolutionary, let me just go and make a new friend.' In academics, there is much posturing that believes itself to pass for political resistance. My goal here is not to add an item to that particular inventory.

Nor do I want to isolate the essence of friendship itself. I will use a definition of friendship, one postulated by Elizabeth Telfer. Moreover, I will offer intersections of my discussion with that of some classic views of friendship, for example, that of Aristotle. But I am not interested here in the particular character of friendship itself. As Liz Spencer and Ray Pahl have sought to show (contra Putnam's argument in *Bowling Alone* that people have become increasingly disconnected from one another), there are a variety of types of relationships, both formal and informal, in contemporary society, and many of them are considered by their participants to be forms of friendship. 'The more we explore in detail the range and quality of people's actual rather than imputed social relationships, the more the intricacy of their micro-social worlds – and the hidden solidarities they contain – are revealed' (Spencer and Ray, 2006, p. 191), What I am interested in instead is the political possibilities of some types of friendships. Moreover, I am interested in them not as a matter of political resistance generally, but as a matter of political resistance to a particular dominant strain of our social, political and economic culture, one that I will call neoliberalism.

I shall proceed in three stages. First, I discuss the character of neoliberalism, particularly as it appears to frame our social relationships. There I make a distinction that often goes missing in discussions of neoliberalism. Second, I briefly canvass the character of friendship, and look to isolate elements of friendship that resist the way in which neoliberalism frames social relationships. Finally, I try to suggest why a certain type of friendship has political implications. That will bring the discussion back to Foucault and Rancière, but I hope with more detail than they offer in their gestures in this direction.

Neoliberalism is as much a movement as an economic view. Considered as the latter, it might be characterized as the view that endorses more or less unrestricted capitalism and open markets as the best economic system, not only nationally but also internationally. David Harvey defines it as

a theory of political economic practices that proposes that human well-being can best be advanced by liberating individual entrepreneurial freedoms and skills within an institutional framework characterized by strong private property rights, free markets, and free trade.

(Harvey, 2005, p. 2)

Considered as a movement, neoliberalism involves a particular set of interventions into various national markets. In particular, supported by the World Bank and especially the International Monetary Fund, it seeks, or has until recently, to promote deregulation, privatization and the withdrawal of the public sector from social services.

There are any number of discussions we might have about the origins, purposes and effects of neoliberalism. I would like here to concentrate on a particular aspect of its operation: the kind of individuals or subjects neoliberalism creates. In other words, recognizing that individuals are formed in particular social, economic and political circumstances, I would like to focus on what kinds of individuals are created in a context dominated by neoliberalism. It is at this level, the formation of individuals in neoliberalism, that I see friendship offering the possibility of political resistance.

In particular, there are two types of individuals, or better, two types of personal formations or figures, that are the product of neoliberalism. We might designate them as the consumer and the entrepreneur. These two have been confused, but if we are to understand neoliberal subject formation correctly, it is worth keeping them distinct. The first, the consumer, has been discussed in depth by many thinkers, for instance Benjamin Barber (2008), Zygmunt Bauman (2007), and from a slightly different angle, Jean Baudrillard. It is probably the figure we are most familiar with. The second, the entrepreneur, emerges in Michel Foucault's late lectures, *The Birth of Biopolitics* (2004). This figure is distinct from, but not contradictory to, the consumer. In fact many of us, inasmuch as we are products of neoliberalism, are some combination or intersection of the two.

The consumer is perhaps best summed up by the phrase, 'I shop, therefore I am.' These are the people who define themselves by what they own or by the activity of purchasing. As Baudrillard has emphasized in his critique of Marx and Marxism, many of us no longer define ourselves as producers (1975: 9–10).[1] We do not ground our identity in what we create, but rather in what we own or buy. We identify ourselves as consumers. This identification was characterized at the turn of the twentieth century by Thorstein Veblen, but has become more central to our culture over the past several decades. This idea has been summed up by Bauman:

> The 'society of consumers'… stands for the kind of society that promotes, encourages or enforces the choice of a consumerist lifestyle and life strategy and dislikes all alternative cultural options; a society in which adapting to the precepts of consumer culture and following them strictly is … a condition of membership.
>
> (Bauman, 2007, p. 53)

The entrepreneur is the figure Foucault defines as *homo oeconomicus*. Foucault writes, in contrast to the consumer view of neoliberalism, 'Not a society of the supermarket – a society of enterprise. *Homo oeconomicus*... is not the man of exchange, he is not the consuming man, he is the man of enterprise and of production' (2004, p. 152). The entrepreneur is the investor, the figure that seeks to place their resources where they will yield the best return. In his lectures, Foucault refers to the American neoliberal Gary Becker, who saw the entrepreneurial figure as a standard for all aspects of personal life and not just economic involvements. Parenthood, for instance, involves an investment of resources in the creation of an individual. That investment requires particular genetic resources – thus the importance of finding a genetically appropriate spouse – the investment of money in day care, school, after-school activities and the investment of time in one or another aspect of a child's life. All this must be balanced against the other investments people have in their other children, their career and so on, in order to assess an overall yield for a parental life.

Neither of these two figures, the consumer or the entrepreneur, are exclusive to neoliberalism. They both appear well before its emergence in the late 1970s and 1980s. What is new about these figures is not their existence but rather their depth in structuring who we are. It would be hard to argue, for instance, that earlier in the last century people saw themselves primarily as either consumers or entrepreneurs. The amount of consumer goods was still too limited and their scope too narrow for the former, and the dominance of industrial production over finance would hinder the development of a self-identity as the latter. People's sense of themselves lay more in their role as producers, a role that intersects with, among other figures, Foucault's analysis of the normalized individual in *Discipline and Punish* (1995), although a full discussion of that would take us too far afield of our current concerns (Pahl, 2000, p. 55).[2]

What has emerged over the past 30 or 40 years is a pair of figures that, we might say, lie on the near and far side of production. On the near side, the entrepreneur invests without yet producing. On the far side, the consumer partakes without having had to produce. These are figures that, I would argue, are not outside of us. They define large swaths of who many of us are. We invest our time and energies in our careers and with certain colleagues in those careers, hoping for a return. We place our personal resources, when we are 'rational actors', in the activities that are most likely to offer the greatest yield. Our competition with others does not so much concern what one or another of us has made or accomplished, but who has had the best return on what has been invested. On the other side of things, our model for noninvested life is consumption. We watch others perform their lives for us on plasma screen televisions while eating foreign take-out food and sipping beer from the newest and smallest microbrewery. And at those moments, when the picture is sharp, the food just so and the beer cold, life is what it is meant to be.

There is, perhaps, no more starkly revealing place to see these figures in operation than in our relationships with others. Our professional relationships are marked by the question of how to position ourselves relative to those who can do us some good. Our sexual relationships are marked by the consumption of pleasure, as displayed by the phenomenon of 'hooking up'. Even many of our friendships are given a silent accounting: who has done what for whom, and when. It is not that these types of relationships have never happened before. Nor is it that they are entirely bad things. Sex for pleasure rather than simple procreation is surely a social advance. Rather, the point is twofold. First, these relationships are currently framed by two particular neoliberal orientations, that of investment and that of consumption. And inasmuch as we embody these orientations, we become the figures of neoliberalism. Second, and related, to the extent that we embody these figures, we become not only the products but also the conduits of neoliberalism. There have always been connivers and pleasure-seekers. What neoliberalism has brought us are entrepreneurs and consumers, not only in our economic lives but also in our lives in general.

The suggestion I want to make here is that there are modes of friendship that can serve as forms of resistance to the two figures of neoliberalism. Otherwise put, there are friendships that can cut against what neoliberalism is making of us. I can only gesture at the idea here, but its importance lies in this: that inasmuch as neoliberalism infiltrates our lives to make of us figures that in turn reinforce its grip, we can use those lives to resist that infiltration and thus create alternatives to whom we are being asked to be. And that, I take it, is the contemporary force of Foucault's claim that society fears friendship as a way of life.

We might begin by asking what is referred to in the idea of friendship. What is a friendship, and how does it differ from other forms of social relationship? For the goals of this chapter, the distinction between friendship and other types of relationship is not crucial, since what I am after is a particular type of friendship, or perhaps better, particular themes within friendships. However, an initial definition will help point us on our way. I take this definition from Elizabeth Telfer's classic 1970 article entitled, simply, 'Friendship' (reprinted 1991). She writes that, 'there are three necessary conditions for friendship: shared activities, the passions of friendship, and acknowledgement of the fulfilment of the first two conditions' (1991, p. 257). The first condition, that of shared activities, recalls of course Aristotle's view that friends share their lives. This seems a fairly obvious criterion of friendship. It is hard to imagine using the term friendship among those who are not engaged in any kind of shared activities. One question that is worth reflecting on, although wide of the purpose of this chapter, is whether contiguity in time and space is also necessary for a shared activity to ground friendship. In other words, can friendship be had solely or mostly along virtual lines? It is not a question that Telfer faced, but it is, I believe, a pressing question for us.

The second condition for friendship, the passions of friendship, involves what Telfer calls an affection for the friend. More than that, however, she adds that affection is not necessarily rooted in the particular character of the friend. In other words, it is not the qualities of a friend that are the object of passion in the affection of friendship, but the friend in person. She adds, not disapprovingly, that, 'Affection is in this sense *irrational*, and because of this may survive radical changes in the character of its object. Thus we often continue to be fond of someone when we no longer like or respect him, and such a situation is not considered in any way odd' (Telfer, 1991, p. 252). We shall return to this 'irrationality' momentarily, but should note in passing that, as Telfer argues, it goes against the Aristotelian idea that true friendships can only be had among good people.

The final condition of friendship is an acknowledgement of these first two conditions. That is, friendship does not simply involve a sharing and a passion, but some recognition that these are in place. Another term she uses for this acknowledgement is commitment. A friendship is not based on the happenstance of sharing and passion, one that seems no more than a stroke of good luck. Rather, it also involves what we might call a tending to, in the sense that people tend to their garden. There is an awareness of the special relationship a friendship involves, one that calls one person towards the other as a matter not simply of passion or affection but also of cognitive commitment.

What Telfer has done is to isolate, among our personal relationships, a set that involves more than passing acquaintanceship or professional engagement. However, there is something else suggested in her view of friendship, something that may not, strictly speaking, be entailed by her definition but would likely be a characteristic that would be hard to exclude from most relationships that meet her criteria. We may begin to isolate this characteristic by calling it other-regarding. That is to say, friendships, at least the ones most of us admire, to one degree or another seek the good of the other for the sake of the other, and not simply for the friend's own sake. This characteristic of friendship is one that Aristotle uses to distinguish true friendships from friendships of pleasure or of utility. It is also found in other accounts of friendship, for instance when Cicero writes, 'we do not exercise kindness and generosity in order that we may put in a claim for gratitude; we do not make our feelings of affection into a business proposition. No, there is something in our nature that impels us to open hand and heart' (1991, p. 90). In some friendships there may be an orientation toward the friend that, we might say, pulls us off the centre of ourselves, allowing us to expend ourselves (if I may be excused for the reference to Bataille here) on behalf of the friend.

It is not the decency or the nobility of this aspect of some friendships that interests me. Rather, it is its non-economic character (and thus the reference to Bataille). There are things people do in the contexts of certain kinds of friendship that are done without calculation. They are done because they are called for, or because they are unexpected, or because they would be useful to the friend. We all know of actions like these, and of the contexts in which they occur. They are the compliments paid to a friend because they are momentarily vulnerable, the rides given because the friend's car is in the repair shop or the friend is drunk or because you are going that way anyway and it would be just as easy. They are the hospital visits, the childcare, the expertise shared, or the spontaneous gifts.

These activities cut against the figures of neoliberalism. They are not simply investments, performed with an eye to the return they will yield. And they are not simply enjoyments to be consumed. People might indeed enjoy doing them because they are for the friend. But this is not the same thing as the consumptive enjoyment promised by neoliberalism. It is a joy that arises from the knowledge of how it will affect the other rather than solely how it feels to yourself. And this, I want to suggest, is one of the things that can make friendship threatening to the neoliberal order. It provides a model of relationships that cannot be subsumed under neoliberalism. It shows us that, in the words of contemporary activists, another world is possible. And it does so not only by envisioning another world, but also by pointing to its existence, already encrusted within this one. We can imagine what a world not dominated by the figures of neoliberalism would look like, because its seeds already exist in some of the most significant relationships we have with others among us.

Now it might be objected that such a relationship cannot exist. In fact, Jacques Derrida has done so. There is no such thing, in his view, as a giving that lies beyond the economy of investment and return

> At the limit, the gift as gift ought not appear as a gift: either to the donee or to the donor. It cannot be gift as gift except by not being present as gift .... The temporalization of time ... always sets in motion the process of a destruction of the gift: through keeping, restitution, reproduction, the anticipatory expectation or apprehension that grasps or comprehends in advance.
>
> (Derrida, 1992, p. 14)

The problem of placing the gift outside of all economies, Derrida claims, is that it cannot be given without the knowledge that it is given, which brings with it the expectation of gratitude or return, in the recipient if not in the donor.

I believe that, in casting the matter this way, Derrida removes the gift from the context of friendship within which it arises. Thought of outside the context of a friendship, a gift, whether physical or of some other kind – a giving or an offering to another – may seem to be caught within an economy of investment and return. However, in the parameters of certain kinds of friendships this kind of giving can come to make sense. Friendship cannot develop an interpersonal realm in which the economy of gift and return begins to lose its grip. My claim here is not that such friendships have nothing of the economic within them. If one person always gives and the other always receives, this puts a strain on the character of the friendship, at least as friendship. However, there is a difference between thinking that a friend will look after you because that person is your friend, and giving to the friend in a particular circumstance because that will foster the friend's looking after you. And from the other side, the gratitude people feel in receiving a friend's gift need not be the payment of a debt. It can, instead, be the joy in inhabiting a relationship that is not reducible to an economy of debts.

The inhabiting of this kind of relationship, although it is not a repayment of debts, is, perhaps ironically, rooted more in the past than in relationships stemming from the figures of neoliberalism. This is not to say that all three temporal modes are not involved in any or all of these relationships. The claim is more specific. There is a certain way in which the consumer privileges the present and the investor the future, while a friendship is rooted in the past, and in the way it is rooted resists the economism of neoliberalism.

The consumerist privileging of the present is not difficult to grasp. Pleasure is a matter of current enjoyment. It is not so concerned with what has happened or with what is going to happen. To have pleasure is to be in the moment in a particular way. For consumers, that particular way of being in the present is rarely one of active engagement. Consumption is a matter of receiving pleasure, of incorporating it, taking it in. You reach out, of course, in order to obtain that pleasure, but the reaching out generally comes in the form of payment rather than active participation, production or creation. The pleasure for which you reach, however, is of the present moment. As Eastern thinkers would have it, you live in the now. However, in contrast to Eastern philosophies, that living rests not upon the shedding of temporal fetters but precisely on the most passing of those fetters. Or, if we think of things from the opposite direction, the pleasure we obtain is only momentary, so we must move from pleasure to pleasure. As Bauman argues, 'Satisfaction must be only a momentary experience, something to be feared rather than coveted if it lasts too long' (2007, p. 98).

The investor's relation to the future is also straightforward. People invest for the sake of future return. To be sure, they envision a present in which the return will be had. But, inasmuch as someone is an investor, that present never arrives. The return that comes to them in the present is either turned into consumption (in which case they have tilted, however momentarily, into the other figure), or else is capital of one form or another to be further invested for the sake of future return.

Friendship certainly enjoys the present and envisions a future. But friendships of the type we are discussing here are often founded on a rich past. Here is where my reply to Derrida is rooted. If Derrida misses the context of friendship in his argument of the necessity for an economy of the gift, that context is largely framed by a past. Recall Telfer's first condition of friendship, shared activities. When a person begins to share activities with another, we would generally be reluctant to call the relationship with that other a friendship. There could be a spark there, as when two people recognize mutual interests, or enthusiasms, or a common way of seeing things. However the friendship itself develops over time. It is a temporal thickness of shared activity that creates a friendship. In contrast to Derrida's view of the economy of the gift, what that temporal thickness does is not so much create a balance sheet of debts, as erase or at least efface the very idea of a balance sheet. It is not difficult to see why. As friendships develop, their participants are often doing one thing or another for the friend in the midst of their shared activities. This doing for one another over time and in the context of shared activities creates a bond, what Telfer calls a passion, that draws the friends to do things for each other, as Aristotle would have it, for the sake of the other. This passion and this doing are sometimes described as an effacing of the borders between the friends. It is often better characterized, I believe, as an effacing of the economy of debts that drives so many other relationships. Sharing a common bond rooted in temporal thickness, friendship does not so much do away with the general borders between individuals as with the specific borders erected by economistic self-understandings.

If this articulation of the possibilities of friendship is right, we may understand Foucault's point about friendship as a way of life as threatening the social order by offering ways to form new alliances and lines of force. These new alliances and lines of force consist in meaningful ways of conducting our lives with one another that resist the reduction to the figures of neoliberalism. They resist the economy of investment and return and the translation of relationships into forms of consumption. This, in itself, offers a vision of social interaction beyond the confines of the neoliberal order, one that is inimical to it precisely because it characterizes some of our most significant relationships. We can, I believe, go a step further in this direction. This next step would lead us from Foucault's suggestion to Rancière's politics. The suggestion I want to make here is that a theme of the kind of friendship I have isolated here may also be a contributant to an egalitarian politics. It is what might be meant by the term 'trust' (the French is *confiance*) we saw in the citation from Rancière at the outset.

Kant writes that, 'The relationship of friendship is a relation of equality. A friend who bears my losses becomes my benefactor and puts me in his debt. I feel shy in his presence and cannot look him boldly in the face. The true relationship of friendship is cancelled and friendship ceases' (1991, pp. 213–14). Kant's argument here is that friendship requires a delicate balance between how much is asked and offered from one friend to another, a point we discussed a moment ago. However, there is another way to take this citation.

Friendships, at least those characterized by the theme we are discussing here, are relations of equality. We might amend Kant by saying that they are relations of equality not simply because of the general balance of giving and receiving but also, and more deeply, because in many cases that balance does not even come into play. That is to say, we look at our friends as our equals, not because they are equal in measure to us but because equality of this type is, to a certain extent, beyond measure. The equality here is an equality of two or more people who take one another not as equals in this or that characteristic but, we might say, as equals, period.

This equality is, in Rancière's view, the basis for a democratic politics. 'Political activity', he writes, 'is always a mode of expression that undoes the perceptible divisions of the police order by implementing a basically heterogeneous assumption ... the equality of any speaking being with any other speaking being' (1999, p. 30). What the assumption of equality accomplishes is to challenge the hierarchical order, what Rancière calls the police order, of most social arrangements. To act democratically is to act collectively on the presupposition of the equality of anyone and everyone. To do so, as the citation we saw earlier notes, is to act with a sort of collective trust. The suggestion I want to make here is that modes of friendship that resist the figures of neoliberalism offer, in some of their elements, both models of and routes toward such a democratic politics.

Rancière claims that 'The essence of equality is in fact not so much to unify as to declassify, to undo the supposed naturalness of orders and replace it with the controversial figures of division' (1995, pp. 32–3). The supposedly natural figures of the neoliberal order are the entrepreneur and the consumer. In taking a friendship as without measure in the way we have described, in seeing friends as those whose own stakes are importantly our stakes, in resisting the reduction of social relationships to pleasures or investments, what emerges is precisely a declassification in Rancière's sense. It is not in the name of something else, unless we want to call that something else either equality or perhaps friendship itself, that the figures of neoliberalism are challenged. It is, instead, for a type of relationship without hierarchy, or with as little hierarchy as our age permits.

Moreover, as Marilyn Friedman points out, the fact that friendship is a 'voluntary choice' allows it to act as an egalitarian type of relationship that cuts across the traditional structures of a police order and allows alternative and disruptive communities to form. She notes that 'Because of its basis in voluntary choice, friendship is more likely than many other relationships, such as those of family and neighbourhood, to be grounded and sustained by shared interests and values, mutual affection, and possibilities for generating reciprocal respect and esteem', adding that 'friendship, more so than many other relationships, can provide social support for people who are idiosyncratic, whose unconventional values and deviant lifestyles make them victims of intolerance from family members and others who are involuntarily related to them' (1993, p. 298). This, she points out, is essential to feminist formations of solidarity, which face steep and often violent resistance to their challenges to traditional sex and gender roles.

We might want to argue here, against Friedman's last point, that it is one of the virtues of neoliberalism that it has undermined traditional gender roles, equalizing everyone in the face of globalized market exchange. This argument, however, would be wrong on two counts. First, women, particularly in less technologically advanced countries, have not so much been liberated from traditional gender roles as shifted from one set of oppressive roles to another. For instance, in many of the export processing zones developed by transnational corporations, women are drawn into exploitative work whose effects are little more than to trade in being at the bottom of a traditional social ladder for being at the bottom of the neoliberal one. David Harvey notes that:

> Accumulation by dispossession typically undermines whatever powers women may have had within traditional household production/marketing systems and within traditional social structures and markets. The paths of women's liberation from traditional patriarchal controls in developing countries lie either through degrading factory labour or through trading on sexuality.
> (Harvey, 2005, p. 170)[3]

Second, the promised equality is not the kind of equality that Friedman thinks of as the basis of feminist emancipation. What she calls 'idiosyncratic' or 'deviant' lifestyles do not consist in buying Goth clothes at Hot Topic. They are, instead, experiments in different forms of non-exploitative personal relationships; as Foucault would have it, friendship as a way of life.

All of this is what allows certain aspects of friendship of this type to be both a model for and a route into a democratic politics. They are a model for such politics because they show what it can look like. Friendship can give a picture of solidarity, which is no mean feat in an era of the individualism characteristic of both consumerism and entrepreneurship. Moreover, it also offers a route toward such a politics. Friendship can be a movement of solidarity. It presupposes the equality of its participants, and thus trains those participants in the mode of political solidarity required by democratic movements. Friendship can provide a know-how that is the ground for progressive political solidarity. By cutting against the figures of neoliberalism, it cultivates an alternative form of social interaction that is the requirement of any movement that would effectively counter neoliberal domination.

This cultivation is a necessary element of building an alternative set of social relationships. In a recent article entitled 'Fetishizing process' (2005), Mark Lance intervenes in the traditional debate among anarchists, regarding whether voting or consensus respects the equality of participants, by arguing that the focus on process misses the significance of the training and self-training of those participants. Lance's claim is that we often expect to design processes that will guarantee respect for persons when in fact the processes themselves only work when that respect has been instilled. 'An anti-authoritarian democratic organization must not understand itself as defined by a set of formal procedures. Rules can be used, as tools of a virtuous community with a largely functional practice, but they should be no more than tools' (Lance, 2005). Although he does not refer to the figures of neoliberalism, we can see why cultivation of the 'virtues' of respect for and solidarity with others is particularly urgent in light of how we are being moulded by current social, economic and political forces.

And cultivation is not all. Friendship is also motivating. Friendships, after all, are among the most rewarding of our social relationships. We would often like other of our relationships with others to share certain characteristics of friendship. Not that we can consider all our social relationships to be friendships: that would require too much commitment to too many people. However, most of us would find it a better world in which we could trust one another a little more, feel a little less in competition with one another, and feel less a means to others' ends. By modelling such relationships, friendship can not only offer the preparation for political solidarity; it can not only show us, in the intimacy of our particular worlds, what a better world looks like; it can also motivate us to achieve such a world.

I would like to close with two objections, both of which can be drawn from Derrida's *Politics of Friendship*. The first objection concerns how far the net of friendship can spread. The second one, following from the first, seeks to question the coherence of the concept of friendship itself. As for the first, Derrida notes that there is a tension between friendship and a democratic politics in that friendship can only extend to a limited number of people:

> it is not possible to love while one is simultaneously, at the same time (*áma*), the friend of numerous others (*to de pollois áma einai phílon kai to phileîn kolúei*); the numerous ones, the numerous others – this means neither number nor multiplicity in general but too great a number.
>
> (Derrida, 1997, p. 21)

Friendship requires spending time and expending emotion on those one befriends; it is impossible to engage in this level of interpersonal concentration with numerous people, especially in the kinds of friendship we have sketched here. For a friendship to move beyond the parameters set by the figures of neoliberalism there needs to be a level of involvement that precludes the possibility of drawing the circle of your friends very wide. As a result, we might see friendship not, as we have suggested here, as a support for an egalitarian politics, but rather in tension with it. There must of necessity be an inside and an outside, the inside including those we have been able to construct friendships with and the outside consisting in everyone else. It would seem difficult to build an egalitarian politics on such a basis.

If what were required of an egalitarian politics were that everyone in it became friends, friendship would indeed be an unpromising basis for politics. What I have argued, however, is not that everyone in a political movement must become friends, but rather that friendship offers several tools, perhaps essential tools, for forming egalitarian political movements. In particular, I have claimed three political virtues for friendship: it offers a model of egalitarian relationships that resist the figures of neoliberalism, it trains people in such egalitarian interaction, and it motivates people to have healthier egalitarian interaction with others. These virtues can be prized apart from friendship, either individually or collectively, and utilized in relationships that are not themselves friendships. It is possible to interact with others without thinking of them as either investments or objects of consumption and yet without developing friendships with them. It is possible to learn to consider others as equals without holding them to be friends. And it is possible to maintain that consideration without it ever turning into friendship. Moreover, all of this can be done with numerous others. It does not require the time and emotional engagement characteristic of a meaningful friendship. What it does require is a commitment to move beyond the parameters of interpersonal interaction that neoliberalism has prescribed for us.

More deeply than the question of numbers, however, Derrida argues that the friend/enemy distinction itself is one that has porous borders, friend becoming enemy and enemy becoming friend, or better, friendship becoming enmity and enmity becoming friendship. 'The two concepts (friend/enemy) consequently intersect and ceaselessly change places' (Derrida, 1997, p. 72). However, as with all Derridean deconstructions, while the terms pass into each other they are not entirely effaced. If this is true, then the use of friendship to ground the equality of anyone and everyone is a project doomed to failure. There will always be others, even intimate others, who are outside the thematic of friendship we have canvassed here, and thus beyond the capacity to be treated entirely as equals, as Rancière would want to have it. Or better, since they would not be entirely beyond that capacity either, we might say more precisely that they would never been entirely on this side of it.

I do not want to claim here that friendship, even friendship strongly characterized by the themes we have described here, is immune to its outside, that is, to some form of enmity. My reasons for reserve, however, are not Derridean but neoliberal. In a society where entrepreneurship and consumerism are everywhere pressed upon us, it is unlikely that we can escape their influence, even in our best relationships. My agreement with Derrida on this matter, then, is not on the basis of deconstruction but rather on the basis of history and context. The question is whether this agreement undercuts the role friendship can play in political solidarity. I believe that it does not. As with my response to the earlier Derridean objection, there is no need to envision a pure friendship in order to envision friendship. Friendship, in its noneconomic mode, presses against the figures of neoliberalism and, in doing so, presses against neoliberalism itself. It is one thing to admit that this pressing is not pure, that it is surrounded and at times infused by that against which it presses. It is quite another to seek to deconstruct it on that basis. To do the latter is to erase the distinction between the figure of friendship and that of neoliberalism, an erasure that would rebound only to the benefit of neoliberalism itself.

Derrida, of course, would not want to accept that neoliberalism would be the beneficiary of a deconstruction of friendship. In his view, the deconstruction leads not to an embrace of neoliberalism but rather to a recognition of democracy as always a democracy-to-come. As he tells us in *Rogues*, 'The "to-come" not only points to the promise but suggests that a democracy will never exist, in the sense of a present existence: not because it will be deferred but because it will always remain aporetic in its structure' (2005, p. 86). What he commends in a deconstruction of the friend–enemy distinction is not an apathy or a yielding to current political relationships, but instead an effacing of the border between friend and enemy that will allow a hospitality to the other to emerge. For Derrida, solidarity is created not through the cultivation of friendship but rather through a deconstruction of the borders between the same of friendship and the other of enmity. This would open a space for a recognition of the other that would seem particularly relevant in light of current movements of exclusion of homosexuals, immigrants and so on. Such a space would not be entirely one of differences, nor entirely one of identical equals. It would instead be a space of the economy between the two. As he writes in *Politics of Friendship*:

> There is no democracy without respect for irreducible singularity or alterity, but there is no democracy without the 'community of friends' (*koína ta philon*) without the calculation of majorities, without identifiable, stabilizable, representable subjects, all equal. These two laws are irreducible one to the other. Tragically irreconcilable and forever wounding. The wound itself opens with the necessity of having to *count* one's friends, to count the others, in the economy of one's own, there where every other is altogether other.
>
> (Derrida, 1997, p. 22)[4]

What we seem to have here, then, is a confrontation of two models of solidarity. One is a broadly Rancièrean model that sees in friendship a model for solidarity, and the other a Derridean model that seeks instead to efface (without, of course, ever entirely erasing) the borders between friendship and enmity. From the perspective of the latter, the former risks excluding others from whatever solidarity is claimed, and thus undercutting the egalitarianism on which it is founded. What is required, from this perspective, is an embrace of a more 'messianic' view of democratic solidarity, one that resists bringing to full presence the character, nature or basis of that solidarity if it wishes to remain democratic. Or, from a different angle, the requirement is to hold together self and other in an unending 'tragic' confrontation.

There are, I believe, at least two things that can be said in response to the Derridean perspective, one in defence of Rancière's view and another in criticism of the Derridean alternative. As for the former, the history of nonviolent struggle and teaching suggests that the building of internal solidarity does not require an exclusion of the other. To see the other as an adversary is not to see them as less than equal, or as prohibited in principle from the group to which you belong. Trouble begins, not when there is resistance but when that resistance hypostasizes the other into an Other, an enemy or a force that must be destroyed or dismantled in order for someone to move forward. It is this idea that Martin Luther King captures in a Christian vein when he writes that the doctrine of nonviolent action:

> Was not a doctrine that made their followers yearn for revenge but one that called upon them to champion change. It was not a doctrine that asked an eye for an eye but one that summoned men to seek to open the eyes of blind prejudice. The Negro turned his back on force not only because he knew he could not win his freedom through physical force but also because he believed that through physical force he could lose his soul.
>
> (King, 1964, p. 35)

Those who subscribe to Derrida's view might quickly and accurately point out that the adversaries addressed by a Rancièrean view are not the others whom Derrida sees excluded from participation. This is true, and is precisely what leads to the criticism of Derrida's perspective. The deconstructionist view addresses those who are beneficiaries of inequality, those who see themselves as among the *included* rather than the excluded. His discourse seeks to discover (and create) pores in the border the self-perceived included might have erected between themselves and those they exclude. Rancière's view, alternatively, is addressed in the first place to the excluded. It is a framework of solidarity for those who seek to struggle, not for those against whom struggle might be directed.

And, given the dominance of the figures of neoliberalism we have canvassed, the kind of friendship we have outlined here is on the side of the excluded rather than the included. Derrida's deconstruction concerns friendship as a movement of internal cohesion among those who would keep at bay what Rancière calls 'the part that has no part' (1999, pp. 8–9). In a neoliberal world, friendship as a movement of internal cohesion can only be one of investment and consumption. At its most cohesive, friendship would be a mutual investment in a collective organization whose goal is to ensure the dominance of those who already have a part. There is no place for friendship's contribution to solidarity, because such friendship can only be threatening to the neoliberal order, for reasons we have seen. Thus, the possibilities of friendship that we have outlined here are not properly the subject of a deconstruction but, if anything, part of the other that is to have a space opened for it by a deconstruction. In attempting to deconstruct friendship, then, Derrida is looking through the wrong end of the telescope. In the name of opening a space for the other, he deconstructs one of the social tools by which that space can be opened. The reason he does this is that his discourse, by addressing itself to those who have a part rather than those who lack it, sees friendship only through the eyes of those for whom solidarity is a threat rather than a promise.

There is, of course, much more to be said about the relation of friendship to our current political order. My suggestion here is that Foucault's quick remark about homosexual friendship offering a challenge to current social arrangements is apt, and apt not only with regard to homosexual friendship. Moreover, friendship can be seen as a model for and a form of cultivation of political solidarity. If we can find ways to bring elements of some of the most significant relationships of our lives into the larger social, economic and political arena, then perhaps we can, to one extent or another, echo the current slogan of so many progressive political movements and say that another world is indeed possible. In fact, if we look in the right place, we will see that it is often already here.

NOTES

1 Baudrillard focuses on the change from production to consumption in his early works, particularly *The Mirror of Production* (1975, pp. 9–10). In that work, as in much of his work, the consumption Baudrillard focuses on is not consumption of goods, but rather consumption of signs. 'What is consumed is not a thing, laden with materiality and the complex cycle that finally derives from labor and nature, but purely and simply an element in a code.'

2 Ray Pahl argues that it was, in fact, the emergence of capitalism that allowed friendship as we know it to begin to thrive, by breaking the traditional, local interpersonal bonds between people in favour of more generalized and less structured forms of relationship. 'Sometime in the

eighteenth century, it seems, friendship appeared as one of a new set of benevolent bonds. This was not as some kind of sharp reaction to the dehumanizing aspects of commercial society but rather as an essential moral and psychological ingredient of new liberal and fraternal values.' I suspect that Pahl is overstating his case here, neglecting the Foucaultian possibility that the new relationships were not simply more liberal but were themselves positively structured by capitalist practices. However, the point that neoliberalism brings with it a new set of interpersonal relationship structures that were distinct from earlier ones remains. See Pahl (2000).

3 For an account of export processing zones and women's place in them, see Klein (1999, ch. 9).

4 We should note here that in this passage Derrida seems to reduce equality to sameness. There is no reason that equality should be thought of in terms of sameness. Although this point would take us too far afield, I address it in the context of Rancière's thought in *The Political Thought of Jacques Rancière: Creating equality.* See Rancière (2008, pp. 56–64).

REFERENCES

Barber, B. (2008) *Consumed: How markets corrupt children, infantilize adults, and swallow citizens whole.* New York: Norton.

Baudrillard , J. (1975) *The Mirror of Production,* trans. M. Poster. St Louis, Mo.: Telos Press.

Bauman, Z. (2007) *Consuming Life.* London: Polity.

Cicero. (1991) 'On friendship', in M. Pakaluk (ed.), *Other Selves: Philosophers on friendship.* Indianapolis, Ind.: Hackett.

Derrida, J. (1992) *Given Time: 1. counterfeit money,* trans. P. Kamuf. Chicago, Ill.: University of Chicago Press.

Derrida, J. (1997) *Politics of Friendship,* trans. G. Collins. London: Verso.

Derrida, J. (2005) *Rogues: Two essays on reason,* trans. P.-A. Nass and M. Nass. Palo Alto, Calif.: Stanford University Press.

Foucault, M. (1989) 'Friendship as a way of life', in S. Lotinger (ed.), *Foucault Live,* trans. J. Johnston. New York: Semiotext(e).

Foucault, M. (1995) *Discipline and Punish: The birth of the prison.* New York: Vintage

Foucault, M. (2004) *Naissance de la biopolitique (The Birth of Biopolitics).* Paris: Gallimard.

Friedman, M. 1993 'Feminism and modern friendship', in N. K. Badhwar (ed.), *Friendship: A philosophical reader.* Ithaca, N.Y.: Cornell University Press.

Harvey, D. (2005) *A Brief History of Neoliberalism.* Oxford: Oxford University Press.

Kant, I. (1991) 'Lecture on friendship', in M. Pakaluk (ed.), *Other Selves: Philosophers on friendship.* Indianapolis, Ind.: Hackett.

King, M. L. (1964) 'The sword that heals', in *Why We Can't Wait*. New York: New American Library.

Klein, N. (1999) *No Logo: Taking aim at the brand bullies*. New York: Picador.

Lance, M. (2005) 'Fetishizing process', Institute for Anarchist Studies. http://zinelibrary.info/files/Fetishizing%20Process.pdf (accessed September 3, 2012).

May, T. (2008) *The Political Thought of Jacques Rancière: Creating equality*. Edinburgh and University Park, Pa.: Edinburgh University Press and Penn State University Press.

Pahl, R. (2000) *On Friendship*. London: Polity Press.

Putnam, R. D. (2000) *Bowling Alone: The collapse and revival of American community*. New York: Simon & Schuster.

Rancière, J. (1995) *On the Shores of Politics*, trans. L. Heron. London: Verso.

Rancière, J. (1999) *Disagreement,* trans. J. Rose. Minneapolis, Minn.: University of Minnesota Press.

Spencer, L. and Pahl, R. (2006) *Rethinking Friendship: Hidden solidarities today*. Princeton, N.J.: Princeton University Press.

Telfer, E. (1991) 'Friendship', in M. Pakaluk (ed.), *Other Selves: Philosophers on friendship*. Indianapolis, Ind.: Hackett.

4

AN-ARCHY BETWEEN
METAPOLITICS AND POLITICS

Miguel Abensour

As the preposition 'between' suggests, our aim is to locate what might not be locatable, that is, *an-archy, or more commonly anarchy, or the anarchic*. The question is then: where can we situate an-archy in Emmanuel Levinas's philosophy? Can we consider it to be somewhere between metapolitics and politics? This question is legitimate, because we know that the Levinasian sense of *an-archy* must be distinguished from anarchism. Anarchy cannot be reduced to its political sense inasmuch as it has to do with the unique intrigue that Levinas calls 'proximity'. However, and this is where the question becomes quite complex, even if we cannot confine anarchy to its political sense, it still somewhat concerns and affects politics. It is as if Levinas's deliberate recourse to such an undoubtedly charged term is linked to one of the most profound aspects of his philosophy.

To help answer our question, three essential texts must be examined:

- 'Humanism and an-archy', the title of a section in *Humanism of the Other*, which was first published in 1968 in *La Revue internationale de Philosophie* (Levinas, 2006)
- the first section of the fourth chapter, 'Principle and anarchy', in *Otherwise than Being; or, Beyond Essence* (Levinas, 1991b), which was first published in *La Revue Philosophique de Louvain*
- 'Subjectivity as anarchy' in Levinas's course on *God, Death and Time* (1976), edited by Jacques Rolland.

To return to our initial question: why state that anarchy can be found somewhere between metapolitics and politics? In essence, it is because anarchy appears at two different levels in Levinas's work. On the one hand, it refers to what precedes all *arche*; it is an absolute beginning and prior to all principles. On the other hand, this relationship with the pre-original does not exclude a certain political sense. An example of the double nature of Levinasian *an-archy* is when Levinas tries to describe the term 'obsession' as an anarchic movement, in the second half of note 3 in *Otherwise than Being*:

> The notion of anarchy as we are introducing it here has a meaning prior to the political (or antipolitical) meaning currently attributed to it. It would be self-contradictory to set it up as a principle (in the sense that anarchists understand it). Anarchy cannot be sovereign like an *arche*. It can only disturb the State – but in a radical way, making possible moments of negation *without any* affirmation. The State then cannot set itself up as a Whole. But, on the other hand, anarchy can be stated. Yet disorder has an irreducible meaning, as a refusal of synthesis.
>
> (Levinas, 1991b, p. 194)

Our question gives rise to others, most notably: what do we mean by metapolitics?

The term 'metapolitics' cannot be found in Levinas's philosophy. We use it, however, in order to conjure up a dimension other than the political by the use of the Greek 'meta': that is, a plurality of meanings. Although the first sense of 'meta' is 'after' or 'behind' (in a topical and technical sense), it also means, as Heidegger points out in *The Fundamental Concepts of Metaphysics* (1995), a movement akin to a turn. In other words, it is a departure from something in order to turn toward something else. This movement or this turn permits a departure from a particular being and a movement toward the Other. Metaphysics therefore signifies a knowledge that goes beyond the senses, a knowledge that is, because of the turn, supra sensible. For Heidegger, this turn is anything but a mere detail; it is what decides the fate of true philosophy in the Western world.

When applied to Levinas's thought, the term 'metapolitics' does not refer to its technical or topical sense – that which comes after politics. 'Metapolitics' cannot be understood in such a way, because, as Levinas writes in a famous text (1961), politics comes *after* ethics, which in turn becomes the first philosophy. Metapolitics would, however, obtain meaning with respect to its content; it would signify the turn that consists of leaving something in order to go towards something else. In this case, metapolitics is a departure from politics, a move away from the particular being that is politics in order to go towards an Other that would be metapolitics. Thus metapolitics attempts to embody such a reversal. When closely examined, this term designates a complex journey. If the 'meta' in metapolitics means a turn or a departure – a leaving of politics in order to proceed elsewhere, or a passageway beyond politics – it nevertheless means a *source* or a *provenance*: that is, an *underneath*. It is as if the effect of metapolitics is to call to our attention an underneath that permits a leaving of politics and that opens a passageway beyond politics.

In defining our responsibility for the Other, Levinas insists on this complex structure, on the trajectory that goes from the underneath to the beyond:

> The other's freedom can neither constitute a structure along with my freedom, nor enter into a synthesis with it. Responsibility for the neighbor is precisely what goes beyond the legal and obliges beyond contracts; it comes to me from what is prior to my freedom, from a non-present, an immemorial.
>
> (Levinas, 1986, p. 67)

Moreover, it is not a question here of founding the practice of politics on a philosophical system in order to do away with its immediacy and its empirical nature. For this would signify that metapolitics is politics based on a principle, or on many principles. By contrast, metapolitics must be put in resonance and in consonance with what occurs in the ethical relationship with the Other, that is, 'a responsibility that is justified by no prior commitment', such that 'the me-ontological and metalogical structure of anarchy takes form, undoing the logos in which the apology by which consciousness always regains its self-control, and commands, is inserted' (Levinas, 1991b, p. 102) It is as if metapolitics was the analogue of this departure from ontology.

Is it not thanks to this reversal that we can better situate anarchy, on the way out of politics, by turning away from politics to reach another dimension? Does this turn, this way out of politics, not affect that from which it detaches itself, that from which it turns away?

It is not, however, enough to situate. We must also describe. Our journey will thus comprise of two elements: first, a description of the intrigue of anarchy, or anarchy and proximity; and second, a critical essay of the effects on politics, or the disturbance of politics.

THE INTRIGUE OF ANARCHY: ANARCHY AND PROXIMITY

Before engaging in the question of intrigue as it is developed in *Otherwise than Being*, it is important to briefly analyse one of the first appearances of the term 'anarchy' in Levinas's thought, in *Totality and Infinity* (*Totalité et infini*), published in 1961.

Very early in the elaboration of his philosophy, Levinas sets forth a pluralist conception of the social. In his conferences on *Time and the Other* (*Le temps et l'autre*), Levinas states, 'we wish to move toward a pluralism that does not amalgamate into a whole' (1991a, p. 20). In *Existence and Existents* (*De l'existence à l'existant*, 2000 – first published 1947), Levinas refuses a social thought that views society in terms of a totality that is different from the sum of its parts (Durkheim) as well as a social thought that sees society in terms of imitation (Tarde). In both cases, although by different means, we end up with the idea of a fusion: either I identify myself with the Other by way of a collective representation, or I become one with the Other by the renewal of a common deed. Levinas also refuses the community of the 'with' which, following Heidegger, brings communities together around something that is commonly shared, such as the truth. In 1947, he wrote:

> To the community of companionship we oppose the community of the 'Me' and 'You' that precedes it. This is not a participation in a third term ... that is to say a communion. The 'Me' and 'You' community is the formidable face to face relationship without intermediary or mediation.
>
> (Levinas, 2000, p. 162)

Levinas reiterates this position in *Time and the Other*, where he critiques Plato for assuming an eleatic notion of being that subordinates the multiple to the One and that reduces the role of the feminine to matter. He accuses Plato of not understanding the specificity of the relationship of one to the other. It is from this perspective that Levinas critiques Plato's *Republic* as being constructed upon the model of the world of ideas, and thus perceives the ideal social order in terms of the ideal of fusion. 'In his relationship with the other, the subject has a tendency to identify himself with the other by way of a collective representation, or by way of a common ideal' (Levinas, 1991b, p. 88). Levinas renews this position in his critique of Heidegger, and thus concludes in a similar yet more profound fashion, since he distinguishes his position from that of Martin Buber. 'Against this side-by-side community, I have tried to oppose the "Me" and "You" community, not in the sense of Buber where the social link is reciprocity and where the inescapable properties of isolated subjects are underestimated' (1991b, p. 89).

In *Totality and Infinity*, Levinas's analysis of the face-to-face relationship is considerably enriched. Against Buber's irenicism, this relationship is now thought as being a one-way relationship, or as being asymmetrical. Levinas insists on the 'curb of inter-subjective space' that includes a dimension of elevation. In addition, he distances himself from Hobbes and goes beyond thinkers who identify the social with the reign of violence (Levinas, 1961, pp. 266–7). To postulate a relationship other than that of violence does not, however, constitute a return to the reign of totality. For Levinas, the face-to-face relationship reaffirms itself as the final and irreducible relationship that 'renders possible the pluralism of society' (1961, p. 267). Being is exteriority: that is, the resistance of the social multiplicity against a logic that totalizes the multiple (1961, p. 268). Against the idea of totality that is the proper of ontological philosophy, Levinas opposes 'the idea of a separation that resists synthesis' (1961, p. 269). The 'selfs', strangely written in the plural form and following the example of La Boétie's 'all ones', do not form a totality.

It is in regard to this resistance of the multiple against totalization that appears the reference to anarchy: 'anarchy essential to the multiplicity', states Levinas. Anarchy, because 'an ultimate plane where the "selfs" could gain self-understanding with regards to their principle does not exist' (1961, p. 270). Yet this anarchy seems ambiguous and temporary. It only exists for lack of a common plan, principle or *arche*. In fact, the multiple can resist totalization precisely because of the lack of an *arche*. Although anarchy is, on the one hand, a form of resistance and thus a manifestation of the pluralism of society, it is also, on the other hand, 'vertigo' and 'shivering'. It is not the war of all against all, but the anomie of free wills: 'we will never know which will, in the realm of free wills, is pulling the strings; we will never know who is playing whom' (Levinas, 1961, p. 270). And this anarchy must disappear, not because of the appearance of a more efficient totality, but because of the coming of a principle, of an *arche*, when the face calls for justice. It is as if the multiple had to take leave and give its place to a pluralism of being that 'comes to be in the goodness that goes from the self to the other' (1961, pp. 282–3).

In this first elaboration in Levinas's thought, anarchy is seen more as a temporary state whose fate is to abolish itself in the face of the call to justice, than as an intrigue born of the enigma of proximity.

Contrary to Reiner Schürmann's arguments in *Heidegger on Being and Acting: From principles to anarchy* (1987), Levinas does not attempt to think of or describe an 'anarchy principle'. The use of this paradoxical term permits Schürmann to oppose the classical metaphysical apparatus and Heidegger's thought, which Schürmann sees as an expression of this new principle, or more precisely, as a new way of thinking through this principle. By traditional structure of philosophy – or archic structure – we mean a structure whose dominant feature is to submit the question of action to an *arche* in such a way that the theories of action inevitably attempt to answer the question 'What should I do?' And the answer is always to be found with regard to that period's ultimate knowledge. Metaphysics would then mean the different attempts to determine an *arche* that subordinates action. Or again, it would be the apparatus 'where action requires a principle that words, things, and actions can be referred to' (Schürmann, 1987, p. 16). This principle is at once foundation, beginning and commandment. 'The *arche* operates with regards to action much like the substance operates with regards to accidents, it gives meaning and telos' (1987, p. 15).

It is in the perspective of the metaphysical and archic structure that we can better understand the new sense that Schürmann gives to anarchy and, at the same time, to Heidegger's thought. In the age of the closing of metaphysics (the thesis of the anarchy principle is closely related to the hypothesis of the closure), the rule that states that the world becomes intelligible and controllable by a 'first' or by a first foundation loses its ascendancy. The derivation between first philosophy and practical philosophy decreases; the obligatory reference to an *arche* disappears at the same time as the 'epochal principals, that in every historical age organize thoughts and actions, fade away' (Schürmann, 1987, p. 15). Hence the articulation of the 'dazzling' paradox that is the anarchy principle. The two terms of this concept imply two opposing sides: one that points beneath the closure of metaphysics and the other that points beyond the closure. The principle at once states and denies itself. In other words, the principle is stated only in order to be denied. It is important to understand the twentieth century, by its critique of metaphysics, as the era in which the derivation of praxis from theory ends. Action is anarchic: that is, without *arche*, foundation, beginning or commandment. It is the era of the principle of the non-principle, or of the principle that requires the absence of principle. In terms of Heidegger's thought, this paradox reveals his work as transitory, for Heidegger is stuck in the classical problematic of the question 'What is being?' He does however manage to disengage this question from the attributive or principle scheme. 'There is still a principle but it is nevertheless an anarchy principle. One must think through this contradiction. In its history and in its essence, a dislocating and 'plurifying' force works the reference to a principle .... Deconstruction is a transitory discourse' (Schürmann, 1987, p. 16).

Is it possible to resolve the inherent contradiction of the anarchy principle? Is Emmanuel Levinas's radicality not a turn away from this paradox (which he envisages, most notably regarding anarchism) and the positing of an insurmountable gap between principle and anarchy? And is it not this contrast that brings Levinas to refuse a purely political conception of anarchy, since anarchy is situated beyond the alternative of order and disorder? In this sense, the notion of anarchy points toward a reality other than the political or anti-political meaning. This refusal of a political conception of anarchy is logical, since such a conception amounts to imposing a principle on anarchy. In order to avoid the transformation of anarchy into a principle, Levinas separates anarchy from politics, anarchy from all principle, and anarchy from anarchism. For the anarchist doctrine is nothing else but the affirmation of the principle of reason over that of authority. The anarchy principle is inconceivable for Levinas. To quote again note 3 of *Otherwise than Being*: 'It (anarchy) would be self-contradictory to set it up as a principle (in the sense that anarchists understand it). Anarchy cannot be sovereign, like an *arche*' (Levinas, 1991b, p. 194). Or note 4: 'Anarchy does not *reign*' (1991b, p. 194). Anarchy is thus separated from a principle, and from any attempt to make it deviate toward a principle. Anarchy, rendered to itself and returning to a certain bareness, touches a profound stratum where we can find the complex entanglement of the underneath (the source or the provenance) and the beyond (the turn). Proto-political, anarchy opens the way beyond politics and ontology. And here there forms the intrigue of anarchy and proximity.

Jean-François Lyotard, at the evening in honour of Levinas that led to the publication of *Otherwise than Knowledge* (Petitdemange and Rolland, 1988), firmly and soberly stated that Levinas's invaluable contribution is the way in which he takes leave of the dominant tradition in Western philosophy:

all thought is not knowledge. That is quite clear. And philosophy is not necessarily, or at least, exclusively ... a type of discourse that has to do with knowledge .... My admiration for Levinas comes from this; suddenly Levinas' thought discovers the realm of experience, or of reflection, which is not an object of knowledge. Yet we can still say something about it, despite the fact that it can never be knowledge.

(in Petitdemange and Rolland, 1988)

To this statement, Levinas answered:

By recalling the possibility of thought that is not knowledge, I wanted to assert that a spiritual – preceding all ideas – exists within the fact of being close to someone. Proximity or sociality itself is 'otherwise' than the knowledge that expresses it. Otherwise than knowledge is not faith. ... This sociality is not an experience of the other; it is proximity to the other.

(Levinas, 1961, pp. 90–1)

Otherwise than knowledge is not faith. It is, however, a source of meaning or of the sensible born of the responsibility toward others. Knowledge is thus only one of the possibilities of the human psyche; it cannot exhaust it. Another form of thought is thus conceivable: 'a thought that is not constructed as a relationship: of the thinking to the thought, with the domination of thought' (Lyotard in Levinas, 1996, p. 22). By forgoing the equivalency between the psyche and the intentional, Levinas attains another side of the human psyche that is far from the mastery or the hegemony of the self of knowledge. Is this not already an entry into anarchism? Levinas states:

The Psyche is the form of a peculiar dephasing, a loosening up or unclamping of identity: the same prevented from coinciding with itself, at odds, torn up from its rest, between sleep and insomnia, panting, shivering. It is not an abdication of the same now alienated and slave to the other, but an abnegation of oneself fully responsible for the other. This identity is brought out of responsibility and is at the service of the other. In the form of responsibility, the psyche in the soul is the other in me, a male of identity, both accused and self, the same for the other, the same by the other.

(Levinas, 1961, pp. 68–9)

This account, beyond the fact that it states the importance of possession (in the case of the psyche, one for the other, 'the soul is already seed of folly'), has the great merit of guiding us toward the right question, in terms of this 'peculiar dephasing'. Indeed, it is not so much a question of resuming the description of the three notions that characterize the relationship to the other – responsibility, proximity and substitution – but of analysing how they are anarchic, or better, by what path and how they participate in anarchy.

The Case of Proximity

Levinas begins by de-objectifying this notion, refusing to reduce it to a purely spatial understanding that would be akin to a reduced interval between close terms. And within the context of this de-objectification, Levinas also refuses to view proximity in terms of an experience of the other. Proximity is rather an exposure to the other. Moreover, regarding proximity, can we not state, to modify Levinas's phrase in *Totality and Infinity*, 'Anarchy is essential to humanity under the auspices of the category of proximity'? Anarchy is thus no longer only a form of resistance of the multiple against a totalizing logic. It is now the 'nucleus' of the human psyche inasmuch as we understand the psyche as being beyond knowledge and one-for-the-other. With respect to proximity, Levinas states, 'Its absolute and proper meaning presupposes "humanity"' (1991b, p. 81). And by a bold reversal of the kind that he has the habit of accomplishing, Levinas goes so far as to ask if spatial contiguity does not depend upon human proximity via the experience of justice. This 'assumption' of humanity, this constitutive bond of humanity, requires that proximity be thought through at a distance from knowledge and from intentional consciousness as 'consciousness of':

> Humanity, to which proximity properly so called refers, must then not be first understood as consciousness, that is, as the identity of an ego endowed with knowledge or (what amounts to the same thing) with powers. Proximity does not resolve into the consciousness a being would have of another being that it would judge to be near inasmuch as the other would be under one's eyes or within one's reach, and inasmuch as it would be possible for one to take hold of that being, hold on to it or converse with it, in the reciprocity of handshakes, caresses, struggle, collaboration, commerce, conversation.
>
> (Levinas, 1991b, p. 83)

To begin with knowledge or with intentional consciousness can lead to a loss, to an overlooking of proximity by transforming it into a thematic. Even worse, it can lead to a repression into the conscious of 'a subjectivity already older than knowing or power' (1991b, p. 83).

Proximity is neither a state nor a respite. It is an inexhaustible anxiety and a 'null site' (a utopia?). Proximity is exterior to a resting-place, for in such a place proximity is not intense enough. It is as if the impulse of proximity was a 'never close enough' (1991b, p. 82). Lacking indifference or fraternity, proximity is not a simple relation; far from being an awareness, it is 'being caught up in fraternity', self-sacrifice, institution of one for the other. (1991b, p. 82). 'The approach' – writes Levinas – 'is precisely an implication of the approaching one in fraternity .... This being caught up in fraternity which proximity is we call *signifyingness*' (1991b, p. 83). Beyond knowledge and beyond a simple relationship, proximity is obsession, that is, the incarnation of non-reciprocity and an irreversible affection for the other which is one-sided, since 'I have always one response more to give' (1991b, p. 84). A self 'at once obliged to', in the accusative form – at once responsible without any possibility of escape.

This obsessed subjectivity, this non-reciprocal obsession, testifies to the exceptional nature of proximity with regards to a rational order that leads to a reversible and symmetrical system of relations. The other summons me. Such is the modality of the obsession. I am always indebted and cannot rid myself of my debt. 'I am as it were ordered from the outside, traumatically commanded' (Levinas, 1991b, p. 87). If consciousness appears, it is only within the context of the prior obligation that consciousness cannot undo. An extreme urgency, which is yet another modality of the obsession, thwarts all attempts at consciousness and at the transformation of representations into themes. Moreover, proximity attests to a different temporality than that of consciousness and of the time of the clocks. Proximity as obsession is disturbance.

An 'Anarchic sense of proximity', states Levinas. His exact words are, 'it [justice] derives from an anarchic signification of proximity' (1991b, p.81). What does this mean?

To follow the excessiveness of this description, proximity is an assault on a rational order. A third party could understand this order by demonstrating how it becomes intelligible inasmuch as the relations that constitute it are, to a certain extent, interchangeable because they are reversible and symmetrical. Thus, with regards to such a conceivable system, proximity is an exception, a 'disturbance'. In addition, proximity leads an additional assault on this rational order through its own temporality. 'The proximity', writes Levinas, 'does not enter into the common time of clocks, which makes meetings possible. It is a disturbance' (1991b, p. 89). Yet another disturbance.

Beyond this tendency to disturb which raises the question of disorder, proximity reveals itself as being anarchic or *an-archy*, since it comes to be without the mediation of an ideality, or of a principle that takes the place of an ideality or of an *arche*. As an involvement, a hold in fraternity, and a signification, subjectivity is at once described as an-archy. Levinas states, 'The subjectivity of the approaching subject is then preliminary, anarchic, prior to consciousness' (1991b, pp. 82–3). Or again, in the course on God and onto-theology, the obsession is presented as 'a delirium that surprises origin, that arises earlier than origin ... that shows itself before any glimmer of consciousness. It is an anarchy that puts an end to the game of ontology in which being loses and discovers itself' (Levinas, 1995, p. 200).

This passion encounters the extremes in three different ways: by this passion, consciousness is affected despite itself; within this passion, consciousness is apprehended without any *a priori*; with this passion, consciousness is affected by that which is not desirable (Levinas, 1995, p. 201). The other as other is not preceded by a precursor that would alert consciousness and thus facilitate the engaging of the irresistible movement of reduction of the other to the Same. Is this not yet another way of staying beneath all *arche*? 'Absolving himself from all essence, all genus, all resemblance,' writes Levinas, 'the neighbor, *the first one on the scene*, concerns me for the first time (even if he is an old acquaintance, an old friend, an old lover, long caught up in the fabric of my social relations) in a contingency that excludes the a priori' (1991b, p. 86). The appearance of the other is even more anarchic, since it is a summoning that forgoes all mediation. It is as if the other claims his belonging to humanity in order to bring forth recognition and encounters. The scenario is completely different, infinitely more abrupt: I am assigned to the other as an other because of his singularity. 'His extreme singularity is precisely his assignation' (1991b, p. 86). Far from being done by an intermediary, this assignation is accomplished directly face to face. 'This way of a neighbor is a face. The face of the neighbor signifies for me an unexceptionable responsibility' (1991b, p. 88). An-archy is here redoubled: assignation before all *arche*, for the call to responsibility is not preceded by free consent, pact or contract. The face 'escapes representation. It is the very collapse of phenomenality'; it is so weak that it is less than a phenomenon. 'The disclosing of a face is nudity, non-form, abandon of self, ageing, dying' (1991b, p. 88).

There is something here akin to a scandal, for this relationship escapes all intentionality and all commitment. I obey the commandment of the other before even hearing it. Hence there is a particular temporality that is no less anarchic since it is situated before all *arche*, before all beginning, and before all initiative.

Moreover, the temporality of proximity is exceptional; not only does it disrupt, it troubles the time of the clocks, it introduces us to another test of time that is different from the time of consciousness or from the temporality that express itself in the Said (*le Dit*). In its own way, temporality testifies to anarchy. In the time of consciousness, an active self assembles the past, recuperates it by memory or by the work of historiography. The proper of proximity and responsibility for the other is that they precede all commitments and do not result from free consent: that is, from any present. Responsibility for the other belongs to a peculiar time that is a time without beginning. Hence it is anarchy that, *by not having a beginning*, cannot be represented (Levinas, 1991b, p. 51). To form a relationship with a past that has never been present, such as an immemorial past, proximity 'takes apart the recuperative time of history and memory in which representation continues' (1991b, p. 88). Once again, proximity is disruption of historical time.

We can also try to show the presence of anarchy in the Levinasian responsibility for the other – 'the irreducible anarchy of responsibility for another', writes Levinas (1991b, p. 76). How does the passage from consciousness *of* to consciousness *for* affect self-consciousness that spontaneously poses itself as origin, beginning, initiative or *arche*? In responsibility for another, 'the self does not pose itself, but loses its place, departs itself or finds itself deported' (Levinas, 1995, p. 181). This is the irreducible anarchy of responsibility indeed, since it is a bond that cannot be reflected upon within the context of foundational rationality, despite the fact that this thought might be in search of another rationality. Even more disturbing is the an-archy found in substitution, a climax of sorts of the anarchic intrigue. The self is not only responsible for the other, but is also the hostage of all others, much like in the image of maternity where the mother is the hostage of the baby that she is carrying and nourishing. 'In the Self's pre-history, the Self is entirely hostage and this precedes the ego' (1995, p. 202). One-for-another is here pushed to the extreme, without a return to the self, to the point where anarchy undermines the *arche* that is Being. It is an 'anarchy that puts an end to the game of ontology in which being loses and discovers itself', writes Levinas (1995, p. 200).

For Levinas, proximity and obsession are not phenomena of consciousness. But this non-consciousness, instead of being the sign of a deficit of some sort (a pre-conscience stage or a repression), is an affirmation of 'their exception from totality, that is their refusal of manifestation', and 'this exception is non-being or anarchy, prior to the still ontological alternative of being and nothingness' (Levinas, 1991b, p. 197, note 26). But the subject as an elected subject, as a substitution, experiences a stunning reversal. Alienation is now seen as the withdrawal into a being that perseveres in its being, *conatus in esse* – while freedom is to be found on the side of substitution. 'A mode of freedom, ontologically impossible, breaks the unrendable essence. Substitution frees the subject from ennui, that is, from the enchainment to the itself, where the ego suffocates in itself' (1991b, p. 124). The unique quality of this liberation is that it does not fall into the game of ontology that consists of beginning, action, perseverance in being and so on. Yet Levinas writes and thus creates a new and paradoxical image of linearity: 'an anarchic liberation, it emerges, without being assumed, without turning into a beginning, in inequality with oneself' (1991b, p. 124).

On many occasions, Levinas defines anarchy as a disturbance: a disturbance of the time of the clocks, of historical time, and of being. Does this mean that, because of this disturbance, we can identify, without qualifying it, anarchy with disorder? Not at all, it would seem. For in his description of obsession, the anarchic movement in the original sense of the term, Levinas states that anarchy is not the fact of a disorder opposed to an order, especially since disorder is, in truth, another form of order. It is important to point out that this is not an affirmation of order or of the omnipresence of order. Rather, Levinas is attempting to preserve a maximal, even emphatic, conception of anarchy. An-archy is beyond the ontological alternative between order and disorder that is still under the hold of 'being *arche*' (1991b, p. 102). Indeed, 'anarchy troubles being over and beyond these alternatives' (1991b, p. 101). It is because anarchy – and anarchy of obsession as a non-intentional enigma – troubles being, that is, puts an end to the ontological game, that we cannot reduce it to a disorder 'that opposes order'. A more complex movement occurs. If anarchy cannot be reduced to a disorder, in an ontological sense, it seems that a disorder subtracted from ontology, conceived in a non-dialectical manner, and beyond its opposition to order, could receive an anarchic force. In other words, a disorder that has to do with an outside, and that stays away from all synthesis can be conceivable. In this sense, Levinas concludes the third note of *Otherwise than Being* by recognizing the virtues of a sort of meta-ontological disorder. 'Disorder has an irreducible meaning, as a refusal of synthesis' (1991b, p. 194). Hence the sixth note that invites us, against Bergson, to distinguish between many types of disorder. All disorders are not just different orders, as testified by the diachronical an-archy that cannot be assembled into an order.

If an-archy cannot be reduced to a disorder that is opposed to an order, then conversely, some disorders – to the extent that they are disturbances of being, or that they undermine 'being *arche*' – have to do with anarchy.

THE DISTURBANCE OF POLITICS

Let us come back to the question of departure: anarchy between metapolitics and politics. In the trajectory that we have just taken, whether it be proximity, responsibility for the other, substitution or obsession, we have been constantly directed toward an underneath of freedom, a pre-original, pre-historic, an immemorial, underneath of the *arche*. In short, we have explored what one could call the *dimensions of the underneath* and, amongst others, the underneath of politics that is found on the side of free action, beginning, principle, Being, and *arche*, is thus on the side of ontology. If we turn, however, to the *meta* – that is, if we turn away from politics, if we take leave of politics and turn to something else, if we turn toward metapolitics – what do we find? Perhaps ethics (without which we know that politics would be tyranny), ethics that is related to infinity and to the glory of infinity? Is this answer satisfactory? To resume this movement, and to embrace it, it seems then that anarchy is to be found either on the side of an underneath or on the side of a beyond or perhaps in the passage that goes from an underneath to a beyond. Levinas speaks of an ambiguity of anarchy in the sense of a self anachronistically late with regards to its present, unable to make up for its lateness. This is a persecuted self, unable to think through that which affects it. The Self can, however, say that this unableness for anarchy leaves a trace. Yet it is only a trace that speech can attempt to reflect. However, regarding anarchy, would its ambiguity not be that it finds itself between a source and a turn, between an underneath that is coming and a beyond that is going? Is it not as if there was a direct 'communication' between 'this pre-historical and an-archic' trace and proximity? Is responsibility for the other, one for the other, irreducibly anarchic?

Nevertheless, to follow such a road, does anarchy not, in its complex trajectories, leave aside politics, since it is well anchored in its tranquillity, in its self-consciousness, and in its equality of self to self? Is this to say that anarchy cuts itself off from politics, which remains under the hold of ontology, logos and *arche*? This is not at all the case: anarchy disturbs politics to the point where we can speak of the *disturbance of politics*.

Admittedly, anarchy does not reign. It cannot be sovereign like an *arche*, and it cannot be stated as a principle without contradicting itself. Hence the anarchists' insurmountable contradiction that would put anarchy in power or that would break power (as domination) in the name of the principle of reason over authority. In short, to follow the anarchist project, anarchy would reign. Hence also the aporia of the anarchy principle which maintains – even while rejecting the classical metaphysical derivation of action – a reference to an *arche* that is no less than Being; 'being *arche*', as Levinas puts it.

To separate anarchy from sovereignty, to separate it from a principle, does not mean that anarchy does not affect politics or leaves it unchanged by abandoning it to its own determinations.

To begin with, in order to better appreciate the disturbance of politics, we should perhaps confront it with what I have called the 'extravagant hypothesis'. It is the hypothesis that Levinas proposes to explain the origins of the State. For Levinas, the State – far from proceeding from the limitation of violence and from the limitation of the excesses of the war of all against all – ensues from proximity, from the human intrigue of responsibility for the other, in the sense that the State is a limitation of the infinity that affects the ethical relationship. Hence there is a legitimate question: what is the relationship between the Levinasian hypothesis and anarchy? Without envisaging the question as a whole, it clearly appears that what Levinas thinks is on the side of anarchy – proximity, responsibility for the other, substitution – is what nourishes the extravagant hypothesis. The establishment of the State corresponds to the limitation of this pre-original and anarchic intrigue. The State is born of the limitation of the pre-original anarchy, in the Levinasian sense of the term: that is, limitation under the category of justice. There is no doubt that this relationship to anarchy creates a disturbance of politics and provokes the disturbance of politics. For even if justice, with the sudden appearance of the third party (*le Tiers*), imposes its measurement upon that which is incommensurable, at no time can it cut itself off from the source that inspired and inspires it.

In much the same way as the extravagant hypothesis, the effect of anarchy is to place the State in a multidimensional space in which it finds itself torn between the extraordinary intrigue from which it proceeds and the ends it pursues, namely justice. In this perspective, the State is permanently submitted to a twofold interrogation in order to determine its legitimacy. On the one hand, is the form of human coexistence established by the State in continuity with the original intrigue? On the other hand, does this form bring forth the end that it pursues: that is, justice? Moreover, this conception is oriented toward a sovereign yet decentred State, a State that is submitted to the determinations that are the proper of a centrifugal movement to the extent that an otherwise oriented effect is superposed on the institution. The recalling of the first intrigue (the anarchic proximity) and the telos of the State (justice) permits the struggle against the natural penchant of the State to close and recentre itself, and to put into place a centripetal logic that brings the State to construct and reconstruct itself as a totality. This begs the question (which we shall leave unanswered): what is the relationship between anarchy in the Levinasian sense of the term and the strange movement that, following Levinas, pushes the State (in certain forms) to go beyond the State?

There is, however, yet another passageway that helps us understand how anarchy disturbs politics. Anarchy does not reign, but it could be said that it can be speech without being sovereign speech. It must be careful not to lose its ambiguous status of an enigma that can manifest itself without unveiling: that is, an exception of the totality which leaves a trace – only a trace. 'This way of passing, disturbing the present without allowing itself to be invested by the *arche* of consciousness, striating with its furrows the clarity of the ostensible, is what we have called a trace' (Levinas, 1991b, p. 100). This *saying as a saying*, that contains the dimension of the one for another, is recognized as the faculty of 'disturbing' the State, the *arche* State. It disturbs the State in a radical way by shaking the State at its roots and its foundation. This disturbance opens the way to a truly 'negative dialectic' in the sense of Adorno. If we refer to the beginning of *Negative Dialectics* (1995), we see another form of dialectic whose specificity is that it is set free from all affirmative essence, since the means of negativity or the game of negativity ceases to produce positivity. Negative dialectics then, for Levinas (even if he does not use the term), because it makes 'possible instances of negation without any affirmation', deliberately underlines 'any affirmation'. Indeed, to go to the affirmative or to the positive register would be to fall back into sovereignty, *arche*, and thus for anarchy to immediately ruin itself. These are only moments, but crucial moments which, in their own fragility, in their non-installation in time, hinder the political manifestation of *arche* which is the possessor of sovereignty, and which reigns as a totality, as a mortal God. A non-dialectical disorder is hence recognized; a disorder not opposed to order, not stuck in the game of ontology, a disorder as disturbance of Being, is recognized an irreducible sense that is the refusal of synthesis.

Does this 'seed of folly', this trace not come back to what Hegel (1965) criticised as 'Jewish folly', the attitude that refuses to let universal history be the tribunal of the world? This thought opens us to an exteriority of history: that is, the space from which we can judge it, a space within which it is possible for a 'saying' to affirm, against the State, that the totality is the non-truth.

Speech against the king, the *arche* that reigns, speech that resolves, prophetic speech. Speech that, in 1968, against contemporary anti-humanism, was able to invent a novel and unusual relationship between humanism and anarchy.

CONCLUSION

From this trajectory there emerges the singularity of Levinas. Many great philosophers of the twentieth century have elaborated their thought with the help of a principle, of an *arche*: Ernst Bloch, the principle of hope; Hans Jonas, the principle of responsibility; Heidegger (if we follow Schürmann), the principle of anarchy. Levinas is the uncommon thinker, resolutely modern, who explores the intrigue of the human, out of any principle, at the outside of any *arche*, in quest of an anarchy essential to humanity.

REFERENCES

Adorno, Theodor (1995) *Negative Dialectics*. New York: Continuum.

Hegel, Georg Wilhelm Friedrich (1956) *The Philosophy of History*, ed. J. Sibree. New York: Dover.

Heidegger, M. (1995) *The Fundamental Concepts of Metaphysics*. Bloomington, Ind.: Indiana University Press.

Levinas, Emmanuel (1961) *Totalité et infini: essai sur l'extériorité* (*Totality and Infinity*). The Hague: Martinus Nijhoff.

Levinas, Emmanuel (1976) 'Subjectivity as anarchy', repr. 2001 as pp. 198–202 in Jacques Rolland (ed.), *God, Death and Time*. Stanford, Calif.: Stanford University Press.

Levinas, Emmanuel (1986) *Of God Who Comes to Mind*. Stanford, Calif.: Stanford University Press.

Levinas, Emmanuel (1991a) *Le temps et l'autre (Time and the Other)*. Paris: PUF.

Levinas, Emmanuel (1991b) *Otherwise than Being: or, beyond essence*. Norwell, Mass.: Kluwer Academic.

Levinas, Emmanuel (1995) *Dieu, La Mort et le Temps (God, Death and Time)*. Paris: Kluwer Academic.

Levinas, Emmanuel (1996) *Transcendance et intelligibilité (Transcendence et Intelligibility)*. Paris: Labor et Fides.

Levinas, Emmanuel (2000) *De l'existence à l'existant (Existence and Existents)*. Paris: Vrin.

Levinas, Emmanuel (2006) *Humanism of the Other*. Chicago, Ill.: University of Illinois Press.

Petitdemange, G. and Rolland, J. (1988) *Autrement que savoir: Emmanuel Levinas avec des études de Guy Petitdemange and Jacques Rolland*. Paris: Osiris.

Schürmann, Reiner (1987) *Heidegger on Being and Acting: From principles to anarchy*. Bloomington, Ind.: Indiana University Press.

PART II

PAINT IT PINK: ANARCHISM AND FEMINISM

5

UNDOING PATRIARCHY, SUBVERTING POLITICS: ANARCHISM AS A PRACTICE OF CARE

Mitchell Cowen Verter

SUBVERTING THE MILITARY LOGIC OF POLITICS

At its roots, anarchism is already deeply feminist. When we consult Greek literature, we learn that the term 'anarchy' was first used in the active, anti-political sense to describe the behaviour of Antigone, a re/sister who rose up against her uncle Creon[1] to rebel against the military logic of fraternity and fratricide, a logic which divides humanity into friends who are loyal to the state and enemies who betray it. Denounced as an anarchist in both Aeschylus's (1991) and Sophocles' (1994) accounts of her tragedy,[2] Antigone opposes this antagonistic logic in the name of a more ethical mode of human interconnection, one that affirms that we must unconditionally nurture each other, even beyond the moment of death.

The link between feminism and anarchism has similarly been noted in the writings of more recent anarcha-feminists, as in Lynne Farrow's 1974 proclamation that 'Feminism practices what Anarchism preaches. One might go as far as to claim feminists are the only existing protest groups that can honestly be called practicing Anarchists' (2002). Taking these examples as our inspiration, we will endeavour to recollect this deep connection between the project of anarchism and the feminist critique of patriarchy.

Before we consider the importance of the feminist critique, let us begin by asking what are the aims and aspirations of anarchism. Anarchism is sometimes defined simply as the refusal of the state. However, anarchism must strive towards a much more profound goal than this. The long history of authoritarian domination has penetrated our ways of thinking and acting so deeply that an anarchist critique must re-evaluate the very roots of political philosophy, of the thinking that considers communality in terms of political association. The feminist scholar Nancy Hartsock argues that Western political thinking has been shaped by the way that the Greek *polis* (city-state) emerged out of what she terms the 'barracks community' (Hartsock, 1982, p. 283). Within this military encampment, the paradigmatic virtues were defined as courage, heroism, glory and the striving for immortality; human relationships were conceived as being fundamentally antagonistic and competitive, as struggles for power and domination. Hartsock claims that war and the masculine role of the warrior-hero have been central to our conception of politics ever since: for example, the warrior's dominance on the physical battlefield has been transformed into the citizen's dominance on the battlefield of rhetoric and into the businessman's dominance on the field of commerce (Hartsock, 1982, pp. 285–6).

The logic of militarism prevails not only within mainstream conceptions of politics, but also within various strands of radical thinking, from Marx's belief that class struggle is the engine of history to Badiou's celebration of the militant as a model for political subjectivity. Most alarming is the way that such militarism runs throughout the writings of the French *Tiqqun* group. Within these texts, we find the standard masculinist warnings against the way one is 'castrated' (Tiqqun, 2010b, p. 18) by mass society, as well as a hostile denunciation of the figure of the 'Young Girl', who represents for them the shallow bitch who succumbs to the idiocy of consumer culture. Worse yet are the recurrent calls to violence. Not only does it cite Clastres's proclamation that 'war is the truth of relations between communities' (Tiqqun, 2010a, p. 22), but the text *Introduction to Civil War* also tells us, 'Only the timid atom of imperial society thinks of "violence" as a radical and unique evil. ... For us, ultimately, violence is what has been taken from us, and today we need to take it back' (Tiqqun, 2010a, p. 10). We are similarly informed that hostility is a primordial relationship and that the 'hostis is a nothing that demands to be annihilate' (2010a, p. 12).

COMMUNALITY AS THE NURTURANCE OF NEEDS

Clearly, some sort of revolution will be necessary to disarm the elite who oppress and immiserate the mass of humanity by their maintenance of power, property and violence. However, it is even more important to recover models of subjectivity and sociality that do not follow this military model. Is the political conception of human sociality sufficient to describe our relationships with each other, and more importantly, should it be the basis for imagining our anarchist future? Part of the problem is that we tend to think of human sociality as being already saturated by politics; that we subscribe either to the Hegelian vision that the state is the transcendental sphere which sustains all other particular affiliations, or to the Foucaultian vision of an immanent micropolitics that determines and disciplines all intimate relationships. But is human existence really so dominated by the political? By submitting to this domination, do we not already foreclose the exploration of other forms of human sociality?

It is important to note that, even in one of the foundational texts of political philosophy, there are already clues that point towards other possibilities. In the first lines of his treatise on *Politics*, Aristotle declares that the *polis* (city-state) is only one among several kinds of human *koinon* (community), another of which is the *oikos* (home) (1996, 1251b1ff). Unfortunately, however, the analysis he offers of the home is the prototypically patriarchal one, a definition that has been influential throughout Western history. Not only does Aristotle claim that the home is encompassed within the state, but he also intersects these two communal spheres in the figure of the patriarch, who establishes his dominion over the domestic sphere through a process of domination and domestication, and who establishes the science of *oikonomos* (economy) to order the household and to acquire property (1996, 1253b1ff). However, Aristotle supplements this patriarchal analysis of the household with a secondary definition. The household is not simply the locus of domination, but more fundamentally, it is the association where people come together to attend to their everyday needs and wants, the communal space where people become companions through the activity of eating together (Aristotle, 1996, 1252b12–20).

How are these two definitions of the home, as the sphere of domination and as the sphere of need, related to each other? Hannah Arendt collapses these two definitions, arguing that the vulnerability of bodily need is our primordial experience of being dominated, and that our need to dominate the needs that dominate us is the reason why we need to elaborate structures of hierarchical political domination (1998, p. 31). Arendt's correlation of dependency with domination is one of the most problematic and most characteristic aspects of patriarchal thinking. This repudiation of dependency becomes so absurd that many patriarchal thinkers even conceal the fact that we are born unto women. Thomas Hobbes, for example, inaugurates the modern conception of citizenship by comparing political subjects with mushrooms that spring out of the ground fully formed, emerging as isolated individuals who can freely establish contracts and submit to rulers (1998, p. 205).

Are there not different ways of understanding the vulnerability experienced in individual and social life? Can we not embrace a non-patriarchal vision of the home as a site for the enactment of responsibility for the needs of ourselves and other people, as a place for caring, refuge and hospitality; as a model for empathetic sociality? Could the affirmation of such social nurturance not subvert the hierarchical and antagonistic logic of the political?

MATERNAL NURTURANCE AS A MODEL FOR CARE

In order to consider these alternatives, it is useful to return to the critical interventions of feminist ethics. These analyses are interesting not because they posit an essence of 'the feminine', but rather because they have engendered a fecund critique of the patriarchal system. According to Nancy Hartsock, the dominant powers in any society promulgate an understanding of social relations that is both partial and perverse, an ideology that not only perpetuates social inequity but also denies the true nature of social life (1983, pp. 287–8). Hartsock argues that a feminist standpoint arises not out of any essential female difference, but rather because women have tended to occupy social roles involving material sustenance and support, and this proximity to materiality allows them to understand how much our everyday lives depend upon the satisfaction of material needs (1983, pp. 291ff). Influenced by Hartsock, Sara Ruddick explains that:

> care workers depend on a practical knowledge of the qualities of the material world, including the human bodily world, in which they deal. This means that the material world, seen under the aspect of caring labor, is organized in terms of people's needs and pleasures and, by extension, of the needs and pleasures of any animal or plant that is instrumental in human caring or is tended for its own sake.
>
> (Ruddick, 2006, p. 130)

Ruddick's research into caring labour is carried out though an investigation of maternal thinking. She defines maternal thinking as the pattern of cognition that emerges out of the practice of mothering, a set of attunements women acquire as they become responsible for meeting the demands of a child. The child confronts the mother as a completely helpless being, one who is totally dependent upon her for the satisfaction of all its most basic needs. The activity of mothering requires that the mother – who according to Ruddick can be of any gender (2006, pp. 40ff) – respond to the material reality of this human vulnerability in a way that does not enforce power relations. Even the weakest mother can overwhelm the fragility of a dependent child, but domination is not what defines the activity of mothering. Instead of establishing rigid control over the child, Ruddick recommends what she terms 'holding' as the best way to preserve its fragility, a practice that maintains safety of the child, promotes its strength, and allows it to flourish without establishing any ownership over it (2006, pp. 78–9). In addition to reconsidering the importance of maternal care, other feminist thinkers have similarly re-evaluated the category of domestic nurturance. For example, bell hooks discusses how black women maintained what she calls 'home place' as a site of resistance against rampant racism, a refuge where people could gather and heal themselves from the wounds inflicted by a hostile society (2001, pp. 41–9).

Many contemporary anarcha-feminists avoid themes such as mothering and the household out of a desire to avoid gender essentialism. However, we do read anarcha-feminist authors arguing that traditionally feminine concerns such as domestic labour, sexuality and child rearing should not be treated as mere addendums to the anarchist project, but must be central to our vision of an anarchist society. This attitude was expressed most strongly in an early essay by Roxanne Dunbar in which she argued:

> If the maternal traits conditioned into women are desirable traits, they are desirable for everyone, not just women. By destroying the present society and building a society on feminist principles, men will be forced to live in the human community on terms very different from the present. For that to happen, feminism must be asserted by women as the basis of revolutionary social change.
>
> (Dunbar, 1970, p. 499)

ANARCHISM AS A PROGRAMME OF NURTURANCE

I would argue that the importance of maternal nurturance is at the very core of the anarchocommunist project articulated by Peter Kropotkin and others. Errico Malatesta once attested to this aspect of Kropotkin's personality, remarking:

> I remember what [Kropotkin] did in Geneva in the winter of 1879 to help a group of Italian refugees in dire straits, among them myself; I remember the small attentions, I would call maternal, which he bestowed on me when one night in London having been the victim of an accident I went and knocked on his door; I recall the innumerable kind actions towards all sorts of people.
>
> (Malatesta, 1965, p. 258)

Beyond this anecdotal evidence, when we read Kropotkin's work, we should be reminded of how much his thinking resonates with Sara Ruddick's characterization of care work as the organization of the material world in terms of people's needs and desires.

The best way to understand Kropotkin's thinking is to see how much it embraces human vulnerability and how much it insists upon the paramount virtue of nurturance. In his writings on mutual aid, Kropotkin repeatedly articulates the value of human dependency. For example, he characterizes solidarity as 'the unconscious recognition of the force that is borrowed by each man from the practice of mutual aid; of the close dependency of everyone's happiness upon the happiness of all' (1902, pp. xliii–xliv). Kropotkin's notion of dependency seems remarkable in several ways. First, he does not equate the notion of dependency with that of domination. Second, his notion of mutual aid emphasizes human dependency more than it does human capacity. That is, he concentrates not on the fact that people possess powers that they can contribute to the common good, but rather that each of us depends radically on the sustenance granted by infinite others. Third, his idea of dependency should not be reduced to the reciprocity of interdependence. While it may be true from an outside perspective that all of our social contributions balance each other out, what is important is that, from my own perspective, I realize how indebted I am to the rest of humanity.

Kropotkin's interpretation of human dependence provides the basis for his critique of property ownership. People depend so utterly upon what other people have already contributed that they never have a foundation to claim anything as their own. Private property is unjust not simply because it fails to recognize the worker's agency as a producer, but rather because it neglects to accept our infinite dependency as consumers. For this reason, Kropotkin declares:

> All things are for all men, since all men have need of them, since all men have worked in the measure of their strength to produce them, and since it is not possible to evaluate every one's part in the production of the world's wealth. That each and every person has a right to well being; there is a right to well being for all.
>
> (Kropotkin, 1995, p. 19)

According to Kropotkin, the problem of satisfying needs is the most essential problem of all revolutionary problems, and the question of how we nurture each other is the most important of all revolutionary questions.

The analysis of human needs also provides the basis for Kropotkin's critique of capitalism and the state. First, Kropotkin argues that capitalism, supported by the state, reorients material life such that it caters to the needs of the rich: rather than providing well-being for all of humanity, production becomes focused on producing luxury items for the wealthy – and by extension, for wealthy countries like our own. Second, he explains that the wealth of the wealthy ultimately derives from the poverty of the poor. Only because people are allowed to suffer such profound material destitution can the capitalist compel them to become labourers, paying them a meagre wage that allows them barely to subsist. Third, one of the alibis that the state employs to justify its existence is its monopoly over the activity of care. The state eliminates autonomous institutions of mutual aid, replacing them with various forms of charity, welfare and health care. While any form of care is significant and should be defended, the care function of the state allows it to mask the fact that the state exists as the institution that facilitates the domination of the rich and powerful and abets the immiseration of the poor and subjugated.

Despite the efforts of the state to monopolize caring, anarchists have persevered in the effort to create a society based on mutual aid. The revolutionary significance of an anarchism based on nurturance can be observed in both institutional and spontaneous settings. Anarchist groups such as Food Not Bombs organize to feed the hungry; the Really Really Free Market organizes to provide a space for free exchange of goods; the Icarus Project organizes to help people with psychological difficulties to give each other support and therapy; various squatting initiatives help people to find shelter.

In addition, we have seen examples of spontaneous anarchist nurturance throughout the uprisings in North Africa. What seems remarkable about these revolutions is not just that people rose up en masse to overthrow their leaders, but also the way that they supported each other throughout. Protesters in Tahrir Square, for example, managed to keep each other fed, tended to each other's bodily needs, and endeavoured to keep each other safe. Reporting from Egypt, Mohammed Bamyeh marvelled at how the occupants of the square:

> established autonomous field hospitals to treat the injured; formed street committees to maintain security and hygiene. I saw peasant women giving protestors onions to help them recover from teargas attacks .... and countless other incidents of generous civility amidst the prevailing destruction and chaos. ... During the ensuing week and a half, millions converged on the streets almost everywhere in Egypt, and one could empirically see how noble ethics – community and solidarity, care for others, respect for the dignity of all, feeling of personal responsibility for everyone – emerge precisely out of the disappearance of government.
>
> (Bamyeh, 2011)

A similar gesture of solidarity was practised by Tunisians who, having consummated their uprising, welcomed refugees from the Libyan conflict with food and shelter. The *New York Times* quotes Abdallah Awaye explaining, 'This is how it is, these are our customs. If there is something to eat, we will eat it together. If there is nothing to eat, we will have nothing together' (Sayare, 2011). Such behaviour constitutes the very greatest example of ethical anarchism.

CONCLUSION

In conclusion, let me reiterate some of my basic points and then comment briefly about what this might say regarding our current state of anarchist thinking. First of all, rereading feminist critiques can help us to remember what has been suppressed by centuries of patriarchal thought: namely, that the nurturance of material needs is more fundamental than the establishment of control. Anarchist thought should focus more on how to nurture and sustain each other. Furthermore, this is precisely what many anarchist initiatives have practised and continue to practise.

Not only should anarchists focus on promoting human well-being, we should be more careful about using the same military logic promoted by the patriarchal state. As stated in my introduction, there is something really terrifying about not only the violence but also the sectarianism promoted by the Tiqqun group. Their various texts urge us to 'find each other' (Invisible Committee, 2009, p. 65). While human solidarity is always a worthwhile goal, the Invisible Committee's notion of communal organization sounds combative to the point of paranoia. The positive task of human affiliation is shadowed by an intense antipathy towards others who are not 'worthy' of being part of the commune (Invisible Committee, 2009, p. 66). The group proclaim:

> To the citizens of Empire, we have nothing to say. That would mean we shared something in common. As far as they are concerned, the choice is clear: either desert, join us and throw yourself into becoming; or stay where you are and be dealt with in accordance with the well-known principles of hostility: reduction and abasement.
>
> (Tiqqun, 2010a, p. 39)

The destructiveness of such a statement is idiotic and reprehensible. In New York and elsewhere, we have seen how this type of sectarian rhetoric has produced very real violence within the anarchist milieu. Once we understand that the goal of anarchism is human nurturance, we should reconsider the priority of our anarchist mission to be not to 'find each other' but rather to 'feed each other'. Once we understand caring as a core principle of anarchism, we will endeavour not to establish coming communities of like-minded friends who are bound together by a common political spirit, but instead to create the 'coming community' as 'the community of those who have nothing common' (Lingis, 1994), one that will spread well-being to all.

NOTES

1 The Greek κρέων translates literally as 'ruler'.
2 In *Seven Against Thebes*, Antigone declares that she is 'not ashamed to act in anarchist opposition to the rulers of the city' (*oud' aischunomai echous' apiston tênd' anarchian polei*) (1035–6). In *Antigone*, Creon condemns her, asserting that 'there is no evil worse than anarchy' (*anarchias de meizon ouk estin kakon*) (673).

REFERENCES

Aeschylus (1991) *Aeschylus II*, ed. D. Grene and R. Lattimore. Chicago, Ill.: University of Chicago Press.

Arendt, H. (1998) *The Human Condition*. Chicago, Ill.: University of Chicago Press.

Aristotle (1996) *Politics*, ed. H. Rackham. Cambridge, Mass.: Harvard University Press.

Bamyeh, M. (2011) 'The Egyptian Revolution: first impressions from the field', Jadaliyya. Accessed July 15, 2011, www.jadaliyya.com/pages/index/561/the-egyptian-revolution_first-impressions-from-the-field-

Dunbar, R. (1970) 'Female liberation as the basis for social revolution', in R. Morgan (ed.), *Sisterhood is Powerful*. New York: Random House.

Farrow, L. (2002) 'Feminism as anarchism', in Dark Star Collective (ed.), *Quiet Rumors*. Oakland, Calif.: AK Press.

Hartsock, N. (1982) 'The barracks community in western political thought: prolegomena to a feminist critique of war and politics', *Women's Studies International Forum*, 5:3/4.

Hartsock, N. (1983). 'The feminist standpoint', in S. Harding and M. B. Hintikka (eds), *Discovering Reality*. Boston, Mass.: D. Riedel.

Hobbes, Thomas (1998) *Man and Citizen*, ed. B. Gert. Indianapolis, Ind.: Hackett.

hooks, b. (2001) 'Homeplace: a site of resistance', in *Yearning*. Boston, Mass.: South End Press.

Invisible Committee(2009) *The Coming Insurrection*. New York: Semiotext.

Kropotkin, P. (1902) *Mutual Aid as a Factor in Evolution*. London: Heinemann.

Kropotkin, P. (1995) *The Conquest of Bread and Other Writings*, ed. Marshall S. Shatz. Cambridge: Cambridge University Press.

Lingis, A. (1994) *The Community of Those Who Have Nothing in Common*. Bloomington, Ind.: Indiana University Press.

Malatesta, E. (1965) 'Peter Kropotkin: recollections and criticisms of an old friend', in V. Richards (ed.), *Errico Malatesta: His life and ideas*. London: Freedom Press.

Ruddick, S. (2006) *Maternal Thinking: Towards a politics of peace*. Boston, Mass.: Beacon Press.

Sayare, S. (2011) 'Thousands fleeing Qaddafi bask in Tunisia's hospitality', *New York Times*, April 28, 2011.

Sophocles (1994) *Antigone*, ed. H. Lloyd-Jones. Cambridge, Mass.: Harvard University Press.

Tiqqun (2010a) *Introduction to Civil War*, trans. J. E. Smith and A. Galloway. Cambridge, Mass.: MIT Press.

Tiqqun (2010b) *Theory of the Young Girl*, Zine Library. Accessed May 1 2011, http://zinelibrary.info/files/jeune-fille.pdf

6

OF WHAT IS ANARCHA-FEMINISM THE NAME?

Cinzia Arruzza

INTRODUCTION

On May 2, 1992, anarchist groups from different countries took part in the International Anarcha-feminist meeting in Paris, organized by the Women's Commission of the Fédération Anarchiste Française, on behalf of the International Federation of Anarchists (IFA). Among the tasks taken up at this meeting was the attempt to define what exactly anarcha-feminism stands for. As noticed in one of the preparatory contributions to this meeting, developing a feminist *and* anarchist thought had as an aim the 'feminization' of the libertarian movement, the introduction within the anarchist movement of different, deeply egalitarian practices, but also the 'anarchization' of feminist practices, via the refusal of the 'totalitarianism of sisterhood'. This refusal, therefore, implied naming the political differences that divide the feminist movement, abandoning the ideas both that women are a homogenous social subject and that the women's movement is a unified political actor (Rosell, 1992).

By stressing the necessity of breaking the 'totalitarianism of sisterhood', the meeting was taking a critical stance with regard to some recent developments of second-wave feminism. In particular, it criticized the second wave's cooptation by political parties, state and other institutions; its concealment of class and race differences behind the notion of universal sisterhood; and most fundamentally, its incapacity to establish a political and theoretical bond between a critique of male power and the denunciation of the state as the patriarchal institution *par excellence* (see Trume, 1992). With the critique of the conception of the feminist movement as a unified totality held together by some kind of automatic solidarity of interests among women, the meeting consistently tried to promote the necessity of defining in a far clearer way the theoretical and political profile of anarcha-feminism as a specific current characterized by the insertion of the critique of male power into a more general opposition to every form of power and domination.

The international anarcha-feminist meeting's effort at self-definition and its published expression of differentiation from other feminist currents has been rekindled since 1992 in more recent publications, like Heller's book, *Ecology of Everyday Life*, published in 1999, or the 2010 monographic issue on anarcha-feminism of the journal *Réfractions*. These publications tried to make good on the striking delay in the theoretical development of anarchist feminist thought.[1] Looking at some writings on women's condition and emancipation by authors like Emma Goldman or Voltairine de Cleyre, or at the documents produced by the Spanish movement *Mujeres libres* in the 1930s, you can find surprisingly modern analyses and political positions, which anticipate second-wave feminism from several viewpoints. It appears, however, that in the following decades these elements were not theoretically developed within the anarchist movement. Of course, the reasons for this under-theorization are numerous, and have to do with both the political marginalization suffered by anarchism and the resistance often offered by the anarchist movement itself to the autonomous organization and political elaboration of women. This resistance was often motivated not only by influence exerted by common sexist prejudices and habits within the anarchist movement, but also by the belief that anarchism did not need a feminist movement, for women's liberation was already implied in the general goals of the anarchist movement. [2]

What I would like to suggest is, on the one hand, that the impact of second-wave feminism on the anarchist movement and the kind of analysis of the feminist movement offered by anarchist feminist activists in the 1970s should be included among the main reasons for the delay in the theoretical development of anarcha-feminism; and on the other hand, that anarcha-feminism should be rethought today in relation to the recent developments in eco-feminist, materialist and queer theory, in order to answer the crucial question about the specific theoretical and political role and nature of anarcha-feminist thought.

In what follows, I try to point out briefly the peculiar aspects of the critique of women's oppression in Emma Goldman's and

Voltairine de Cleyre's articles, and the way in which these aspects coalesce to produce an original view that anticipates second-wave feminism.[3] I then focus on a series of articles written in the 1970s on the specific question of the relation between anarchism and feminism, and finally I try to delineate the new challenges raised by poststructuralist feminism for the theoretical development of anarchist feminism today. In this way, I hope to contribute to elucidating the question of the specificity of anarcha-feminism in the context of the flourishing of gender and sexuality theories from the 1970s onwards.

THE ORIGINALITY OF EMMA GOLDMAN AND VOLTAIRINE DE CLEYRE

In Goldman's and de Cleyre's articles on women's liberation (see Goldman, 1970; de Cleyre, 2005), it is possible to find a very peculiar combination of three elements: first, a class perspective on women's condition; second, a critique of emancipationist feminism, particularly with regard to the questions of suffrage and of economic equal opportunities; and third, a focus on sexual liberation and the development of a critique of bourgeois morality and its institutions, such as marriage.

The article 'The traffic in women' (in Goldman, 1970), in which Goldman articulates her anti-prohibitionist position on prostitution, combines class analysis, denunciation of the sexual reification of women, and a critique of bourgeois morality. As Goldman underlines, bourgeois public morality, while contributing to the view that women are sex objects, simultaneously instils in women a deep ignorance about their own sexuality, thereby rendering many women incapable on the one hand, of having control over it, and on the other, of separating it from biological reproduction. While she explains the phenomenon of prostitution as having its origin in class exploitation and poverty, Goldman denounces the hypocrisy of bourgeois society displayed in prohibitionist policies, for a number of reasons. The public condemnation of prostitution is hypocritical, first, because it is a facet of the very system of class exploitation on which bourgeois society relies – for bourgeois society creates the increased necessity of prostitution as a means of survival for the women it economically exploits. Second, it is hypocritical because the primary alternative option open to economically disenfranchised women – that is, the institution of marriage – is nothing but the legal ratification of an economic transition that compels women to offer sexual services in exchange for a living. Goldman's appraisal of marriage echoes the analysis of the economic basis of monogamous families already articulated in several socialist writings, and theoretically developed particularly in Engels's pages on monogamy in *The Origin of the Family* (1996, pp. 95–118). From this point of view, marriage is not seen as particularly different from other forms of prostitution that are morally and legally condemned by society. To quote a passage from Goldman's 'Marriage and love':

> Marriage is primarily an economic arrangement, an insurance pact. It differs from the ordinary life insurance agreement only in that it is more binding, more exacting. Its returns are insignificantly small compared with the investments.
>
> (Goldman, 1970, p. 38)

In her article, 'Those who marry do ill', Voltairine de Cleyre underlines the disadvantages of long exclusive relationships, particularly when they imply economic dependence (de Cleyre, 2005). This prolonged and permanent economic and sexual relation between a man and a woman, by developing a strong interdependence through its method of home keeping, has a fundamentally negative effect both on the free development of the individual and on love. The conclusion is therefore clear, and it implies the separation of sexual desire from reproduction, the questioning of individual child-raising, the absence of any economic bond between the partners, and the radical rethinking of what a love union is in general, for the sake of the full development of women's personalities and of the liberation of their sexual desire:

> That love and respect may last, I would have unions rare and impermanent. That life may grow, I would have men and women remain separate personalities. Have no common possessions with your lover more than you might freely have with one not your lover. Because I believe that marriage stales love, brings respect into contempt, outrages all the privacies and limits the growth of both parties, I believe that 'they who marry do ill'.
>
> (de Cleyre, 2005, p. 206)

The third reason why, according to Goldman, prohibitionism is hypocritical, is that it conceals the fact that prostitution is itself thinkable only as a result of the sexual objectification of women, an objectification that lies at the very root of a social and patriarchal division of gender roles:

Nowhere is woman treated according to the merit of her work, but rather as a sex. It is therefore almost inevitable that she should pay for her right to exist, to keep a position in whatever line, with sex favors.

(Goldman, 1970, p. 20)

As noted above, this denunciation of bourgeois hypocrisy concerning marriage and sexuality is combined with a class analysis. In two articles on suffragism and emancipationist feminism, 'Woman suffrage' and 'The tragedy of woman's emancipation', Goldman endorses a class perspective in order to underline the constitutive limits of suffragist demands within the liberal feminist movement. On the one hand, suffragism is, in fact, detached from the vast majority of working-class women and does not take into account their economic needs and interests. On the other hand, the achievement of equal suffrage does not imply any improvement in working conditions and wages, or the overcoming of the wage difference between men and women. On the contrary, combined with the demand for equal economic opportunities (that is, the possibility of choosing a career), it contributes to the illusion of the possibility of a full emancipation of women within a society based on class exploitation and domination.

It is particularly in her critique of a narrow view of emancipationism and of the effects that this has on the concrete lives of women, that Goldman anticipates the critique of emancipationist feminism that will be developed several decades later in second-wave feminism. Goldman shows, at a very early stage, how emancipationism makes the mistake of thinking that what is needed is nothing more than independence from external tyrannies, while the internal tyrants – social and ethical conventions – are problematically left in their place. The result is that in a situation in which the totality of social and human relations remains unchanged, the emancipated woman is pushed to become a vestal, and to sacrifice her desires and the possible development of a free and authentic sexuality for the sake of her independence.[4]

Both de Cleyre and Goldman point out how the sexual division of labour, social conventions, institutions like marriage, public morality and normative motherhood all contribute to block the free development of women as human beings. The result of this process is a mutilated human being, one who is made dependent, reckless, cowardly, sexually repressed, unable to struggle and lacking social consciousness (Goldman, 1970, pp. 42–3). What we are accustomed to calling a 'woman' is the result of this set of social conventions, rules and institutions which, in addition to exerting an external pressure, have been interiorized. Through this process, the possible horizon for the development of women's human nature has been dramatically curtailed.

What needs to be noticed here is that behind such a denunciation of women's condition there is the idea of a human nature and a sexuality given before power relations. The domination and exploitation implied in power relations is therefore responsible for the oppression and mutilation of a human nature, that is always already given. In other words, human nature plays the role of an historical invariant that, exactly in virtue of this invariance, offers the possibility of a critical stance with regard to existing political, economic and social conditions. These conditions, indeed, are criticized, for they are an obstacle to the full development of capacities that are already, un-historically, implied in women's humanity.

ANARCHA-FEMINISM AND SECOND-WAVE FEMINISM

Goldman and de Cleyre did not develop a theory of women's autonomous political organization. They anticipated – as we have seen – some arguments that were later endorsed by second-wave feminism. They did not anticipate the centrality that would later be acquired by the question of the processes of women's subjectification through forms of separatist or autonomous self-organization. In this sense, a fundamental contribution would rather come to be offered by the experience of *Mujeres libres* in Spain.[5] However, Goldman's and de Cleyre's view on women's liberation, with its combination of the three elements I quoted above – class perspective, critique of emancipationism and centrality of the question of sexuality – occupied an original and peculiar position with regard to both liberal emancipationist feminism and socialist feminism. In other words, the seeds of anarcha-feminist thought distinguished from other feminist currents were already present.

The flourishing of second-wave feminism in the 1960s and 1970s, and the way in which it was welcomed by anarcha-feminist authors, contributed to blocking the growth of these seeds, instead of encouraging it. Under several aspects, second-wave feminism appeared to anarchist authors and activists to be a sort of practical application of anarchist organizational principles. Its refusal of leadership and hierarchy, its critique of centralism and delegation, its support of small-sized groups, and its willingness to strongly relate the public

and private – focusing on personal behaviours, practices and liberation – all contributed to blunting critique from an anarchist direction.
The question of organizational forms, and of the strong solidarity
between radical feminism and anarchist feminism, is the central
topic in the few theoretical anarcha-feminist writings of the 1970s,
particularly in the United States. I am referring here in particular to
a set of essays that appeared between 1974 and 1979 in magazines
like *Aurora*, *Second Wave* and *Black Rose*: Peggy Kornegger's
'Anarchism: the feminist connection' (2008), Lynne Farrow's
'Feminism as anarchism' (2002), Marian Leighton's 'Anarcho-
feminism' (1974) and Carol Ehrlich's 'Socialism, anarchism and
feminism' (1979).

The shared assumption of these writings was the existence of
a natural affinity between the feminist movement, particularly in
its radical version, and anarchism. Whereas for Lynne Farrow,
'Feminism practices what Anarchism preaches' (2002, p. 15), for
Peggy Kornegger, it was not only the case that the feminist movement
decisively contributed to libertarian thought, but further, feminists
had been unconscious anarchists in both theory and practice for
years, and needed only to become aware of the natural connection
between anarchism and radical feminism (2008, pp. 21–31).

This unconscious anarchism revealed itself first in the concrete
ways in which the feminist movement was organized: small-sized
groups, the focus on problem-solving projects, the development of
alternative forms of organizing the reproduction of material life,
and the attempt to reshape interpersonal interactions, thereby immediately changing social relations and forms of life, starting with
everyday practices (Ehrlich, 1979, p. 44).[6] Second, the unconscious
trend towards anarchism was evidenced in the critique of the male
domineering attitude, of the hierarchical subordination of both
sensuality to rationality, and intuition to mind (Kornegger, 2008, p.
27; Farrow, 2002, pp. 18–19).

The emphasis on the natural affinity between radical feminism
and anarchism led Kornegger, Farrow, Leighton and Ehrlich to
slightly different conclusions. For Farrow, what the feminists were
doing was exactly what they were supposed to do: not having a
programme, not elaborating big social narratives, having concrete
community-based projects – that is, not planning a revolution. In a
manifestation of suspicion of male-dominated 'logic and its rituals',
she endorsed a blanket anti-intellectualistic position, claiming that
women do not have interests in theoretical assumptions at all. As she
put it:

Because women have no vested interest in theoretical assumptions and their implications and hence no practice in the arts of verbal domination, they will not easily be drawn into its intricate mechanisms.

(Farrow, 2002, p. 19)

For Kornegger (2008), the point was recognizing the need to verbalize the 'subsurface' anarchism underlying the feminist movement: only after the recognition of its unconscious anarchist roots could feminism legitimately proclaim itself the 'ultimate revolution'. A similar view was suggested by Leighton, a founding member of Black Rose Anarcho-Feminists in 1971, when she explicitly raised and answered the question of meaningfully using the 'anarcha-feminism' denomination:

Since anarcho-feminism's primary commitment is and should be made to the radical feminist movement with only marginal participation in anarchist movement politics, does the term 'anarcho-feminist' possess any functional significance, or is it only a confusing label laden with semantic difficulties? My own feeling is that the refining distinction from radical feminist to anarcho-feminist is largely that of making a step in self-conscious theoretical development. Having perceived that there are 'natural' anarchist tendencies in the women's movement, an anarcho-feminist is one who intellectually identifies with major aspects of the intellectual tradition of anarchist radicalism.

(Leighton, 1974, p. 258)

In this view, anarchism became not much more than the explicit, conscious expression of the unconscious anarchist nature of radical feminism. In other words, it gave voice to the conscious expression of the unavoidable relation between a critique of male power and a critique of power *per se*. In this perspective, an autonomous anarchist elaboration on the nature of male power became redundant, as the theorizations of patriarchy articulated by radical feminism were taken at face value, the problem now becoming how, through the development of its critique into a more general critique of power *per se*, to realize their revolutionary potential.

Some 20 years later, in a critical essay on Kornegger's and Farrow's articles, L. Susan Brown underlined how their optimist and simplifying view had not only been contradicted by the following development of the feminist movement, but itself relied on a fundamental disregard for the plurality of feminist perspectives (1996, pp.149–55). I would go one step further, and suggest that this theoretical and political overlap relied on a fundamental misunderstanding about the nature of the motivations of the radical feminist critique of male power. This misunderstanding was made possible by a certain fetishism of the social and organizational forms that led anarchist feminists to mistake the political content of radical feminism. While these anarcha-feminist authors saw in radical feminism the seeds of a general opposition to all forms of power and domination as oppressing and disfiguring human nature, they overlooked the fact that it was rather the demand to empower a specific subject which was constituting itself through a discourse of difference and separation, and was progressively finding expression in it.

Even if it is true that consciousness-raising, project-focused, small-sized groups, combined with a critique of male hierarchies, showed some similarity with anarchist concerns about the consistency between means and end, the other side of the coin is that these practices were part of a project of creating and empowering 'women' as a new subject. This tendency towards identity politics would in the end come to obliterate both the tendency to question domination and power *per se* – which was still present in the foundational texts of radical feminism – and the relationship between women's oppression and class exploitation.

From a theoretical point of view, this process has been overlooked by the anarcha-feminist authors quoted above because of the application of a general and simplistic equation: as specifically male power and male domination are species of the genus power and domination, so too is the feminist movement a species of the general movement against all forms of power and domination. Simply put, the task of the anarcha-feminists would be just making this genus–species relation explicit. This attitude somehow revealed a kind of Enlightenment approach to social and political struggle, according to which anarchism would be the conscious, enlightened and self-aware expression of the unconscious impulses of the feminist movement. The further development of the second-wave movement would soon reveal that the relation between conscious and unconscious is, also in the case of social and political struggle, more complicated than this.

ECOFEMINISM, MATERIALIST FEMINISM AND QUEER THEORY

Some decades later, the few more recent anarcha-feminist writings that have been produced show a much more critical approach to the experience of radical feminism, to its evolution, and a greater awareness of the political and theoretical differences between anarcha-feminism and radical feminism. However, the impressive flourishing of gender theories in the last 30 years raises the question of what should be the specific theoretical space for anarcha-feminism. The definition of this space, in fact, would imply a new, less simplistic exchange with, and analysis of, the current trends in feminist and gender theory.

From the end of the 1990s onwards, a few writings have tried to deal with this issue, confronting in particular ecofeminism, materialist feminism and queer theory. Among the most accomplished attempts in this sense is Chaia Heller's book *Ecology of Everyday Life*, published in 1999. Whereas Heller does not renounce claiming the presence of an 'anarchist impulse' both in the feminism of the 1960s and 1970s, and in the emergence of ecofeminist activism in the 1980s, she also points out the limits of their anarchism. In particular, she criticizes their tendency to abstraction and their romanticizing of both nature in general and women's nature in particular, the loss of 'degrees of immediacy and historicity' (Heller, 1999, p. 46), the tendency toward an individualist account of subjectivity, the increasing absence of a critique of capitalism and of the state rooted in a historical analysis, and with a few exceptions, the erasure of the question of race.[7] Starting from this critical appraisal, Heller tries to delineate the grounds for a new anarchist ecofeminist perspective.

The value of this project lies in its refusal to resort, on the one hand, to a romantic or nostalgic view of nature, and on the other, to a standard opposition of spirituality and rationality. Heller rather insists on the possibility of building an anarchist ecofeminism on the phenomenology of what she calls the 'socio-erotic': a spectrum of social desires oriented toward collectivity, sensuality and non-hierarchy, which are not opposed to rationality but are, on the contrary, rationally informed. In fact, according to Heller, the dichotomy between rationality and spirituality (which informs a large part of ecofeminist theory), and the equation between what is rich, deep and meaningful with what is not rational, fails to take into account the possibility of using reason in order to create structures and ways of life in which social desires can find a meaningful and cooperative expression (1999, p. 115).

For Heller, these social desires are rooted in human nature understood in its sociality. Desires are the product of the social life of human beings, but at the same time affect – in a dialectic relation between individuality and society – the forms of sociality. While

Heller refuses to rely on a simplistic view of the goodness of human nature, insisting – along with Kropotkin – that human nature entails both the impulse to sociality and its opposite, she nevertheless relies on the idea of human nature and its potentialities in order to ground her notion of social desire. As in traditional anarchism, human nature remains a resource of resistance to social power relations.

Resorting to the notion of human nature, however, is among the crucial assumptions anarcha-feminism would need to challenge today, in the light of the radical questioning of such a presupposition by materialist feminism and queer theory. As I tried to show, the idea that the relations of exploitation and domination prevent women from realizing themselves as full human beings is at the core of the first anarchist critiques of women's oppression. But should this idea still be at the core of anarcha-feminism today? Should the task of anarcha-feminism be to gender the notion of human nature, or to move beyond this very idea? This question is particularly compelling, as both materialist feminism and queer theory have challenged the idea of any natural basis for the division of sexes, arguing that gender as a social construct precedes and causes the sexed body. The point, therefore, is not developing a notion of human nature capable of including the specificity of gender and sex, but rather renouncing 'human nature' as both the grounds for a feminist critique of women's oppression and the source of a politics of liberation.

This problem is debated, among others, in the very recent monographic issue of the journal *Réfractions, Des féminismes, en veux-tu, en voilà*, which confronts the anarchist tradition (focusing particularly on anarcho-communism and anarcho-syndicalism) with the current political practices within anarcha-feminist and libertarian milieux, and with contemporary feminist theories. All its articles share common perspectives concerning the critique of individualist anarchism, the centrality of class exploitation and its relation to race and gender oppression, the collective strategies of women's emancipation and their bond with other collective struggles; however, the appraisal of the contribution of deconstructionism to feminist theory looks more problematic.

Françoise Picq, for example, considers that queer theory represents a new form of avant-gardism, which not only dissolves the women as a subject, but further does not show any political solidarity with women as an oppressed group. She therefore insists on the fact that the relationship man/woman is the 'subject and the object of the feminist project', against both the obliteration of maternity in materialist feminism, and that of the subject and of gender in queer theory (Picq, 2010, pp. 5–13). In her article, 'Être anarchiste et féministe aujourd'hui', on the contrary, Irene Pereira welcomes the deconstruction of the biological difference between the sexes carried out by materialist feminist authors like Elsa Dorlin. As she notices, considering sex as a class differentiation and not as a biological one leads to an interrogation of anarchist anthropology. The question is, indeed, whether anarchist anthropology leads to the deconstruction of the sexual biological difference or not, and whether it is capable of contributing fruitfully to the debate on the relationship between social and biological categories (Pereira, 2010, pp. 68–9).

This debate, although still very embryonic, shows a willingness to deal theoretically with issues as fundamental as the role of nature in women's oppression, the relation between different systems of domination, and the role of the interaction between class, gender and race in the processes of subjectivation and strategies for collective liberation. This marks a fundamental difference from the anarcha-feminist writings of the 1970s. These writings, in most cases, confined themselves to reminding the feminist movement – and particularly radical feminism – of the need for binding the struggle against gender oppression to the more general struggle against domination, without questioning radical feminism's analysis of the reasons and origin of male domination.

NOTES

1 On the necessity of filling this gap also from the point of view of gendering anarchist historiography, by developing a specific and adequate methodology, see Greenway (2010).

2 For an analysis of the underestimation of the specific character of women's oppression, within individualist anarchism, see Steiner (2010). For an analysis of 'anarcho-sexism' see Dupuis-Déri (2010).

3 For a presentation of Emma Goldman's thought see the recent book by Ferguson (2011), in particular chapter 4, 'Gender and genre', in which the author challenges the psychological approach in the scholarship on Goldman's feminism, which is inclined to stress the contradictions between Goldman's political positions and her dependence on male lovers.

4 Like Engels, and after him Bebel, Zetkin and Kollontaj, de Cleyre insisted on the fact that the other side of the coin of wage slavery was the new possibility for women of economic independence and reinsertion into the society, opened by capitalist development. As she noticed, bread is the basis of all independence and individuality. See 'The case of woman versus orthodoxy', in de Cleyre (2005, pp. 209–19).

5 On the history of *Mujeres libres* see Ackelsberg (2004).

6 Jo Freeman (1972–3), on the contrary, criticized the very idea of the existence of informal structures: the informality of women's groups in fact conceals decision-making processes which are often based on hidden hierarchies and power dynamics within the group. This is why formal structures which embody clear principles of democratic structuring are preferable, as they make decision-making processes accountable and not rooted in interpersonal relationships and preferences. See also Cathy Levine's response (1979).
7 In particular, Heller points to the WomanEarth Feminist Peace Institute's operations between 1984 and 1989.

REFERENCES

Ackelsberg, Martha A. (2004) *Free Women of Spain: Anarchism and the struggle for the emancipation of women*. Oakland, Calif.: AK Press.

Brown, L. Susan (1996) 'Beyond feminism: anarchism and human freedom', in Howard J. Ehrlich (ed.), *Reinventing Anarchy, Again*. Edinburgh and San Francisco, Calif.: AK Press.

De Cleyre, Voltairine (2005) *Exquisite Rebel: The essays of Voltairine de Cleyre, feminist, anarchist, genius*, ed. S. Presley and C. Sartwell. Albany, N.Y.: State University of New York Press.

Dupuis-Déri, Francis (2010) 'Hommes anarchistes face au féminisme. Pistes de réflexion au sujet de la politique, de l'amour et de la sexualité', *Réfractions*, 24, pp. 107–21.

Ehrlich, Carol (1979) 'Socialism, anarchism and feminism', repr. (2008) as pp. 41–50 in *Quiet Rumors: An anarcha-feminist reader*. San Francisco, Calif.: AKA Press/Dark Start.

Engels, Friedrich (1996) *The Origin of the Family, Private Property, and the State*. New York: Pathfinder.

Farrow, Lynne (2002). 'Feminism as anarchism', repr. (2008) as pp. 15–20 in *Quiet Rumors: An anarcha-feminist reader*. San Francisco, Calif.: AKA Press/Dark Start.

Ferguson, Kathy E. (2011) *Emma Goldman: Political thinking in the streets*. Lanham, Md.: Rowman & Littlefield.

Freeman, Jo AKA Joreen (1972–3) 'The tyranny of structurelessness', repr. (2008) as pp. 54–61 in *Quiet Rumors: An anarcha-feminist reader*. San Francisco, Calif.: AKA Press/Dark Start.

Goldman, Emma (1970) *The Traffic in Women and Other Essays On Feminism*. New York: Times Change Press.

Greenway, Judy (2010) 'Remembering women, reminding men: the gender politics of anarchist history', paper given at the panel on Anarchism and Feminism, PSA Conference, Edinburgh 2010 (available on www.judygreenway.org.uk/anarchfem.html).

Heller, Chaia (1999) *Ecology of Everyday Life: Rethinking the desire for nature*. Montreal, New York and London: Black Rose.

Kornegger, Peggy (2008) 'Anarchism: the feminist connection', pp. 21–31 in *Quiet Rumors: An Anarcha-feminist reader*. San Francisco, Calif.: AKA Press/Dark Start.

Leighton, Marian (1974) 'Anarcho-feminism', repr. (2001) as pp. 253–8 in *Reinventing Anarchy, Again*. Edinburgh and San Francisco, Calif.: AK Press.

Levine, Cathy. (1979) 'The tyranny of tyranny', repr. (2008) as pp. 63–6 in *Quiet Rumors: An anarcha-feminist reader*. San Francisco, Calif.: AKA Press/Dark Start.

Pereira, I. (2010) 'Être anarchiste et féministe aujourd'hui', *Réfractions*, 24, pp. 63–72.

Picq, Françoise (2010) '"Vous avez dit queer?" La question de l'identité et le féminisme', *Réfractions*, 24, pp. 5–13.

Rosell, Thyde (1992) 'Anarcha-féminisme', *Actes de la Rencontre Internationale Anarcho-féministe*, 2 May.

Steiner, Anne (2010) 'De l'émancipation des femmes dans les milieux individualists à la Belle Époque', *Réfractions*, 24, pp. 19–29.

Trumel, Nelly (1992) 'Les raisons de l'anarcho-féminisme', *Actes de la Rencontre Internationale Anarcho-féministe*, 2 May.

7

BLACK, RED, PINK AND GREEN: BREAKING BOUNDARIES, BUILDING BRIDGES

Laura Corradi

INTRODUCTION

From 1990 onwards, new social movements have been expressing different forms of agency in terms of collective action, mobilization capacity, and self-reflection, re-elaboration of their own goals, limits and methods. Their relevance, contextual to the economical and ecological crisis, has been highlighted by a growing popular sympathy. So-called masses seem to be outraged by social inequality, the evidence of degenerative forms of patriarchy, and spontaneously take part in multifaceted processes of delegitimization of political parties and institutions.

The new social movements' antagonism to the status quo has been expressed at different levels: social, political and economic; it also includes, to certain degrees, critical issues related to gender, sexual orientation and the relationship between humans and the rest of nature. Interestingly enough, new social movements show several forms of engagement in radical discursive practices – in an intermittent way, often alternating dissimilar types of tactics and approaches to institutional politics in unpredictable ways. As stated by Laraña, Johnston and Gusfeld, what is significant for sociologists 'is the inability of these movements to be clearly understood within the European-American traditions of analysis. They constitute the "anomalies" of Kuhnian normal science' (1994, p. 3). If such anomalies can give birth to a new paradigm, they need to be a special focus of our interest as both scholars and activists.

The purpose of this chapter is to share empirical results and propose a new way to look at different kinds of oppositional political identities acting today within new social movements – which have somehow different roots and common intermittent practices. The empirical research discussed here focuses on the individual perception of constitutive elements of the four main components of contemporary social movements: the older 'historical' ones – anarchism and communism – and the younger ones, feminism and ecologism, which emerged in a powerful way during the social and political struggles of the 1960s and the 1970s. My research aimed to understand the activists' representations of anarchism, communism, feminism and ecology within the new social movements. By using chromatic terms, the object of the project was the individual perception of how black, red, pink and green have played a role in the making of each activist's political life. This sociological project – which may be considered unique in its genre in the new social movements milieu – has been inspired by Ilvo Diamanti's work *White, Red, Green and Blue* (2003), a masterpiece of politology in the context of Italian institutional parties, in which he discusses the political positions of Christians, communists, communitarians – that is, the 'green' Lega Nord – and the new Berlusconi party Forza Italia, whose choice of colour fell on a tranquillizer – heavenly, sky azure. In a nutshell, colour matters, even when boundaries between them get blurred. The results of my research were presented at the International Conference on 'Black and Red' at the University of Nottingham in 2008. Given the interest expressed by colleagues and friends, I felt encouraged to pursue more data.

Today in Western countries, mobilization against neoliberalism for health, environment, for social justice, against all types of exploitation and exclusion, has created a plethora of groups and associations as protagonists. They can be seen as hosting diverse traditions and mixed heritages: eco-anarchists, eco-feminists, eco-Marxists, anarcha-feminists, Marxist feminists, libertarian communists and so on. An amazing trend of combining old and new lines of thought can be identified both in the literature and in the realm of social and political praxis where this research found its context of relevance.

Some methodological remarks will be useful. In my work, anarchism, communism, feminism and ecology have been treated as large *signifiers*. All subjects interviewed have been asked to give definitions of what anarchism, communism, feminism and ecology meant to them. In so doing, they personally engaged with their – often unquestioned – significance, on the basis of individual and social experience, readings and sharing: digging in their own biography. Much silence, density of thinking and concentration have been involved in the interviews. The research subjects took quite seriously the task of defining themselves and decoding those signifiers – understanding how their activism has been nourished by different theories and ideas – in the reconstruction of how the attribution of a certain meaning has occurred, and in analysing how much of 'the others' is present in us, given the deep *metissage* of political praxis and milieux.

I had some expectations in this investigation. One was to encourage a spontaneous process – through the decoding of subjective political identities and discursive practices – in the direction of facilitating the awareness of an ongoing practice of breaking boundaries and building bridges in terms of better cooperation. This course of action is already taking place in several struggles of our social reality, while the reflection amongst scholars and activists seems to be not yet geared toward the necessity of shifting the attention from differences to commonalities.

There are several arenas where blacks, reds, pinks and greens are found together, such as antifascism and antiracism, in social movements against neoliberal globalization and 'humanitarian' wars; against nuclear energy and genetically modified organisms (GMOs); in lesbian, gay, bi and transexual (LGBT) associations, autonomous groups and grassroots organizing for health, environment, animal rights; in precarious workers' unions, students' collectives and indigenous rights organizations; in new waves of peasants living in communes, and in anti-authoritarian kindergartens. There are so many places where communists, anarchists, feminists and ecologists coexist. And I found more than that: such different identities tend to overlap within the subjects themselves.

LOCATED KNOWLEDGE: UNVEILING THE PERSPECTIVE

This work has been carried out with a reflexive sociology (Bourdieu, 1992) approach. If I am allowed to situate my research in terms of located knowledge, I should first confess a radical feminist methodology. Scandalously, I started from myself, having grown into diverse political environments since my childhood, with a Gramscian grandmother, who had been a partisan *staffetta*. The other one was a *curandera* in her peasant community. I had a self-defined anarchist, despotic and repressive father, who deeply loved his own freedom and the idea of masses, and turned later into a fan of the Italian communist party, and a Gandhian mother, who believed in women's liberation. My adolescence was spent as a factory worker, full-time on a production line, where the study of Marxism was the only mental survival option. After the late achievement of a high school degree, I gained access to college and worked as a part-time janitor and babysitter. I was a fresh working-class student in a petit bourgeois, 'autonomous' university in Padua, where Negri's theory was hegemonic in an authoritarian way.

During my PhD years at the University of California at Santa Cruz, and then as a scholar-activist, I always had the feeling that different political ideas were finding space in my own way of thinking, merging in a non-dichotomous manner. Through the years, libertarian authors and practices have influenced me. Since 1990, I have studied Afro-centric and Native American theories, and had the opportunity of an early and intense political experience with the Zapatistas (1994–6), which included being a participatory observer at the *Acuerdos de San Andres de los Pobres* between the EZLN and the Mexican government. The *Intercontinental Encuentros Contra El Neoliberismo y Por la Humanidad* (1996–7) – organized first by the indigenous Mayan populations – highlighted the divisions and conflicts among Western activists (which have never been properly addressed or resolved) and also established the awareness of the need to create global venues of debate. The *Encuentros* stimulated the birth of an embryo of consciousness, which led eventually to the constitution of the World Social Forum – which, despite the internal bureaucracy, in its early years represented an important arena for attaining more contamination among different components, for producing a discussion geared toward action (leaving aside Western unproductive ideological debates, which suddenly didn't make much sense in the context of the world).

My quest for a non-Eurocentric political perspective in the last two decades has been deeply affected by postcolonial and subaltern studies. Eco-feminism and aboriginal sociology, as well as Adivasi indigenous standpoints and struggles, helped to re-educate me, in combination with my living for some time in jungle contexts. Reading about primitive subversions (Kulchyski, 1992) and gaining a theoretical and practical understanding of native cosmogonies made an important difference in my own existence and as a political militant.

Surprisingly enough, most of the interviewees did not make explicit reference to indigenous or aboriginal people's theory and practice, even though those who identified themselves with ecological thought used several concepts that can be traced back to indigenous cultures. This is one of the reasons why, in this chapter, I have chosen to offer, as a qualitative research sample, an interview with a native feminist scholar activist. I felt such a perspective was missing amongst the (mostly white) interviewees.

My central hypothesis is that subjects who are committed to social change and engaging in a radical questioning of the status quo – regardless of their ideological identifications – are inspired both theoretically and practically by different sets of ideas and social/political praxis. Overall, we may say today that social movements can nourish themselves from a common heritage, which is at times contradictory. The research project does not aspire to obliterate the value of differences and a history of conflicts among the four components examined. However, the goal is to focus on today's social representations, a synchronic perspective which may help to look further at the real state of the relations among the components themselves. As we shall see, the research results point out how heterodoxy is widespread among activists of different ages, who seem to have built their identities as colourful patchworks.

I decided to work with no other hypothesis than a larger one based on the assumption of commonalities between different components, and the existence of different ideas and concepts (taken from different traditions) in each subject. I asked the interviewees, 'What do "anarchism", "communism", "feminism" and "ecology" mean to you?' The body of empirical data that emerged consists of five in-depth interviews of privileged witnesses and 30 questionnaires administered with an oil-splash type of recruitment. Most of the subjects involved in the research seemed to be happy about having the opportunity to focus on their own political identity. Someone even told me it never occurred to them to look at themselves in such a deep way.

I now present my research results, beginning with an interview with Roxanne Dunbar-Ortiz, political activist and author of the introduction to *Quiet Rumors: An anarcha-feminist reader* (2002). She was chosen as a privileged witness, as a person who has been studying and writing on the subject of intersections – in particular, between anarchism and feminism.

INTERVIEW WITH ROXANNE DUNBAR ORTIZ

Her self-definition is the following: 'feminist, historian, revolutionary'. She considers these to be super-identities, self-identifications, gifts.

Other identities pertain to whom she is materially: 'a working class person with a poor family background', a 'Native American from Oklahoma'.

Communism, for Roxanne, is 'the only force challenging capitalism; the dedication of communists I met, [they were] as models in my life and activism; the seeming irrationality of anti-communism [made me think of] the fragility of capitalist ideology; [and today I feel] the lack of communist analysis and organizing, in the US.' Also in her account of communism, there are 'national liberation movements and Maoism – which weren't always positive', yet she feels some of these ideas are to be considered part of her background.

In talking about anarchism, Roxanne starts with a preface about significant persons in her family. Her grandfather was 'a Wobbly in Oklahoma, where farmers had been kicked off the land'. Her father had a strong class consciousness, but anti-union feelings, 'a Scotch-Irish man who was convinced all [unionists] were sold out'. Her mother, a Native-American who embraced the Baptist Evangelical religion, was a 'very mystical' woman. A quite mixed heritage started to interweave her identity at an early age. Then, as a young adult:

> during Civil Rights movements in Oklahoma ... [the idea of] freedom and African American oppression ... I made my choice which side to be .... I have a very strong anti-authoritarian personality, with individualism and without selfishness. The essence of anarchism (differently from communism) is trusting the awareness of people to be out for the community.

For her, anarchy is mostly 'refusing to be a follower and to be a leader. Never trust leaders.' She ends by commenting how 'anarchism can exist without the analysis of capitalism and imperialism. It questions the state, but it does not change the state. It has a flow but it is an expression of freedom.'

Her account of feminism starts with a self-reflection: 'I never thought of myself as a female; I was so conscious of class. I was discriminated because poor not as a girl. [Then] Simone's [De Beauvoir] *Second Sex* in 1963... I was a teenager in the 50s and read everything translated!' In a sex-segregated social context where she lived, feminism at first meant, 'Understanding how women do act out the roles of patriarchy', which had to do with the 'common resentment toward the mother'. Her mother had become an alcoholic and died from it. Anger and bitterness were 'part of the feeling of sisterhood with other women ... at that time Valerie Solanas shot

Andy Warhol [which allowed us to] understand the "crazy woman" and the source of one's violence'.

While she was doing her doctorate, 'anti-militarism and anti-violence led to feminism, mutual support and mutual assistance, health centers, challenging the state, and the Vietnam War'. In that period, the writing of 'William Hanton, *Fan Chen Village*' was crucial. 'During [the] cultural revolution [the book[helped us for our own organizing – so young feminists picked up also anti-imperialism'. Then it was the time of '*Daring to be Bad* in the 80s – the divide between cultural and political feminists, and lesbian feminism, the purple menace with the pink triangle.'

Roxanne's ecological awareness started during the anti-Vietnam war activism, with the information about 'Agent Orange and chemical warfare' and in the anti-nuclear movement, later in promoting pesticide awareness. For her what is very important is the struggle for 'health and environment, [since] the beginning chapter of Marx's *Capital* – [the parts on] deforestation, pollution, slums, colonialism] ... the less known ecological part of Marxism' is the one she refers to as the most useful.

Finally, ecological thought played a crucial role in her decision of 'becoming a vegan, aware of animal rights, and politicize my behavior about how to respect the planet – which is related with my being a Native.' At the end, her Native identity, her familial heritage, became an identity choice encompassing even her recent choices. Her very roots, enriched with the consciousness she acquired during her life (through personal experience, readings, sharing with others) closed the circle of the interview in a meaningful way.

GIVE ME FIVE: DEFINITIONS

Now let us look at eight interviews of students (who also engage in precarious work) and manual workers, followed by eight interviews of intellectual workers (scholar-activists). This part of the research was named 'give me five'. I asked the subject to provide five definitions for each signifier (anarchism, communism, feminism, ecology). The following results should be read as synthetic narratives, as semi-precious raw stones excavated from the mine of individual and social memory. I have underlined the most frequent definitions, while the self-identification definition of the subject is highlighted in bold characters.

The first three interviewees considered here were participants at a 'no nuke camp' in the Puglia region, in southern Italy, where I delivered a feminist leadership workshop in the summer of 2008. A student, a young woman of 25, defined herself as a **libertarian communist** and gave the following definitions:

Communism: sharing; clarity; rationality; method; goals

Anarchy: freedom; self-liberation; fun; creativity; autonomy

Feminism: revolution here and now; many girlfriends and women comrades; self-consciousness and self-government of the body; irony; pleasure

Ecology: future beyond myself; new generations; overcoming personal ego and anthropocentrism; harmony; relationship with the territory.

Her girlfriend, a militant in the same group, was also a student, 27 years old, who described herself as a **queer feminist**. She gave a definition in which the concept of 'consciousness' played a pivotal role:

Communism: a family against the family; training; utopia; experimentation; songs

Anarchy: consciousness of individuality; importance of small things; mental openness; equal and horizontal relationships; radical oppositional consciousness

Feminism: consciousness of myself; different relationships with family, other women and people; belonging; solidarity; personal self-determination

Ecology: consciousness of being an element of a living organism; anti-speciesism; vegetarianism; hope; projects.

A self-defined **communist feminist**, a woman student aged 27, gave the following classification, highlighting the concepts of self-determination and responsibility across the traditional ideological boundaries:

Communism: equality; sharing; self-determination; hope; resources

Anarchy: responsibility; direct action

Feminism: consciousness of myself and my relationships with others; self-determination; strength; rage

Ecology: will of living well; participation; responsibility; ecological action.

A 55-year-old activist and shoe-maker, mother of three, whom I interviewed in the communal house she had founded in Calabria, described herself with a political slogan: **no vote**. Here the definitions she offered tended to cross old ideological boundaries:

Communism: respect; sharing property; cooperation; freedom; a circular form of communication and decision making

Anarchy: love, trust, altruism of service; happiness of communion; the spirit of the village

Feminism: Magics; the strength of expressing myself and avoiding male authoritarian energy; fighting subalternity; having children; finding my male energy

Ecology: relationship between theory and praxis in everyday life; earth as rest; intuition and creativity; direct action; working outside and passing my experience to others.

In the same household, which is commonly identified as an anarchist milieu, a 42-year-old male farmer described himself as a **post-Marxist ecologist**, and gave the following definitions:

Communism: analysis of society; class relations; capital-labour and capital-nature; history of evolution of capitalism; the commodification of human relations

Anarchy: solidarity; laicism; power of the state; critique of bureaucracy; freedom

Feminism: the differences in the physical relationship between males and females; legal and economical inequalities; gender solidarity; analysis of the gender differences

Ecology: different approach to the economy; different development; change in priorities; global environmental emergencies; resources.

Another occasional guest of the house, a manual worker and self-defined **anarchist**, male, 37 years old, gave the following characterization. It is interesting to notice the similarities between keywords chosen to define communism and anarchy at one end, and feminism and ecology at the other:

Communism: solidarity; equality; idealism; social justice; organization

Anarchy: freedom; solidarity; equality, social justice, eco-sustainability

Feminism: respect of women's freedom; consciousness in the couple relationship; diversity; awareness of gender oppression; power

Ecology: against the state; respect for nature and environment; energy; sobriety; self-production.

A man aged 37, who belonged to the same anarchist federation as the above interviewee, defines himself as a **libertarian**. Curiously, he attached the word 'freedom' – which is emotionally loaded – to communism and feminism, while for defining anarchy he chose more rational types of meanings:

Communism: equality; collective work; literature, Gramsci; struggle against dictatorships and for freedom

Anarchy: self-management; self-production; self-government; self-esteem; self-sufficiency

Feminism: refusing submission; more sexual freedom; equality and responsibility; gendered anti-authoritarianism; critique of the command and gender violence

Ecology: respect of living beings; vegetarianism; contact with the earth; lifestyle and example as consciousness building.

Another man, a nomadic craftsman aged 52, defined himself as libertarian and attached the word freedom to communism, while reserving the key word 'respect' for anarchy and ecology:

Communism: freedom; equality; independence; sharing, co-operating and helping with no private property; transparent relationships in couples

Anarchy: revolution from within; giving value to people around you; respect for humans and nature; talking to people and giving information; avoiding self-exclusion i.e. staying in 'reservations'

Feminism: victories around the body and work

Ecology: respect for nature, exchange; cleaning forests and rivers; change the system; stop consumerism.

The first intellectual worker I interviewed was a Colombian mother, aged 37, a researcher who defined herself as a **feminist libertarian**. In her descriptions, she attributed freedom to communism and feminism, and used the keyword 'desire' for anarchism and feminism, and 'spiritual' for ecology, which was quite common among the interviewees:

Communism: understanding; freedom; joy; togetherness; praxis

Anarchism: playfulness; spontaneity; desire; importance of the individual; rupture

Feminism: liberation; freedom; subjectivity; the unity of intellectuality and desire; the body

Ecology: balance; non-human otherness; spiritual; metaphysical; groundedness.

A young assistant professor, aged 34, mother of two, defines herself as a **libertarian feminist post-Marxist anarchist ecologist**. She placed 'freedom' in what is usually considered to be the right spot and combined 'liberation' with feminism twice:

Communism: fight against alienation; solidarity; liberation; fight against capitalism; human emancipation

Anarchism: freedom; emancipation; critique of established authority; self-government; autonomy

Feminism: women's liberation; equality between sexes; liberation of the body; creativity; struggle

Ecology: relation with nature and environment; rediscovering our being as part of nature; respect for the others; future generations; saving the planet from ultimate disaster.

A Greek researcher, male, 39 years old, defined himself as **anti-authoritarian** and gave the following definitions:

Communism: romanticism; simplicity; modesty; self-sacrifice; pride

Anarchism: against money; no power; no showing off; love; ecology

Feminism: respect; understanding; non violence; love

Ecology: food; water; air; sun; rain.

A British professor, male, aged 66, chose **anarcho-Marxist** as a way to portray himself. In his descriptions, 'freedom' combined with anarchism, while 'equality' was the common keyword for communism, feminism and ecology:

Communism: utopia; discipline and order; orthodoxy; education; equality

Anarchism: spontaneity; freedom; self-organization; art; imagination

Feminism: gender equality; opposition to violence; sexual equality; lesbianism; anti-hierarchy

Ecology: balance; anti-industrialism; anti-globalization; environmentalism; species equality.

A young researcher, female, aged 25, defined herself as an **anarchist feminist**. She saw the ethics of relationships as a link between anarchism and feminism, while equality and egalitarian relationships connect communism and anarchism. Expressive values were dominant in her account of the contribution ecology gave to her political identity:

> Communism: multifaceted theory and practice; communal living; equality for women in the workplace; the work of Marx; strong economical analysis and proposal

> Anarchism: freedom; responsibility; counter-normativity; philosophy of everyday life; ethics of relationship

> Feminism: ethics of relationships; queer theory; specific oppression of women; provides tools for creating egalitarian relationships; useful tool for people of all genders and sexual orientation

> Ecology: sustainability; love for nature; the importance of future; putting humans into context; the circle of life: death, birth, growth.

A scholar from Cyprus, a woman, aged 40, defined herself as an **anarchist** and gave the following characterizations. Interestingly, the concept of freedom links communism and anarchism; the concepts of imagination and 'the embodiment of theory and practice' connect anarchism and feminism. Organization describes both her idea of communism and ecology, which is mostly characterized by rational types of concept:

> Communism: organization; resistance; protection of working class; imagination; discipline

> Anarchism: self-government; fearlessness; freedom; embodiment of theory and practice; imagination

> Feminism: freedom; way of life; protection of women; resistance; embodiment of theory and practice

> Ecology: organization; future oriented action; globality; creativity; commitment.

A researcher, male, aged 30, defined himself as a **critical anarchist-communist**. He offered the following descriptions, also based on equality and freedom, acknowledging that feminism contributed an important aspect to his own identity:

Communism: equality; cooperation; the material basis of freedom; historical movement; care for others

Anarchism: participation; substantial freedom; non-dogmatism; necessity for action; critique of moralism

Feminism: deconstructing masculinity; questioning myself and my sexuality

Ecology: the transcendence of nature; notion of gift; respect; transience: the ephemeral, beauty.

A young intellectual worker, male, aged 24, defined himself as a **revolutionary** and gave the following definitions, where the rational aspect is attributed to ecology. For the previous interviewee, it was described in opposite terms:

Communism: common property of means of production; revolution; conflict; class struggle; organization

Anarchism: self-management; emancipation; struggle; freedom; education

Feminism: sex equality; sexual freedom; gender consciousness; deconstruction of dominating relations; emancipation

Ecology: respect for the world; rational relation to environment; respect for nature; green technology; questioning productivity.

A COMMENTARY

The richness of the data offers the reader some evidence for an ideological miscellaneousness which calls for some remarks. Regardless of how the interviewees represented themselves, their statements appear to resemble each other. In other words, it does not matter that much if the self-definition is primarily as anarchist or communist, feminist or ecologist – which at times is difficult to assess, given a wide range of original self-definitions. Since they were asked to focus on the positive aspect of each line of thought, they tended to offer similar visions and display a feeling of satisfaction afterward.

Beyond the positive methodological edge – which was a native suggestion – communism seems to have lost much of the authoritarian features of the past. While anarchism finds its proverbial individualism downplayed, it still keeps an uncontaminated aura of creative chaos. Being a radical feminist, I was expecting to find clear signs of how feminism has been changing the two main ideologies in a prevalent way. Instead, what I found is a high degree of contamination in all directions. Concepts that are commonly attributed to feminism and ecology seem to have influenced the representation of each interviewee's personal history and experience (among those with both communist and anarchist backgrounds). Feminist and ecological perspectives appear to have inspired and stimulated in a similarly powerful way both manual workers and intellectual workers, males and females.

The research data is prone to be submitted to further analysis. A slight difference seems to emerge between feminism and anarchism, showing inward types of concepts, while communism and ecology were mostly associated with outward-type concepts. They seem to be located on a continuum, between poles of subjective and objective, in a non-dichotomous way.

A comment on similarities in the personal dictionaries used by the interviewees: most definitions could be easily swapped with each other, since the political identity of the signifying subject is not at all indicative of the attributed meanings. Moreover, if we look at the words chosen by the interviewees, there is a recurrence of terms usually considered to be non-political: love, beauty, desire, body, sex(uality); and other terms which are also found in different political areas, such as solidarity, respect, equality, here combined with a revolutionary vocabulary, as in the case of self-determination, autonomy, liberation, direct action. In reality, words seem to not belong to specific political arenas, and tend to be exchanged and appropriated in different expressions and meanings by the subjects, even changing their sign. For example, features like 'idealism' are given an unquestioned positive sense. In the connotation of the signifiers, the main difference I found between manual workers and intellectual workers seemed to be more conformity of the latter to the standard ideological boundaries, in face of more 'poetic' and unconventional types of description in the first group.

CONCLUSIONS

Overall, the interviewees seemed to offer what I would call 'post-ideological' representations. There is no evidence of correlation between the types of self-definition and the ways in which conceptual terms are allocated in reconstructing what each interviewee has been taking from each set of ideas in order to define a personal political identity and agency.

The research results seem to confirm that activists involved in global justice mobilization tend to have multiple identities. As new social movements theorists Della Porta and Diani wrote, the phenomenon has been often left uninvestigated: 'little attention has been given to the systems of relationships in which actors are involved, and this has prevented the multiplicity of identities and allegiances among militants and movement groups from being recognized' (2006, p. 98). Also within the same group or association, 'collective identification is rarely expressed through integrated homogenous identities'. This can be explained, because identity is a fluid matter, 'a social process, not a static property'. In other terms, the identities of people who actively engage in social movements today do not have a hierarchical structure; they can be defined as multiple identities (Calhoun, 1994) or polycentric identities: 'identifying with a movement does not necessarily mean sharing a systematic and coherent vision of the world; nor does it prevent similar feelings from being directed to other groups and movements as well'. Therefore group identities 'can be seen as a meeting point of histories, personal needs and heterogeneous representations' (Della Porta and Diani, 2006, p. 99), which clearly emerges from the research results. One of the reasons for the permanence and appeal of new social movements, despite differences and contradictions, may be the fact that 'global justice activists have so far displayed a great tolerance toward each other's combination of identities' (Della Porta and Diani, 2006, p. 100) – a positive output, a sign of complexity awareness, may be an encouraging feature of the post-modern condition (Harvey, 1990).

The interviewees' statements made me think about Alberto Melucci's early works on new social movements (e.g. Melucci, Keane and Mier, 1989), where he discovered that a small group can experience multiple orientations within itself, being like a reflection, a microcosmos, of the movement as a whole. In my research, located in the political crossroads of communism, feminism, anarchism and ecology, in questioning how different concepts inform similar political identities (and how similar concepts affect different political identities) several issues remained unaddressed. An important one about blurring boundaries between communism, feminism, anarchism and ecology has a strategic value: what are the minimum common denominators in the collective political representations of communism, anarchism, feminism and ecology?

I found an unexpected correspondence between the representations of communism and anarchism – maybe the sign of a reciprocal influence which is, in the world of politics, unrevealed to some extent: anarchists who feel the need for Marxist economic analysis, and communists who are aware of the need to respect individual freedom, who deeply question the authoritarian drifts. All interviewees seem to be in different ways impacted by feminism and ecology in terms of self-reflection as wo/men and as human beings, as a part of the natural/social environment. Maybe boundaries have been broken and bridges have been built while we were still looking at ideological divisions. Perhaps we should look more at new realities in a non-dichotomous way – far from dusty books, with fresh eyes, and with a strong will for learning from the realm of social praxis.

BIBLIOGRAPHY

Babcock, B. A. (1980) 'Reflexivity: definitions and discriminations', *Semiotica*, 30, pp. 1–14.

Biehl, J. (1996) *Finding our Way. Rethinking ecofeminist politics*. Montreal, Canada: Black Rose.

Bourdieu, P. (1992) *Invitation to a Reflexive Sociology*. Chicago, Ill.: University of Chicago Press.

Brown, S. (1993) *The Politics of Individualism: Liberalism, liberal feminism and anarchism*. Montreal, Black Rose.

Buechler, S. M. (1995) 'New social movement theories', *Sociological Quarterly*, 36(3), pp. 441–64.

Calhoun, C. (1994) *Neither Gods Nor Emperors: Students and the struggle for democracy in China*. Los Angeles, Calif.: University of California Press.

Castells, M. (2004) *The Power of Identity*, 2nd edn. London: Blackwell.

Della Porta, D. and Diani, M. (2006) *Social Movements: An introduction*. Oxford: Wiley Blackwell.

Diamanti, I. (2003) *Bianco, rosso, verde ... e azzurro. Mappe e colori dell'Italia politica. (White, Red, Green and Blue)*. Bologna, Italy: Il Mulino.

Dunbar-Ortiz, R. (ed.) (2002) *Quiet Rumours: An anarcha-feminist reader*. London: Dark Star/Rebel Press.

Eisenstein, Z. R. (1995) *Capitalist Patriarchy and the Case for Socialist Feminism*, cited in Nancy Tuana and Rosemarie Tong (eds), *Feminism and Philosophy: Essential readings in theory, reinterpretation, and application*. Boulder, Colo.: Westview Press.

Harvey, D. (1990) *The Condition of Postmodernity*. Oxford: Blackwell.

Holmstrom, N. (ed.) (2002) *The Socialist Feminist Project: A contemporary reader in theory and politics*. New York: Monthly Review Press.

Kornegger, P. (1996) 'Anarchism: the feminist connection', in Howard J. Ehrlich (ed.), *Reinventing Anarchy, Again*. Edinburgh: AK Press.

Kulchyski, P. (1992) 'Primitive subversions: totalization and resistance in Native Canadian politics', pp. 171–95 in *Cultural Critique* 21, University of Minnesota.

Laraña, E., Johnston, H. and Gusfield, J. R. (1994) *New Social Movements*. Philadelphia, Pa.: Temple University Press.

Maurer, D. (2002) *Vegetarianism: Movement or moment?* Philadelphia, Pa.: Temple University Press.

Mcadam, D., Tarrow, S. and Tilly, C. (2001) *Dynamics of Contention*. Cambridge: Cambridge University Press.

Melucci, A. , Keane, J. and Mier, P. (1989) *Nomads of the Present: Social movements and individual needs in contemporary society*. London: Hutchinson Radius.

Meulenbelt, A. (1980) *A Creative Tension: Key issues of socialist-feminism*. Cambridge, Mass.: South End Press.

Mies, M. and Shiva, V. (1993) *Ecofeminism*. London: Zed.

Mohanty, C. T. (2003) *Feminism Without Borders: Decolonizing theory, practicing solidarity*. Durham, N.C.: Duke University Press.

Oberschall, A. (1995) *Social Movements: Ideologies, interests, and identities*. Somerset, N.J.: Transaction.

Pepinsky, H. (1978) 'Communist anarchism as an alternative to the rule of criminal law.' *Contemporary Crises*, 2, pp. 315. Repr. in Charles E. Reasons and Robert M. Rich (eds), (1978) *The Sociology of Law: A conflict perspective*. Scarborough, ON: Butterworths.

Price, W. (2007) *The Abolition of the State: Anarchist and communist perspectives*. Bloomington, Ind.: Author House.

Plumwood, V. (1993) *Feminism and the Mastery of Nature: Environmental culture: the ecological crisis of reason*. London: Routledge.

Salleh, A. (1997) *Ecofeminism as Politics*. New York: Palgrave.

Salleh, A. (2006) 'Edited symposium: 'Ecosocialist-Ecofeminist Dialogue', *Capitalism Nature Socialism*, 17(4), pp. 32–124.

Tarrow, S. (1998) *Power in Movement: Social movements and contentious politics*. Cambridge: Cambridge University Press.

Tilly, C. (2004) *Social Movements*. Boulder, Colo.: Paradigm.

PART III

GEOGRAPHIES OF ANARCHY

8

THE ANARCHIST GEOGRAPHY OF NO-PLACE

Stephen Duncombe

What does anarchist space and place look like? We have models for imagining the geography of other politico-economic formations: feudalism is local and static, tied to land and rooted in tradition; capitalism, with its dynamic global flows of capital, labour, materials and goods;[1] imperialism's asymmetric relationship between the metropole and the colonies; the homogeneous space and monumental place of fascism;[2] and communism's world-spanning space of proletarian solidarity and reciprocity, directed by a vanguard party. But how do we, or rather how *should* we, imagine an anarchist geography?

UTOPIA IS NO-PLACE

In an attempt to address this question, I am going to take us on a trip to a far away place, a long time ago: Thomas More's mythic island nation of Utopia. There is much for an anarchist to admire in Utopia. There is no money, or private property or privately held wealth. There is a democratically elected government and priesthood, and women can attain positions of power. Living and labour are rationally planned for the good of all, and there is public health and education. Utopians are guaranteed freedom of speech and religion; and, perhaps best of all, there are no lawyers in Utopia. But Utopia is far from an anarchist ideal: slavery is widely practised, and women, even those in power, are decidedly second-class citizens. Political power is hierarchical, and personal liberty is nonexistent. What makes Utopia useful for thinking through an anarchist geography, however, is not the features of the island or the qualities of the society; rather, it is the curious nature of More's description of this idyllic place.

Figure 8.1 Woodcut map of *Utopia* included in the first, 1516, edition

Utopia, written by More in 1515 and 1516, is actually two books (as well as a lot of ancillary material). Book I is fascinating, being about the failure of rational criticism, however it is Book II that is the most appropriate for this discussion, as it involves a description of Utopia with regard to its place and space:

The island of Utopia is in the middle two hundred miles broad, and holds almost at the same breadth over a great part of it, but it grows narrower towards both ends. Its figure is not unlike a crescent. Between its horns the sea comes in eleven miles broad, and spreads itself into a great bay, which is environed with land to the compass of about five hundred miles, and is well secured from winds. In this bay there is no great current; the whole coast is, as it were, one continued harbor, which gives all that live in the island great convenience for mutual commerce.

(More, 2011a)

Throughout *Book II* More goes to great lengths to convince the reader that Utopia does, indeed, exist. There are detailed descriptions of the economic, social and political relations of Utopians. And there are myriad physical descriptions of the country, the cities, the meeting and dining halls, and the houses of Utopia.

Every house has a door to the street and another to the garden. The doors, which are made with two leaves, open easily and swing shut of their own accord, freely letting anyone in (for there is no private property).

(More, 1949, p. 31)

Nowhere is this concern for the veracity of geography more evident than in one of the letters that accompanied the first four printings of *Utopia*.[3] It is a letter from More to the Flemish humanist and book-smith Peter Giles, his real-life friend and a fictional character in his book. In the letter, More worries that he may have gotten a fact wrong about the geography of Utopia. He remembers hearing that a certain bridge was 500 paces long, but his servant (who was present when the island was described) recalls hearing that the river was only 300 paces wide. To resolve this question, More asks Giles to ask Hythloday himself – either by letter or in person when he sees him next – for the true measurement. Through this and many other instances, More convinces us that there is a geography of Utopia (albeit perhaps inaccurately recorded). Utopia exists as a place within space, although an unfortunately timed cough, we are told, keeps More from hearing exactly where it is located on a map of the world.

However, More's description of Utopia is problematic. Indeed, *Utopia* is full of contradictions, riddles and paradoxes. The grandest, and best known, is the name of the place itself. Utopia (composed by More from the Greek *ou* and *topos*) is a place that is, literally, no place. In addition, the storyteller of this magic land is called Raphael Hythloday (or Hythlodaeus), from the Greek *Huthlos,* meaning nonsense. So here we are being told a story of a place which is named out of existence, by a narrator who is named as unreliable.

Read through this lens, More's concern with geographic detail takes on a different meaning. Think back to his conversation with Peter Giles over the specific measurement of a bridge and his request to his friend: Ask Raphael when you see him next. The joke here is that Giles will never ask Raphael anything; there will be no fact checking, because there is no fact-checker, as Raphael only exists in, and as, fiction. In another letter to Giles – this one attached to the second (1517) edition of *Utopia* – More defends the facticity of his account, arguing that if it was merely fiction, he would have had the sense and wit to offer clues to tip off his audience. 'Thus,' he states,

> If I had put nothing but the names of prince, river, city and island such as might suggest to the learned that the island was nowhere, the city a phantom, the river without water, and the prince without a people, this would not have been hard to do, and would have been much wittier than what I did; for if the faithfulness of an historian had not been binding on me, I am not so stupid as to have preferred to use those barbarous and meaningless names, Utopia, Anyder, Amaurot and Ademus.
>
> (More, 2011a)

The irony here, that the 'learned' reader would certainly get, is that this is exactly what More has done in his book. Utopia, the name of the island, means nowhere. Amaurot, the Utopian city described, means phantom (a play on the Greek word *amauroton*, meaning dim or obscure) and so on. So much for the binding 'faithfulness of an historian.'

And so begins the scholarly debate: is the entirety of More's *Utopia* an earnest effort to map out an imaginary Utopian geography? Or is it meant as satire, an exercise demonstrating the impossibility of such a place and space? I think this orthodox debate about whether More was satirical or sincere obfuscates rather than clarifies, and actually misses the genius of *Utopia* entirely. It is both. Written in the tradition of *serio ludere*, or 'serious play', that More admired so much in classic authors, the story presents itself as both fact *and* fiction, sincere *and* satirical, earnest *and* absurd. Utopia is someplace *and* no-place.

More takes pains to convince the reader that Utopia is a real place, and it is through the veracity of the description that they can start to imagine a someplace that is radically different than the world they presently inhabit. In reading *Utopia*, we experience a sense of radical alterity: what is foreign becomes familiar and what is unnatural is naturalized. An alternative vision is provided and then destabilized.

This destabilization is the key. It is the presentation of Utopia as *no place*, and its narrator as nonsense, that *opens up* a space for the reader's imagination to wonder at what their vision of an alternative *someplace* might be. That is, More imagines an alternative to his sixteenth-century Europe which he then reveals to be a work of imagination (it is, after all, no-place.). The reader has been infected; another option has been shown. They cannot safely return to the assurances of their own present, as the naturalness of their world has been disrupted.

The opening lines of a brief poem attached to the first printings of *Utopia* read:

> Will thou know what wonders strange be,
> in the land that late was found?
> Will thou learn thy life to lead,
> by divers ways that godly be?

> (Graphey, 2011)

Once an alternative ('divers ways that godly be') has been imagined, to stay where one is or to try something else becomes a question that *demands* attention and a choice. Yet the choice More offers is not an easy one. By destabilizing his own design of an ideal society, he keeps us from short-circuiting this imaginative moment into a fixed imaginary, a realizable future. We have to generate our own plans, *because* the plan offered up is untenable, unrealizable.

The problem with many social imaginaries is that they posit themselves as a realizable possibility. Their designers imagine a future or an alternative and present it as *the* future or *the* alternative – 'Actually Existing Socialism,' for instance. But what if impossibility is incorporated into the design in the first place? This is exactly what More does. By positioning his imaginary someplace as no-place, he escapes the problems that typically haunt imaginaries. The alternatives More describes are sometimes absurd (a place called no-place?), but this conscious absurdity is what keeps *Utopia* from being a singular and authoritative narrative, a closed act of imagination to be either accepted or rejected. The book, moving metaphors from one medium to another, functions as a sort of source code, providing the core of what can, and must, be modified by us in order to create a functioning Utopian program (for as a program itself, it repeatedly crashes). In the last analysis, Thomas More's *Utopia* is far more than a book, and more ambitious even than a blueprint for a Utopian society. It is not the plan of Utopia that makes *Utopia* a model of anarchist geography. Rather, it is the work that the book enables and encourages. *Utopia* is a design for what Hakim Bey has identified, and Stephen Shukaitis has been calling an imaginal machine: a technology for enabling others to become cartographers of their own dreams.

NEW BABYLON

Let me provide you with another example of this machinery in action: New Babylon as it is currently being constructed, virtually, in, on and over New York City. The original New Babylon was created by Constant Nieuwenhuys (better known as Constant), a Dutch artist and one of the founders of the Situationist International (who, like most members of the SI, left the group soon after). Constant spent a good chunk of his life – from 1956 to 1974 – creating a model for what can best be described as an anarchist geography: a built space for free association and creative play (Nieuwenhuys, 1974).[4] As Mark Wigley evocatively describes in the introduction to an exhibit of Constant's work, New Babylon was meant to be:

> A vast network of enormous multilevel interior spaces propagates to eventually cover the planet. These interconnected 'sectors' float above the ground on tall columns. While vehicular traffic rushes underneath and air traffic lands on the roof, the inhabitants drift by foot through the huge labyrinthine interiors, endlessly reconstructing the atmospheres of the spaces. Every aspect of the environment can be controlled and reconfigured spontaneously. Social life becomes architectural play. Architecture becomes a flickering display of interacting desires.
>
> (Wigley, 1998a)

Platforms, and platforms on top of platforms, joined by hallways, opening up onto rooms that could be transformed at will into other rooms, ad infinitum. Homo ludens, humans-at-play, would wander nomadically through the structure, freely and continuously transforming their relationships to one another and their space, in turn transforming the physical and social geography.

Constant's blueprint for a society of freedom was, however, severely

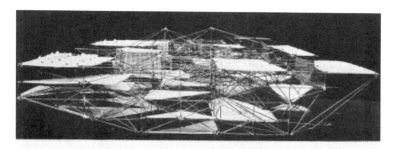

Figure 8.2 Model of New Babylon, Constant Nieuwenhuys

Photographer unknown.

shackled by its mediums. Sequestered to drawings and paintings, and a massive model on display at the Haags Gemeetenmuseum in the Netherlands, his plans for voluntary association and reassociation were fixed in paper, canvas, wood and Plexiglas, the vision of a singular creator frozen in time and space. Constant realized this limitation himself, and writing in a 1974 exhibition catalogue that accompanied his model in The Hague, he explained that:

> Any three-dimensional representation would, in itself, only have the value of a snapshot, since even admitting that the model of each sector may be reduced to several planes and sections of the different levels, and that one manages thereby to constitute a sort of detailed atlas of the sectors, it would still be necessary, from one instant to the next, to record, using symbolic notations as in a ship's log, all the topographical modifications that are produced.

In the next sentence, Constant offers a solution to the immense difficulty of keeping track of the shifting form of New Babylon: 'Recourse to a computer,' he writes, 'will doubtless be necessary to resolve such a complex problem' (Nieuwenhuys, 1974).

In January 2011, New Babylon finally went digital.[5] Its new location was Betaville, a virtual urban planning environment developed by artist/programmer/professor Carl Skelton and used to render lower Manhattan and South Brooklyn in three dimensions.[6] Betaville operates on an open-source software development model, wherein individuals and groups create buildings, artworks and landscapes which are then open for discussion, appropriation, transformation, and re-creation. Using simple and freely available modelling software like Google SketchUp, people build their own structures – terraced housing projects, public art pieces, alternate bikeways, futuristic towers – and then add them to the New York skyline. These structures are then open to visitors to navigate around, over and through. But what makes Betaville a truly liberatory environment is the ability of these visitors, or 'users', to become creators. Every new structure in Betaville can be altered by user/creators who have the ability to add or subtract features and try out new forms, simply by editing the original structure. Like an open source program or a Wikipedia article, all iterations are retained, so you can always revert back to the original source or, moving forward, explore and modify the potentially limitless permutations. Working within this virtual environment and working from Constant's original designs, McKenzie Wark and Ali Dur, two members of the New School community, created New Babylon 2.0.[7]

Visiting New Babylon 2.0 in Betaville is a revealing experience. Clicking on nodes floating in the New York Harbor and hovering over the Brooklyn Bridge, New Babylon unfolds before your eyes, covering large swaths of Brooklyn and Manhattan with multi-hued geometric planes. Manipulating the navigation controls, you can rise above the immense structure or swoop down and explore its sectors, wander its hallways and enter rooms (some with atmospheric music provided by the reigning DJ of the hip and erudite, DJ Spooky), passing though walls and ceilings like a spectre. If you desire, you can remodel the space, coding a new addition or deleting a wall, and saving your version as a new iteration. New Babylon 2.0 finally realizes, albeit virtually, what was forever illusive in Constant's static models.

New Babylon 2.0 works as an anarchist geography in several ways. While Constant proposed that the inhabitants of New Babylon would be able to act spontaneously to reconfigure the space in which they lived and wandered, the initial 'figuring' (that is, the design itself) was to be done by an authoritative individual: Constant himself. It was obviously hard to reconcile such power and authority with

Figure 8.3 New Babylon in Betaville

Source: McKenzie Wark and Ali Dur.

anarchist principles. Betaville, as an open-source platform, however, opens up the planning process itself to collaborative play. What was once a possibility only when New Babylon was built is now integrated into its very creation. To cite Wigley's description again: 'Every aspect of the environment can be controlled and reconfigured spontaneously.' In addition, through the versioning process that is standard in any software development, the element of time, and transformation over time, is introduced. Constant created New Babylon between 1956 and 1974, and Wark and Dur built New Babylon 2.0 over 2010 and 2011. These are done. However, the ability to easily create versions 2.1, 2.2, 3.0 and so on ad infinitum ensures that New Babylon is never done. Flux and change and a responsiveness to new dreams of new peoples are integrated into the geography from the very beginning. There are two, three, many New Babylons.

The most profound way that New Babylon 2.0 realizes an anarchist geography is, perhaps, less intentional. Hovering over its expanse and gliding through its structures, I realized something I had not gleaned during all my time spent studying Constant's sketches, paintings and models of New Babylon: I would not want to live there. It is too big, too imposing, too alienating. When exploring New Babylon 2.0, you get the sense that the nomadic wandering that Constant valorized would, in practice, become an anxious searching as you got lost in a constantly shifting desert of planes and angles. Constant, in an interview in 1962, called his New Babylon 'a labyrinth, inexhaustible in its variations, a palace with a thousand rooms' (Nieuwenhuys and Seyforth, 1962). Kafka's castle comes more to mind. Furthermore, the scale is all wrong. Instead of facilitating and empowering humans, the structure's immensity looms over them; the size of New Babylon announces its sovereignty over the individual. When Le Corbusier sketched his infamous Plan Obus for a new Algiers that would have dwarfed and decimated a city that had grown organically over millennia, he was merely expressing the ideology of an arrogant, elitist Modernism. For Constant, guided by his ideals of unlocking the creativity of ordinary humans and the desirability of free association, to plan something much the same is hard to understand, much less justify.[8] In a word, New Babylon fails.

Yet it is in the very failure of Constant's plans that New Babylon also succeeds. The more dissatisfied I was with Constant's vision of a liberatory geography, the more I was driven to mentally explore and creatively imagine what such a space might look like.[9] New Babylon transported me to a place where I could imagine a geography radically different from the one I inhabit today, yet at the same time the problems with this space kept me from fully 'losing myself' in the pre-packaged imagination of an other. We are continually cast out of the Garden and so must imagine our own. New Babylon, in its failure, finally succeeds in becoming a geography, in Constant's words, 'for playing, for adventure, for mobility' that engenders 'an uninterrupted process of creation and re-creation' (Nieuwenhuys, 1974). Its anarchist potential is unlocked.

Constant noticed that the closer he came toward modelling New Babylon, the less his vision was accepted by others. As he explained in a lecture nearly a decade after he had stopped working on his plan, 'My models appeared to sow confusion instead of fostering understanding for my efforts to visualize a world that was so fundamentally different.' His response was to retreat into more impressionistic representations that would suggest rather than reflect: 'In the end I resorted once more to brush and paints as the most effective way of depicting the unknown' (Nieuwenhuys, 1980). He seems to have recognized the inherent flaw in presenting a fully realized blueprint of a liberatory society, but his move was in the wrong direction, softening his presentation in the hopes that his audience will walk away with a favourable impression. What Constant failed to realize is what More understood: it is precisely the confusion and misunderstanding that allows the audience to develop their own creativity. No longer content to play within a playground designed by someone else, the user, now creator, begins to play with the very ideals of place and space themselves. Contrary to Constant's intentions, New Babylon creates an opening to ask, 'What If?' by not closing down this free space with a convincing answer of, 'This is what!'

By digitizing New Babylon, and rebuilding it on a platform like Betaville, this latent, open quality of New Babylon is made manifest. In Betaville, Constant's vision of an anarchist geography is no longer just a plan, but instead functions as a prompt – a prompt for further imagination on the part of the virtual visitor. Acting as an individual, I am free to edit and rebuild New Babylon; as a collaborative project we create and communicate our vision(s) of what an ideal Anarchist geography might look like. As Thomas More understood, Utopia is No-Place, and it is therefore left up to all of us to find it.

NOTES

1 Ironically, capitalism's dynamic globalism is nowhere better described than in the *Communist Manifesto*: 'In place of the old local and national seclusion and self-sufficiency, we have intercourse in every direction, universal inter-dependence of nations' (Marx and Engels, 1978, p. 476).

2 As Hitler's architect, Albert Speer, described it: 'an architectural stage set of imperial majesty' (cited in Spotts, 2003, p. 364).

3 These four editions: 1516 at Louvain, 1517 at Paris, and two 1518 printings at Basel, were the only editions of *Utopia* in which More had a direct hand, and contained an extensive – and changing – roster of epistles, letters and commendations from More's friends and acquaintances from the European literati.

4 Constant once described New Babylon as a 'Marxist kingdom of freedom', but, like the libertine Marxism of many of the Situationists, his philosophy was a lot closer to Anarchism than Marxist orthodoxy (Nieuwenhuys, 1974).

5 Given the primary function of computers in 1974, Constant could only imagine using them for indexing and inventory: that is, for essentially quantitative operations. The technical and social explosion of computing in the intervening 35 years has demonstrated the computer's use for creative and qualitative endeavours as well, not just ordering and

accounting what has already been imagined and built, but as a tool for imagining and creation itself. Betaville is just such an example.

6 http://betaville.net/. Betaville was initiated at an 'International Urban Media' Symposium at the Media2Culture (M2C) Institute for Applied Media Research at the Hochschule Bremen, in July 2008. The first public demonstration was given at the Summit for the Future of New York City in October 2010.

7 Not coincidentally, Wark, at the same time he was creating New Babylon 2.0, was working on an – excellent – book on the Situationists, *The Beach Beneath the Street* (2011).

8 New Babylon's monstrosity was recognized even in its 'old' form. Zack Winestine, in his unpublished manuscript on the Situationists and the politics of passion, remarks that, '[t]he scale, both of the individual spaces and the overall project, seems inhuman. One gets the sense that New Babylon would be a catastrophe not only for the environment in which it was built, but for the unfortunate people who had to live in it' (2011, ch. 3, p. 18).

9 My disappointment in and disenchantment with New Babylon gave rise to such issues as:

- the desirability of ambitious planning, both its past failures and its absence today
- the role of the planner in relation to those who must reside in the planned space
- the appropriate scale for human habitation
- the relative values of stability and nomadism
- the importance of personal place within social space
- the essential value of nature and organic form within a built society.

All of this sent me on a mental mission to imagine what sort of a world I would like to live in.

REFERENCES

Graphey, C. (2011)'To the Reader,' Open Utopia. http://theopenutopia.org (accessed September 3, 2012).

Marx, K. and Engels, F. (1978) 'Manifesto of the Communist Party', in R.C. Tucker (ed.), *The Marx–Engels Reader*, 2nd edn. New York: Norton.

More, Thomas (1949) *Utopia*, ed. H. V. S. Ogden. New York: Appleton-Century-Crofts.

More, Thomas (2011a) *Utopia, Book II*. Open Utopia. http://theopenutopia. org (accessed September 3, 2012).

More, Thomas (2011b). 'Thomas More to Peter Giles, II'. Open Utopia. http://theopenutopia.org (accessed September 3, 2012).

Nieuwenhuys, C. (1974) 'New Babylon,' exhibition catalogue. The Hague: Haags Gemeetenmuseum.

Nieuwenhuys, C. (1980) 'New Babylon – ten years on', lecture to the Faculty of Architecture, University of Technology, Delft, May 23.

Nieuwenhuys, V. and Seyforth, M. (1962) Interview with Constant. Included in *New Babylon de Constant* (2005), film directed by Victor Nieuwenhuys and Maartje Seyforth.

Spotts, Frederic (2003) *Hitler and the Power of Aesthetics*. London: Pimlico/ Random House.

Wark, McKenzie (2011) *The Beach Beneath the Street: The everyday life and glorious times of the Situationist International*. London and New York: Verso.

Wigley, Mark (1998a) 'Introduction to Constant – New Babylon,' exhibit at the Witte de With Center for Contemporary Art, Rotterdam, November 1998–October 1999. www.wdw.nl/event/constant-new-babylon/ (accessed September 3, 2012).

Wigley, Mark (1998b) *Constant's New Babylon: The hyper-architecture of desire*. Rotterdam: Witte de With, Center for Contemporary Art: 010 Publishers.

Winestine, Zack (2011) *The Politics of Passion*, unpublished manuscript.

9

THE FIGHTING GROUND

Alberto Toscano

The effort to draw intellectual and strategic resources for present anti-capitalist praxis from anarchism and Marxism seems jeopardized from the start by the dispiriting alternative between the production of sterile doctrinal hybrids, on the one hand, and the neurotic revisiting of the primal scene of separation, on the other. Turning to communist lineages, be they 'libertarian' or 'scientific', in geographical thinking is one of the more promising avenues available to those wishing to avoid the commonplaces of dull polemic. Whether this will define new frontlines or forge unexpected alliances is a question I here leave open. A geographical perspective can, among other things, serve to problematize the canonical distinction between the anarchist repudiation of state authority and Marxist arguments for the necessity of planning, by turning our focus toward the broader spatial dynamics, inextricably social and natural, that impinge on any discussion about the organizational forms taken by anti-capitalist politics or by post-capitalist social forms. My starting point here will be the affirmative reference to anarchist geography and specifically to the writings of Peter Kropotkin and Elisée Reclus as we find them in some of the writings of David Harvey, the foremost historical materialist geographer of our time.

Harvey's salutation of the work of these two remarkable protagonists of the nineteenth-century anarchist movement has come at moments when the political vocation of geographical thought was foremost in his mind: in his historical materialist manifesto of 1984, published in *The Professional Geographer* (reprinted as Harvey, 2001), and in recent talks on the right to the city. In the 1984 text, Harvey provides a succinct definition of geography, binding action to explanation:

Geographical knowledge records, analyzes and stores information about the spatial distribution and organization of those conditions (both naturally occurring and humanly created) that provide the material basis for the reproduction of social life. At the same time, it promotes conscious awareness of how such conditions are subject to continuous transformation through human action.

(Harvey, 2001, p. 108)

As Harvey details, this knowledge, while not reducible to the mere status of ideology or instrument, has for much of its history played an important role in serving patterns of action aimed at the reproduction and expansion of a constitutively exploitative, oppressive and geographically disruptive social form, capitalism. Whether mapping the globe for the purposes of navigation and territorial appropriation, describing 'the earth's surface as a repository of use values', inventorying the diverse 'human resources' exploitable as labour, tracing geopolitical horizons and frontlines, rationalizing planning and location, or bolstering through cartography imaginaries of racial and civilizational supremacy, geography has been of signal importance for a social system in which the production, differentiation, localization and destruction of space (and place) is of crucial moment. The utilization of geography, like that of other social and natural sciences, has of course gone hand-in-hand with a dynamic of specialization and professionalization, restricting the scope for reflection and critique.

Harvey's invocation of Kropotkin and Reclus as forerunners of a geography that could think capitalism against the grain is intended to outline an intellectual practice capable of treating the total or planetary reality of space as a condition for social reproduction, and consequently to link this understanding of space to potentially emancipatory political action. Kropotkin and Reclus show that geography 'can become the vehicle to express utopian visions and practical plans for the creation of alternative geographies' (Harvey, 2001, p. 112), and it can do so by treating human, spatial and natural diversity not as a mere resource to be subsumed, mined or capitalized upon, but as the basis for forms of collective life not subsumed by capitalist valorization. For Harvey, it was this spirit that lay behind the emergence, spurred by the insurgent movements of the 1960s and 1970s, of a variegated radical geography centred on 'the process of becoming through which people (and geographers) transform themselves through transforming both their natural and social milieus' (Harvey, 2001, p. 115). While ultimately in no doubt that, to paraphrase Fredric Jameson, Marxism subsumes antagonistic or incommensurable critical perspectives without thereby replacing them, Harvey attends to the contrasts and shortcomings within the anti-capitalist camp. He writes:

> Advocates for community cannot justify a stance of 'community right or wrong' if one community's gain is another's loss any more than environmentalists can reasonably proceed oblivious of employment consequences. Humanists, if they are to avoid the trap of narcissistic radical subjectivism, need a more powerful theory than agency and structure to grapple with macro-problems of money power, inflation and unemployment. Anarchists, while sensitized to ecological and communitarian concerns, lack the social theory to understand the dynamics of capitalism in relation to state power. Marxists come armed with a powerful theory but find it hard to cope with ecological issues or with a subject matter in which highly differentiated activities of individuals and social groups within the particularities of space and place are of paramount concern.
>
> (Harvey, 2001, p. 115)

Political and theoretical integration, 'a common frame of discourse', is the cognitive and political imperative for Harvey, as radical geographers are faced with the restoration of class power – with its spatial and disciplinary dimensions – on a planetary scale. While never forgetting the spaces of hope for alternative geographical futures, the primary task here is one of realism (the absence of which Harvey faults dogmatic Marxism for) about the spaces of capital: 'The world must be depicted, analyzed, and understood not as we would like it to be but as it really is, the material manifestation of human hopes and fears mediated by powerful and conflicting processes of social reproduction' (Harvey, 2001, p. 116). It is on this terrain that the invocation and critique of anarchist geography, and specifically of the work of Reclus, becomes especially interesting. I shall consider it specifically in terms of the question of geographical *difference*, and how this difference is articulated in terms of explanatory theories and political orientations.

Where Marx's own work, and that of most of his heirs, tended to treat geographical differentiation as a form of concreteness that does not impinge constitutively on the theory of the capitalist mode of production – a shortcoming that Harvey has spent some decades rectifying, namely with his theory of the 'spatial fix' – Reclus played a pioneering role in the kind of human and social geography capable of linking economic and political dynamics to geographies of difference. Harvey rightly notes the importance of Reclus's anarchist orientation to his geographical practice. The political belief in the desirability and viability of a 'vast federation of autonomous self-governing communities' (2001, p. 118), and the emphasis on free and spontaneous development against arbitrary territorial authorities, translates into a 'profoundly geographical' and highly decentralized thinking linked to self-management, community control, ecological sensitivity and respect for freedom.

This anarchist lineage within geography, Harvey's argument suggests, is vital both epistemologically and politically; it brings social and geographical differentiation into the purview of social science, and affirms the importance of militant particularisms and local spontaneities against the temptation of homogenizing solutions. But for Harvey it is accompanied by a politically debilitating shortcoming: a tendency to empiricism about differences, which translates into the lack of a totalizing political strategy. So while the theoretical power of Marxism is unmatched by an equivalent sensitivity to placedness (and its politics), attention to freedom and difference in anarchism is betrayed by a theoretical deficit. Whence Harvey's pointed question: 'what would our political and intellectual world be like if Marx had been a better geographer and the anarchists better social theorists?' (2001, p. 120). To integrate geographical sensitivities into a historical-geographical materialism that would also be a partisan and popular practice turns out then to demand some kind of reckoning with the kind of anarchist thinking embodied in the figure of Reclus. I want to turn now to Reclus and ask whether and to what extent Harvey's framing of the geographical tension and eventual complementarities between anarchism and Marxism is perspicacious.

That Reclus's work attends to the wealth of difference in physical and 'social geography', to use his term, is a considerable understatement. Aside from numerous articles, political pamphlets and travel guides (including one of London), Reclus produced a trilogy comprising the two-volume *La terre* (1868–9), the 19-volume *Nouvelle géographie universelle* (1878–1894) and the six-volume *L'homme et la terre* (1905–8, published posthumously). These books, resting on Reclus's emphasis on first-hand observation and his drive to comprehensiveness, more than fulfil Harvey's description of geography as 'record[ing], analyz[ing] and stor[ing] information about the spatial distribution and organization of those conditions (both naturally occurring and humanly created) that provide the material basis for the reproduction of social life' (2001). Their articulation of the geological, morphological, biotic and urban dimensions of geography, especially in the *L'homme et la terre*, is formidable, especially with regard to their attention to what Harvey calls the question of 'becoming'. In Reclus's words, 'geography is not an immutable thing; it is made and remade everyday: at every instant, it is modified by the action of man' (1990, p. 94). The importance of history to Reclus's account is of particular interest inasmuch as he affirms both the multiplicity of trajectories and a unifying 'evolution'. Here the problem of the geographer is indissociable from that of the historian: how are they to establish what – employing an expression used before by Engels in *Anti-Dühring* – Reclus calls the 'parallelogram of forces' (1990, p. 478), which gathers a swarm of processes and wills into a global development or tendency?

In terms of Harvey's claim about the coupling of an attention to difference and a deficit of theory in anarchist geography, it is worth stressing that Reclus does not shy away – as the titles of his works make plain – from thinking in a planetary or a totalizing way. *L'homme et la terre* incessantly acknowledges a global convergence, an emancipatory globalization which it is the task of the geographer to understand, and of political agitation to both assume and enact. A 'revolution in thought' (Reclus, 1990, p. 30) is needed to break with the political-geographic fetishism and ethnocentrism that treats borders and their authorities as given. This thinking is at once ecological and political. Reclus, in a rather dated organicist metaphor, famously referred to humanity as 'the consciousness of nature', but this translates into something much more sophisticated and of contemporary relevance than a sub-Hegelian holism. Human beings have 'become, by force of association, veritable geological agents [who] have transformed in different ways the surface of the continents, changed the economy of rivers, and modified climates themselves' (Reclus, 1864). As a recent commentator remarks, this entails a 'dialectical responsibility' towards nature, linking social organization to the management, reparation and even beautification of nature (Pelletier, 2009).[1] It also involves moving beyond empiricism to a theoretical grasp of 'the globe as an historically and spatially interrelated system subject to discoverable laws' (Fleming, 1988, p. 115).[2] If Reclus can be said to belong to the world of nineteenth-century positivism, this is a positivism that combines 'an investigation of the laws contributing to the maintenance of the existing order and a search for the laws which challenged it' (Fleming, 1988, p. 118).

The context for this assumption of geological agency is an understanding of planetary unification as a social process, currently
evolving under the aegis of capitalism but perverted by this very
motor. As Reclus writes in *L'homme et la terre*:

> The theatre expands, because it now embraces the entirety of
> lands and seas, but the forces that were struggling within each
> particular state are equally those that struggle throughout the
> whole earth. In each country, capital tries to control workers;
> likewise, on the world's greatest market, capital, grown beyond
> measure, indifferent to all the ancient borders, tries to make the
> mass of producers work for its profit, and to guarantee for itself
> all the consumers of the globe, savages, barbarians, as well as the
> civilised.
>
> (quoted in Giblin, 2005, pp. 26–7)

This opens up the important question, raised by Harvey, of whether
Reclus has a theory of capitalism's geographical operation. Though
the emphasis on observation is paramount in his work, and
capitalism is treated more as a form of authoritarian expropriation
than as a more systemic mode of production and exploitation,
Reclus's work does contain some remarks that prefigure the kind
of geographical treatment of the concrete effects of capitalism's real
abstractions, namely the value-form, which we encounter in Harvey.
Reclus will write of the dollar as 'the master of master: it is by
virtue of it that men are differently distributed on the surface of the
earth, distributed here and there in towns and countryside, in fields,
workshops and factories, that they are pushed and pulled from job
to job like the pebble from shore to shore' (1990, p. 546). Not
just the distribution and circulation of human beings is involved,
but the very transformation of the earth, 'All economic oscillations
of society which affect the classes of workers and capitalists,
noble or bourgeois, are represented in the soil and modify the
network of dividing lines' (1990, p. 568). He is also attentive to
the transformations in capitalist forms which affect geography
and urbanization, for instance the increasing deterritorialization
of property, less and less attached to territory and increasingly
subsumed by finance (1990, p. 582). In all of these domains, as well
as in that of the ecology itself, it is the 'social question' as a whole
that demands the attention of both the geographer and the militant.
For this very reason science and revolution cannot be sundered: 'We
now know that there is a social science and we count on using

it against our enemies to hasten the day of liberation' (Reclus, 2008, p. 46).

In sum, it is possible to say that while both his positivism and his anarchist politics may have made Reclus sceptical of the kind of movement from the abstract to the concrete delineated by Marx's method, he nonetheless recognized – in a way not fully acknowledged by Harvey – the need to integrate geography and the study of capitalism in an understanding of the production of both nature and social difference by a human race now become, in his increasingly pertinent formulation, a 'geological agent' (an agency that, echoing Marx, precludes any concessions to Malthusian theories of eco-scarcity).

Neil Smith's claim, that the 'geography of capitalism is more systematically and completely an integral part of the mode of production than was the case with any earlier mode of production' (2008, p. 134), can find some support in Reclus's work. Indeed, it could be argued that the treatments of urbanization, territorial change and capitalist globalization contained in Reclus's 'social geography' are better accounted for precisely by the kind of theory of uneven development and the nature/society dialectic proposed by Marxist geographers such as Smith and Harvey, than by Reclus's own three laws of development: the 'class struggle', the search for equilibrium and the sovereign decision of individuals. What is more, Reclus's focus on increasing solidarity as the only real motor and mark of 'progress' dovetails with much Marxist thinking on cooperation and the socialization of production, just as it refuses any seclusion of liberation to zones separated from planetary development. As he wrote, reflecting on his own attempt to live under no authorities in Colombia, 'Never will we [anarchists] separate ourselves from the world to build a little church, hidden in some vast wilderness. Here is the fighting ground, and we remain in the ranks, ready to give our help wherever it may be most needed' (quoted in Fleming, 1988, p. 48).[3] Reclus's critique of anarchist colonies and *milieux libres* is of particular interest today, when some strands of insurrectionary thought are returning to the idea of the 'commune'.

A case in point is the Invisible Committee's text *The Coming Insurrection* (2009), the object of intense attention on the part of libertarian activists, the French state and the American media (in the surreal 'product placement' of which it was the focus on Glenn Beck's Fox show). The book's capacity to catalyze and renew the debate on the collective experimentation of everyday life is to be welcomed, especially in contrast with nebulous figures of messianic transfiguration. *The Coming Insurrection* also raises some important questions for a radical left that conceives of capitalism as an unacceptably destructive system and views crisis management as an unappetizing and doomed vocation. Rather than an ephemeral image of a glorious tomorrow or a utopian enclave, the commune is envisaged simultaneously as a collective experimentation of politics and as an instrument for a political action which is not merely instrumental but existential, or ethical. Among other things, the emphasis put on the density of real relations – as against the issues of identity and representation that allegedly bedevil parties, groups, collectives and milieux – gives a concrete political meaning to friendship, over against the obsession, whether prudish or prurient, with the commune as the site of sexual exchange. Another classic motif, that of self-reliance, is given a contemporary inflection in *The Coming Insurrection*: the commune is presented as a way of gaining and practising the kind of know-how (medical, agricultural, technical) to allow people to depend no longer on the metropolis and its forms of 'security' – in other words, to ready themselves for real crisis, as communistic survivalism prepares for capitalist apocalypse.

It is impossible to gainsay the force and interest of concrete utopias, however minimal or marginal, or to deny the all too familiar truth – once again laid bare by this case – that the modern capitalist nation-state does not suffer alternatives gladly. The case of Tarnac (see note 4) has certainly shown that even very simple experiments with egalitarianism and emancipation can sow real political relations and solidarities. But especially at a moment when the political question of the public is so crucial, whether we are speaking of universities, hospitals, banks or indeed trains, the opposition between the commune and the metropolis is a false one, as is, to borrow another dichotomy from *The Coming Insurrection*, the one between hegemony and horizontality. It is precisely on this question, framed in terms of the opposition between the commune and the city, that the geographic determinants of insurrectionary projects and strategies, or the wilful absence thereof, become crucial.

The Coming Insurrection formulates, in a compellingly abrasive way, a widespread conviction that contemporary struggles against capital have shifted from the point of production to those of circulation, distribution, transport and consumption. In other words, arresting the flow of this homogenized society is a *conditio sine qua non* for the irruption of non-capitalist forms of life:

The technical infrastructure of the metropolis is vulnerable.

Its flows amount to more than the transportation of people and commodities. Information and energy circulate via wire networks, fibers and channels, and these can be attacked. Nowadays sabotaging the social machine with any real effect involves reappropriating and reinventing the ways of interrupting its networks. How can a TGV line or an electrical network be rendered useless?

(Invisible Committee, 2009, pp. 111–12)[4]

Behind this statement lies an anti-urbanism that regards contemporary spectacular exploitation and conformity as products of the capillary management of everyday life. Cities are stripped of any life not mobilized for the commodity, and pre-empted from any behaviour at odds with a tautological drive for systemic reproduction:

The metropolis is not just this urban pile-up, this final collision between city and country. It is also a flow of being and things, a current that runs through fiber-optic networks, through high-speed train lines, satellites, and video surveillance cameras, making sure that this world keeps running straight to its ruin. It is a current that would like to drag everything along in its hopeless mobility, to mobilize each and every one of us.

(Invisible Committee, 2009, pp. 58–9)

The interruption or sabotage of the infrastructure of mobilization is the other side of *The Coming Insurrection*'s conception of communes not as enclaves for beautiful souls, but as experiences through which to develop the collective organs to both foster and endure the crisis of the present, and to do so in a fashion that does not sever means from ends. The book's catastrophic optimism lies in advocating that interruption as somehow generative of anti-capitalist collectivity (rather than passing irritation or mass reaction). It is also founded on a repudiation of the inauthenticity of massively mediated, separated and atomized lives in the metropolis.

There are inadvertent echoes of the traditional anti-modernist polemics in the scorn against 'indifferent' modern housing and the idea that with 'the proliferation of means of movement and communication, and with the lure of always being elsewhere, we are continuously torn from the here and now' (Invisible Committee, 2009, p. 59). Real communities that do not rest on the atrophying of bodies into legal identities and commodified habits are to emerge out of the sabotaging of all the dominant forms of social reproduction, in particular the ones that administer the ubiquitous mobilization of 'human resources'. Materialism and strategy are obviated by an anti-programmatic assertion of the ethical which appears to repudiate the pressing critical and realist question of how the structures and flows that separate us from our capacities for collective action could be turned to different ends rather than merely brought to a halt.

The spatial vocabulary articulated in *The Coming Insurrection* is, to employ a well-worn dichotomy, not one of revolution but one of revolt. This spatial distinction between negations of the status quo was beautifully traced through the relationship between Rimbaud and the Paris Commune by the Italian critic Furio Jesi. Jesi begins with the evident temporal distinction between revolution, conceived in terms of the conscious concatenation of long- and short-term actions aimed at systemic transformation in historical time, and revolt, as a suspension of historical time. Revolt is not the up-building but the revelation of a collectivity. It is, to borrow from Malraux's *Hope*, an organized apocalypse.

In this abrogation of the ordered rhythms of individual life, with its incessant sequence of personal battles, revolt generates 'a shelter from historical time in which an entire collectivity finds refuge' (Jesi, 1996, p. 22). But the interruption of historical time is also the circumscription of a certain ahistorical or anti-historical space, a space torn from its functional coordinates:

> Until a moment before the clash ... the potential rebel lives in his house or his refuge, often with his relatives; and as much as that residence and that environment may be provisional, precarious, conditioned by the imminent revolt, until the revolt begins they are the site of an individual battle, more or less solitary. ... You can love a city, you can recognise its houses and its streets in your most remote and secret memories; but only in the hour of revolt is the city really felt like an haut-lieu [a high place] and at the same time your own city: your own because it belongs to you but at the same time also to others; your own because it is a battlefield you and the collectivity have chosen; your own, because it is a circumscribed space in which historical time is suspended and in which every act has its own value, in its immediate consequences.
>
> (Jesi, 1996, p. 23–4)

The collective experience of time, and of what Jesi calls symbols (such that the present adversary simply becomes the enemy, the club in my hand the weapon, victory the just act, and so on), means that the revolt is an action for action's sake, an end (as in the Invisible Committee's reflections on the ethics of sabotage and the commune) inseparable from its means:

> It was a matter of acting once and for all, and the fruit of the action was contained in the action itself. Every decisive choice, every irrevocable action, meant being in accordance with time; every hesitation, to be out of time. When everything came to an end, some of the true protagonists had left the stage for ever.
> (Jesi, 1996, p. 24)

Abiding with the interruptive paradigm of an intransitive and intransigent revolt, we can wonder whether, and if so to what extent, the historical space that revolt intervenes in inflects its character. It is no accident that the kind of sabotage envisioned in *The Coming Insurrection* is on lines and nodes of circulation, and not on the machinery of production itself.

It is worth reflecting on what the anarchist Jura Federation wrote of these experiments in 1877:

> The Jura Congress considers the communist colonies as incapable of generalising their action, given the milieu in which they develop, and further to realise the social revolution: as propaganda action, the fact of these communist colonies has no importance due to the failures they are all too often bound to suffer in contemporary society, and remains unknown by the masses just like the numerous attempts of this type already carried out in previous epochs. The Congress therefore does not approve these experiments, which can take the best elements away from revolutionary action.
> (quoted in Maitron, 1975, p. 407)

Returning to Reclus, his criticism of the *milieux libres* did not take away from the fact that he was as firm as his friend and comrade Bakunin in his repudiation of what he perceived as the authoritarian socialism of Marx and his followers. Without delving into the history of the dispute, can we say something about these political questions on the basis of how they impinge on the question of geography? After all, as Harvey's own remarks intimate, the Marxist critique of a theoretical deficit in anarchism is also the critique of a political limitation. Perhaps the point at which Reclus is closest to Marx is in his anti-voluntarist concern – despite the belief in individual sovereignty – with the link between material trends and radical change, or in his terminology, between evolution and revolution. As he declared in a speech from 1880, 'Revolutions are forced consequences of the evolutions that preceded them' (2008, p. 38) – a view not so far removed from Marx's remarks about productive forces breaking the integument of relations of production. But can this revolution bypass the state? For Reclus, it signals a passage to a new mode of evolution, marked by 'direct action by the freely expressed will of men who associate themselves for a determinate work, without preoccupying themselves with the borders between classes and between countries' (1990, p. 512). But is this freedom of association so straightforward? Attention to certain ecological and geographical aspects of Reclus's own reflection suggest otherwise. One of his main points of condemnation of capitalism, shared with contemporary ecosocialists, lies precisely in its unregulated and haphazard character. Under capitalism, Reclus suggests, we are governed by chance, incapable of planning and managing our metabolism with nature in a scientific way. The use, maintenance, reparation and conservation of the earth cannot be left to the destructive whim of profit-seeking. 'All this apparent chaos of forces in struggle, from the humble farmer with his furrow to the opulent capitalist with harvest in a thousand corners of the globe at his disposal, has as its fatal result to lead to a disordered production, without rule or method' (Reclus, 1990, p. 586)

If social relations are indeed determinant of the relation and use of the environment, a view in which Reclus anticipates the likes of Harvey, Smith and John Bellamy Foster, then the question of the political forms adequate to challenging and overcoming capitalism becomes far more complex than the seizure or not of state power, the repudiation or not of authority. It is also here that the question of theory comes into greater focus. Not only is it necessary, as Smith lays out, to understand the contradictory dynamics of differentiation and equalization that determine capitalism's mode of production and its geographical and natural impacts, it is also important to treat political authorities and institutions as themselves geographical entities, veritable components of our ecosystems that cannot be ignored or bypassed in the search for liberation. The state, conceived to include not just a monopoly of violence but also public services, infrastructures and so on, is not just a crucial factor in the reproduction of capital and its associated social forms, it is also a geographical fact of no little political importance. Harvey points this out as a crucial political problem for any geography of freedom:

The proper management of constituted environments ... may therefore require transitional political institutions, hierarchies of power relations, and systems of governance that could well be anathema to both ecologists and socialists alike. This is so because, in a fundamental sense, there is nothing unnatural about New York city and sustaining such an ecosystem even in transition entails an inevitable compromise with the forms of social organization and social relations which produced it.

(Harvey, 1996, p. 186)

Viewed in this light, geography can not just serve as an inventory of social differences and an understanding of their reproduction (as well as an explanation of the production of social homogeneity), it can also operate as a realist science of the spaces of capital that any attempt to generate spatial strategies of liberation cannot but contend with. Neither dogmatically scientific nor complacently utopian, such a geographical view of emancipatory politics can also allow us to ask questions of anti-capitalist strategy and alternatives to capital which are not mired in debates about authority and freedom that, whatever their original merits, are related to different geographies, ecologies and political economies than the ones we are confronted with today.

ACKNOWLEDGEMENTS

An earlier version of this paper was delivered under the title 'Geography against capitalism' at the Is Black and Red Dead? Conference held at the University of Nottingham, September 7–8, 2009. See also Toscano (2011).

This paper is dedicated to the memory of Neil Smith.

NOTES

1 Similar themes can be encountered in John Bellamy Foster's idea of an ecological revolution repairing the metabolic rift generated by capitalist accumulation. See Foster (2009).
2 See also Dunbar (1978).
3 See also Maitron (1975).
4 These reflections prolong those initially spurred by the so-called Tarnac affair, which saw this anonymous argument for sabotage transformed into the flimsy basis for a prosecutorial campaign at once vicious and spurious. See Toscano, (2009, pp. 2–7). Available at: www.radicalphilosophy.com/

commentary/the-war-against-pre-terrorism (accessed September 3, 2012).

REFERENCES

Dunbar, G. S. (1978) *Elisée Reclus: Historian of nature*. Hamden, Conn.: Archon.

Fleming, M. (1988) *The Geography of Freedom: The odyssey of Elisée Reclus*. Montreal, Canada: Black Rose.

Foster, J. B. (2009) *The Ecological Revolution: Making peace with the planet*. New York: Monthly Review Press.

Giblin, B. (2005) 'Élisée Reclus: un géographe d'exception', *Hérodote*, special issue on Elisée Reclus, p. 117.

Harvey, D. (1996) *Justice, Nature and the Geography of Difference*. Oxford: Blackwell.

Harvey, D. (2001 [1984]) 'On the history and present condition of geography: an historical materialist manifesto', in *Spaces of Capital: Towards a critical geography*. Edinburgh: Edinburgh University Press.

Invisible Committee (2009) *The Coming Insurrection*. Los Angeles, Calif.: Semiotext(e).

Jesi, F. (1996 [1972]) *Lettura del 'Bateau ivre' di Rimbaud*. Macerata: Quodlibet.

Maitron, J. (1975) *Le mouvement anarchiste en France,* Vol. 1. Paris: Maspero.

Pelletier, P. (2009) 'La géographie sociale d'Elisée Reclus', *Le Monde diplomatique*, January.

Reclus, E. (1864) De l'action humaine sur la géographie physique. L'homme et la nature', *Revue des Deux Mondes*, 34(140) (December 15).

Reclus, E. (1990 [1905]) *L'homme et la terre: Histoire contemporaine*, ed. B. Giblin. Paris: Fayard.

Reclus, E. (2008) *Évolution et révolution*. Paris: Le Passager clandestin.

Smith, N. (2008) *Uneven Development: Nature, capital, and the production of space*, 3rd edn. Athens Ga.: University of Georgia Press.

Toscano, A. (2009) 'The war against pre-terrorism', *Radical Philosophy*, 154.

Toscano, A. (2011) 'Logistics and opposition', *Mute*, August. www.metamute.org/editorial/articles/logistics-and-opposition (accessed September 21, 2012).

10

REINER SCHÜRMANN'S FAULTLINE TOPOLOGY AND THE ANTHROPOCENE

Stephanie Wakefield

INTRODUCTION

Anarchism is difficult to encapsulate, but in spite of its reluctance to be pinned down and its heterogeneity as a theory and practice, David Graeber succinctly and accurately sums up the politics of contemporary anarchism as 'the horizontalist, direct-action oriented wing of the planetary movement against neoliberalism' (2008). Simon Critchley's definition mirrors that of Graeber; for Critchley, 'anarchy is the creation of interstitial distance within the state, the continual questioning from below of any attempt to establish order from above' (2007, p. 123). In both definitions, one of an anthropologist and another of a philosopher, anarchism is inextricably bound to a horizontal spatial imaginary that posits an 'up-down' power from above against a power from below.

This spatial imaginary pervades most conceptual frameworks associated with anarchism. It is a vocabulary of decentralization and decentralized networks opposed to the perceived centralization of power or authority, seen for example in the anti-globalization movement's demands to disperse economic and political decision-making power among 'everyone' (as opposed to a centralized few). And as with strains of anarchism that posit creative and autonomous action in opposition to oppression or repression, so too anarchism's ethical proponents oppose this top-down domination in all forms, whether at the level of society, individuals by other individuals, or groups of individuals over nature. Whether framed as collective self-organization without centralized authority, anti-hierarchy, anti-centralization, anti-state, anti-state-form, anti-totalitarian or pro-participation and pro-self-management, spatial modifications of an existing plane of reality composed of hierarchical and horizontal collections of *things* are always both a means and an end for anarchism.

Like all scalar frameworks, anarchism operates with a set of prefabricated scalar levels into which accounts of the world can be inserted and frameworks for politics deduced. Thus it typically envisions the world through an up there versus down here, local–global, small–big, community–power set of relations. Through this implicit deductive reasoning, anarchism's foundational premise of power as hierarchical leads to the principled positing of its perceived opposite, the horizontal.

But what happens when these foundational grounds are falling away? For such fissuring of the ground is the claim at the heart of a different way of thinking space, that of Reiner Schürmann's faultline topology. The faultlines Schürmann reveals have destabilizing consequences for history and politics alike. The purpose of this chapter is thus to index the faults and ask about their consequences. Ultimately, anarchist spatial frameworks, by positing new principles of legitimation for those with which it finds fault, seek to suture the fissures and to close the faults, when today, in every sense, they cannot be closed.

FAULTLINE TOPOLOGY

Reiner Schürmann's backwards reading of Martin Heidegger, elaborated throughout all of his writings, including *Heidegger on Being and Acting: From principles to anarchy* (1990) and the later *Broken Hegemonies* (2003), is entirely topological. The explicit reading of faultline topology itself is laid out over a series of four essays that each focus on Heidegger's *Contributions to Philosophy* (Schürmann, 1991, 1992, 1993, 1994).

Topology, from the Greek *topos*, looks at *topoi*, places. In its generic usage, 'place' often means location, *a here*, where locations are understood as extensions in the container of space. But this is the Cartesian version of topology, which up until the last several decades dominated geography and which, to be sure, absolutely dominates anarchist spatial imaginaries (Lefebvre, 1991). Against this 'Cartesian spatial order' (Mitchell, 2000) composed of 'tribes of grids, binaries, hierarchies and oppositions' (Genocchio, 1995, p.

35), the faultline topology of Schürmann, animated at every step by a Heideggerian thought of space and place, is something else.[1]

With faultline topology, Schürmann is drawing upon Heidegger's renaming of his entire project in the 1969 seminar in *Le Thor* as the 'topology of be-ing' (Heidegger, 2003, p. 41), a renaming which, importantly, was part of an explicit attempt to move away from the perceived subjective structure of *Being and Time*, where the 'project' of 'understanding of being ... is then taken to be a structure of subjectivity' (Heidegger, 2008). If, for Heidegger, the topology provided the ability to move away from the anthropocentrism of *Dasein*, then it is not surprising that such a method would be compelling for Schürmann, whose interest was, in many ways, to read Heidegger backwards in an anti-humanistic fashion.

Although Schürmann refers to sites as 'coordinates', they are not merely cartographic, like lines of latitude and longitude on a map. Rather they mark a place in space, time and presencing. Instead of what (or why), sites pose questions of how, such as, 'how do things come to presence today, actually, materially, in everyday experience?' As Schürmann puts it:

> In Heidegger, [topoi, places] are the epochs in our history as they have led up to the age of technicity. Topology shows the deep historical roots of today's global reach. As it traces the places that have been ours, are ours, and can be ours, it is recapitulatory, critical, and anticipatory.
>
> (Schürmann, 1993, p. 196)

Topology, then, is the specifically Heideggerian method that designates a site, the archic–anarchic site. It locates a historical moment irreducible to discourse, empiricism or subjectivism. *Faultline* topology also asks about places, or *topoi*, as those to which we belong, spatially and temporally – but it does so by tracing their grounds, faults and fissures. Speaking geologically, a fault is a boundary between tectonic plates, an extensive, planar and relatively flat fracture in the layers of rock that make up the ground beneath us. Unlike joints, faults are never clean-cut lines, neatly separating plates, but rather complex and hazardous zones of deformation, where rocks have broken and become mobile. According to Schürmann, history should be understood as the successive rise, sway and decline of grounds. Moreover, the place in which we find ourselves today will need to be described quite specifically as just such a fault.

Faultline topology refers to two trajectories of thought, two tasks, that is, which converge together to make up a third. This third Schürmann calls the 'anarchy principle', that singular, contemporary fault that assigns us our place on the 'borderline where action is uprooted from being' (1993). In order to arrive at this 'dazzling', paradoxical condition that is today ours, topology conducts two initial tasks.

FIRST TASKS: BEING

The first task of faultline topology is to 'retrieve the event of disparate, conflictual truth', what Schürmann calls the 'originary double bind' (1993) – that fissured ground as the originary condition that replaced Heidegger's earlier trope of 'originary rootedness' (2008). With this move being is redefined: from concealing–unconcealing, (Heidegger, 1998, p. 183) to the strife of world and earth (Heidegger, 1971, p. 17) and the autonomous play of the fourfold (Heidegger, 1971, p. 163). Presencing–absencing is reconceived as an infinite and endless game, oriented not toward ending the conflict but rather toward preserving strife for its own sake. Thus, it is suggested that each element in the world – earth, sky, divinities and mortals – belongs together intimately, in a manner comparable to that shared by opponents in battle. What is more, the intimacy shared by these four elements is not that to which we are accustomed today, for the four do not exist in isolatable particularity. They do not, as it were, 'stand side by side singly' (Heidegger, 1971, p. 180).

Expressing this intimacy of strife in the language of *The Thing*, we could say that in thinging, there is a sense of contingency and chaos and in worlding, there is a sense of binding and attachment. Outside of this context, neither word has any *sense*. Of gods and dignity, splendour and stone, plants and humans – each elements of the world – there is reciprocal constitution, but even this wording is insufficient to express the indissoluble intimacy of elements of the world that exist *beyond* the threshold of relation.

The dynamic element of fissuring with which topology is concerned must be contrasted with the idea of being as temporal or spatial static presence. Unity only makes sense here as a combination of elements that each involve extension and location, but not exclusively; and which are each not just 'standing next to one another'. Here being is always connected to the possible, to its possibilities, meaning that it can *never* be only constant presence.

SECOND TASK: THE MANAGEMENT OF BEING

As its second task, faultline topology traces the rise, the sway and the decline of a mode of presence held to a first principle, according to which beings appear, speak, move and relate in specific ways. This second task is not separate from the first in its evocation of originary strife; rather, topology reveals the relationship between the two – it asks not only 'How do things come to presence differently in any given period?' but also 'What is the relationship between a mode of presencing and originary strife?' In Schürmann, the modes of presencing are explicitly understood as *modes of managing* the world. Thus, 'what interests the topologist ... is the conflictuality glimpsed, then infallibly repressed at the inception of every single epoch in our past' (Schürmann, 1993, p. 207). Put simply, if metaphysics, according to Heidegger and Schürmann, in each of its instances must extract, out of the dynamic rhythms of the interplay of worlds, a certain ordering, then conversely, the topologist traces the orderings and extracts from them the dynamic rhythm of worlding.

So faultline topology recalls being as presencing–absencing, and the need, against this, to assert an ordering ground, thus suturing over the 'conflictuality without sublation which is truth' (Schürmann, 1993). The second task of topology is decidedly methodological: it traces the 'epochal stamps', those measure-giving grounds esteemed highest for an age, which anchor all that we can say, know and do in a given period. In each case, Schürmann shows, the stamps appear everywhere by 'dimming down' the profusion of presencing, of concealing–unconcealing. Tracing the ancestral lineage of these epochal grounds 'establish[es] the filiation that leads from "the Greek dawn" to "the night of the world" in which – according to Holderlin, modernity is engulfed' (Schürmann, 1990, p. 11).

Taking up the burden of the modern epochal principle is of course Man, what Peter Sloterdijk describes as the outcome of that historical process of *taming* 'through which man became the being who could pull himself together in order to speak the totality of Being' (2009, p. 20). Together Man and Technicity make up *Gestell* which, importantly, is 'the denial of world' (Heidegger, 1977, p. 49). What is denied with *Gestell* is the dynamic interplay of world in its gathering and play. This is achieved by capturing all that is from out of world and bringing this content forth as constantly present subjects and objects in a what may only *then* be understood as a Cartesian terrain. In this way, *Gestell* manages the world *spatially*.

Let me return now to anarchism, to see the implications of these first two topological findings.

From this perspective, in anarchism's positing of a verticality of power with horizontality in opposition and in its creating a historical showdown between the two, it conjures a decidedly *Gestell*-like topography. On both sides are imagined a collective of *cogitos*, who inhabit a space made up of those elements that we typically assume to be a part of any order: subject, object, each fully present and settled. This is the space of the Kantian split between subject and world: measurable, an endless array of nodal beings arranged in a surface of neutral space. Concretely, with *Gestell*, representations take the place of even their referents and what is left is only spatial localizable coordinates and their ordering as such. Schürmann:

> Turning outward, we find but natural resources to be harnessed, and turning back upon our past, only cultural curiosities to be marketed. Turning inward, I no longer find, as did Augustine, the immutable light of truth, but rather neuroses awaiting treatment; and turning upward, more resources – perhaps uranium on Mars – awaiting exploitation.
>
> (Schürmann, 1993, p. 210)

The spatial imaginary of anarchism and citizenist movements relies on this *Gestell* surface monism and would really only like to reorient it through an indefinite rehashing of its management. By advocating horizontalism as a solution to the verticality of oppressions, anarchists remain mired in a Cartesian landscape that no matter how much it is rearranged merely reproduces the world as it has been denied via Gestell.

But the topology reveals an additional problem for anarchism. As Luc Boltanski and Ève Chiapello (2005) and more recently Nancy Fraser (2009) have shown, such a rearrangement has in fact long been underway in Western societies for at least four decades, as the discourses of horizontalism and self-organization which emanated from 1960s and 1970s cultural and social movements have been brought into the service of a massive project of social and economic restructuring that ultimately reshaped life, work and social relations as we know them today. These discourses dovetailed with the practices of cybernetics,[2] early ecology[3] and New Urbanism (Mumford, 1961;

see also Vaneigem, 2001), each of which departed from a celebration of networks and horizontality, to contribute to a thorough reorganization of the social field including managerial science, urban planning, workplace organization and even counter-insurgency. Thus, even worse for anarchism is that it imagines hierarchy as the enemy, the *form* to be combated, when in reality hierarchy as an organizing form of power has long passed out of predominance. As a result, in theory and practice, anarchists furthermore entangle themselves in a binary that fundamentally misunderstands the functioning of power today, resulting in a senile celebration of forms long since adopted by institutions and organizations that horizontalists claim to oppose.

Let me now turn to the final condition in which anarchism finds itself, for it is, I think paradigmatic of the present, and what Schürmann calls the anarchy principle.

THE ANARCHY PRINCIPLE

In topological terms, we find ourselves inscribed within one horizon, one 'time-space,' and then suddenly reinscribed within another. This perplexity involves nothing but singulars: a terra deserta that is no longer ours, a terra incognita that is not yet ours, and a transition in which an entire collectivity lives as if holding its breath. No encompassing nomos governs this nomadism where allocations, assignments to discontinuous planes, follow one another without warning or mediation.

(Schürmann, 1993, p. 198)

Thus at the crossroads of the two tasks already mentioned – recalling being and tracing its management – we arrive at faultline topology's third and final aspect: locating fissuring grounds and breaks. The concern here is with 'reversals of history' and the crises that set upon each principle – in short, the decline of civilizations and their regimes of truth. If the fissures dividing and cleaving epochs interest Schürmann most of all, it is because in these breaks in history, where principles are absent or in decay, 'the double bind once glimpsed ... today appear[s] imminent' (Schürmann, 1993, p. 197). Thus the topologist speaks from a caesura, a faultline, a site described by Schürmann as possessing 'the singular feature, never before seen, of archic anarchic monstrosity ...[where] what disappears is the very possibility of obliterating orginary strife' (1993, p. 197).

Today we stand upon just such a fault, in which our decline appears as the crisis of Man, the subject, and creates a situation that Schürmann calls 'the anarchy principle':

> The anarchy that is at issue here is the name of a history affecting the ground or foundation of action, a history where the bedrock yields and where it becomes obvious that the principle of cohesion, be it authoritarian or 'rational,' is no longer anything more than a blank space deprived of legislative, normative, power. Anarchy expresses a destiny of decline, the decay of the principles to which Westerners since Plato have related their acts and deeds in order to anchor them there and to withdraw them from change and doubt. It is *the rational production of that anchorage* – the most serious task traditionally assigned to philosophers – that has now become impossible.
>
> (Schürmann, 1990, p. 7)

With the anarchy principle, the 'night's world' is something far more monstrous than the reign of Man. For finally, in late *Gestell*, the subject too becomes object, absorbed in the midst of the orderless. Although humans continue to perceive themselves as 'orderer', the opposite is in fact the case; far from possessing any kind of control over *Gestell*, humans have themselves been placed into the realm of the orderable itself. Historically, this development is closely tied to the horizontal reorganization of power referred to above. As many have noted (such as Dupuy), in championing ecology and self-organization, cybernetics has displaced the subject that was modernity's centre with a centreless organizational framework. As management cybernetics founder Stafford Beer put it, 'to people reared in the good liberal tradition, man is in principle infinitely wise... to the cybernetician, man is part of a control system' (quoted in Pickering, 2009, p. 188). With the proliferation of this approach over the past 40 or so years, Western societies have undergone an apparent and profound shift from 'disciplinary' to 'control society', in which power no longer produces subjects but rather desubjectified, 'larval' life (Agamben, 2009).

What does it mean to be living on a fault? It means that all that exists is tied up in principial forces and is also at once unbound. It is thus discordantly binding–unbinding. 'With the transitional now', Schürmann says, 'the rallying point of moderns, their home and focal point – the *I think* – undergoes displacements somewhat in the manner of ... a childhood memory wandering off in a conversation, continuing, in the new site, but no longer going without saying' (2003, p. 562). When the great sheet of constellations that fix things in constant presence folds up, closes in on itself, the principial reference still exists, we still have the sense of identity of self with self, but it is dislocated, plurified and decaying: the figure of the human is One and nothing. In this context, 'to ask what ought I to do? is to speak in the vacuum of the place deserted by the successive representations of an unshakable ground' (Schürmann, 1990).

THE ANTHROPOCENE

To illustrate, let us speak geologically once more. Recently *The Economist, Nature* and the *New Left Review* have each heralded the arrival of the Anthropocene, the new geological epoch designating the period in which humans became 'geological agents' (Oreskes, 2004, p. 93) and began leaving a stratigraphically significant impact in the bedrock of the earth. Literally 'the recent age of man', the Anthropocene dates from the mid-to-late eighteenth century's radical detachment of human life from the biological old regime by way of industrial production and urbanization (Crutzen, 2002). This geological–historical christening points directly to the figure of the modern subject, that principial referent-made-concrete under whose sway the nineteenth and twentieth centuries were held tight. As Dipesh Chakrabarty has noted, 'the geological agency that human beings were acquiring [was] at the same time as and through processes closely linked to their acquisition of [Enlightenment] freedom' (2009, p. 208). Through the realization of the Cartesian project of man's becoming master of nature (Descartes, 1985), the modern subject inaugurates the gap between human and world, between 'nature' and 'culture' (Bacon, 2000; Locke, 2003; Kant, 1999; Smith, 2010).

What the naming of the Anthropocene obscures is the collapse described above. 'Obscures' may be incorrect; perhaps Anthropocene describes perfectly the monstrous faultline, for it names the principial referent *only in the time of its collapse*. Subjective presence registers in earth systems at the same moment the subject has become obsolete. Alongside the Anthropocene's positing of ecological crisis lies the deepest crisis: that of the subject, which now lies in ruins, unable to control that which it wrought.

'The rallying point of the moderns is dead', wrote Schürmann. We could take Fukushima Daiichi[4] as the example.

CITIZEN CONTROL

To say that the grounds are in crisis does not mean that it is just the self alone that is in crisis, but also the relation of this self to what it calls the natural world. Equally in crisis are the dreams of mastery upon which these two Kantian figures, self and world, were separated. Thus the material experience of the anarchy principle will be an experience of this relation as a systematic failure. And nowhere today can we see more clearly this cataclysm of ground than along the eastern coastline of Japan, where the friction of geological faults has nightmarishly unveiled the monstrous Schürmannian site.

In hopes of suturing over the fracture of being exposed, the French journal *Multitudes* has deployed a horizontalist call for CITIZEN CONTROL OF NUCLEAR POWER PLANTS. Evoking again the horizontal imaginary, it protests that 'the general interest should prevail over managerial and State forms of reasoning and power. It is high time that citizens play a role at the international level in the technical evaluations which legitimize installations that compromise our living conditions' (*Multitudes*, 2011).

All parties involved, 'multitudes' and Tokyo Electric Power Company (TEPCO) technicians alike, seek to manage this literal faultline, and each fails. Fukushima is now a melt-through (*Guardian*, 2011). In Tokyo, the government calls for voluntary blackouts as an experiment to test the capacity of the Japanese people to self-manage. Citizens invest in Geiger counters and become accustomed to radiation in their lunch, while Tokyo parks are empty installations, the leaves of their trees covered in a fine dust of radioactive particles.

Once the ground of an epoch and Promethean master of the earthly world, today Man is only master of ruins. At the point of objectlessness, the figure of the human too, whose lived experience was the basis upon and against which the technological edifice was originally erected, is brought into orderability and even the subject–object dyad collapses. No longer a Promethean project of mastery, but instead one of survival, a desperate attempt by the human subject to salvage itself in the midst of its historical decline as the great sheet of constellations that fix things in constant presence folds up. The human, then, is one and nothing, orderer of a mode of presencing that lies in ruin.

Schürmann would say that this is only the nature of such a time. To point to the literal disaster management underway in Fukushima is to be precise about the anarchy principle. Ultimately, this is because, when the bedrock opens up, the world is revealed. Schürmann notes that Heidegger is cautious about this fault, and tends to move around on it, rather than truly crossing it. But Schürmann was not Heidegger, and went further than he did. What we learn from Schürmann is this: hasten the withering away of all epochal grounds, follow the sole injunction contained in worlding; in other words, *cross the fault.*

NOTES

1 For other recent takes on Heidegger's topology, see Malpas (2008) and Ryan (2011).
2 Jean Pierre Dupuy: 'What I have tried to show is that cybernetics, far from being the apotheosis of Cartesian humanism, as Heidegger supposed, actually represented a crucial moment in its demystification, and indeed in its deconstruction. To borrow a term that has been applied to the structuralist movement in the human sciences, cybernetics constituted a decisive step in the rise of antihumanism' (2008).
3 See the See *Whole Earth Catalog*, 1968–1986.
4 'The Fukushima Daiichi nuclear disaster was a series of equipment failures, nuclear meltdowns, and releases of radioactive materials at the Fukushima I Nuclear Power Plant, following the Tōhoku earthquake and tsunami on 11 March 2011. It is the largest nuclear disaster since the Chernobyl disaster of 1986' (Wikipedia, 'Fukushima', accessed October 17, 2012).

REFERENCES

Agamben, G. (2009) *What is an Apparatus? And Other Essays*, trans. D. Kishik and S. Pedatella. Stanford, Calif.: Stanford University Press.
Bacon, F. (2000 [1690]) *The New Organon*. Cambridge: Cambridge University Press.
Boltanski, L. and Chiapello, È. (2005) *The New Spirit of Capitalism*. London: Verso.
Braun, B. (2011) 'A green apparatus? Design, habit and the sustainable everyday'. Talk given at Nordic Geographers Meeting, Roskilde, Denmark.
Chakrabarty, D. (2009) 'The climate of history: four theses', *Critical Inquiry*, 35.
Critchley, S. (2007) *Infinitely Demanding: Ethics of commitment, politics of resistance*. New York: Verso.
Crutzen, P. (2002) 'Geology of mankind', *Nature*, 415, p. 23.
Deleuze, G. (1992) 'Postscript on the societies of control', *October*, 59.

Descartes, R. (1985) *The Philosophical Writings Of Descartes*, trans. J. Cottingham, R. Stoothoff and D. Murdoch. Cambridge: Cambridge University Press.

Dupuy, J.-P. (2008) 'Cybernetics is an antihumanism: advanced technologies and the rebellion against the human condition', paper prepared for the 'Transhumanism and the Meanings of Progress' workshop, ASU, Tempe, Az.

Economist (2011) 'The anthropocene: a man-made world', *The Economist*, March 26.

Foucault, M. (2007) *Security, Territory, Population*. New York: Palgrave Macmillan.

Fraser, N. (2009) 'Feminism, capitalism, and the cunning of history', *New Left Review*, 56, March–April.

Genocchio, B. (1995) 'Discourse, discontinuity, difference', pp. 35-46 in S. Watson and K. Gibson (eds), *Postmodern Cities and Spaces*. Oxford: Blackwell.

Graeber, D. (2008) 'The shock of victory', *Rolling Thunder*, 1(5).

Guardian (2011) 'Fukushima nuclear plant may have suffered "melt-through", Japan admits,' *Guardian*, June 8.

Heidegger, M. (1962). *Being and Time*, trans. J. Macquarrie and E. Robinson. San Francisco, Calif.: Harper Collins.

Heidegger, M. (1971) *Poetry, Language, Thought*, trans. A. Hofstadter. New York: Harper & Row.

Heidegger, M. (1972). *On Time and Being*, trans. J. Stambaugh. New York: Harper & Row.

Heidegger, M. (1977) *The Question Concerning Technology and Other Essays*, trans. W. Lovitt. New York: Harper & Row.

Heidegger, M. (1998) *Pathmarks*, ed. W. McNeill. Cambridge: Cambridge University Press.

Heidegger, M. (2000) *Contributions to Philosophy (From Enowning)*. Bloomington, Ind.: Indiana University Press.

Heidegger, M. (2003) *Four Seminars,* trans. A. Mitchell and F. Raffoul. Bloomington, Ind.: Indiana University Press.

Heidegger, M. (2008) *Being and Time*. New York: Harper Perennial.

Heidegger, M. (2009) 'Bremen Lectures: insight into that which is', in G. Figal, *The Heidegger Reader*, Bloomington, Ind.: Indiana University Press.

Kant, I. (1999 [1781]) *Critique of Pure Reason*. Cambridge: Cambridge University Press.

Kolbert, E. (2011) 'Enter the anthropocene: age of man', *National Geographic*, March.

Lefebvre, H. (1991) *The Production of Space*. Oxford: Wiley-Blackwell.

Locke, J. (2003 [1690]) *Two Treatises of Government and A Letter Concerning Toleration*. New Haven, Conn.: Yale University Press.

Malpas, J. (2008) *Heidegger's Topology: Being, place, world*. Cambridge, Mass.: MIT Press.

Mitchell, D. (2000) *Cultural Geography: A critical introduction*. Oxford: Wiley–Blackwell.

Multitudes (2011) 'Fukushima: putting the catastrophe under citizen control.' http://eipcp.net/n/1302701158 (accessed September 21, 2012).

Mumford, L. (1961) *The City in History*. New York: Harbinger.

Oreskes, N. (2004) 'The scientific consensus', *Science* 3: 306(5702), p. 1686.

Pickering, A. (2009) 'Beyond design: cybernetics, biological computers and hylozoism', *Synthese* 168, 469–91.

Ryan, S. (2011) 'The topology of being', *Parrhesia*, 11.

Schürmann, R. (1931) 'What must I do?' At the end of metaphysics: ethical norms and the hypothesis of a historical closure', in W. L. McBride and C. O. Schrag (eds), *Phenomenology in a Pluralistic Context*. Albany, N.Y.: State University of New York Press.

Schürmann, R. (1990) *Heidegger on Being and Acting: From principles to anarchy*. Bloomington, Ind.: Indiana University Press.

Schürmann, R. (1991) 'Ultimate double binds', *Graduate Faculty Philosophy Journal*, 14(2)–15(1).

Schürmann, R. (1992) 'Riveted to a monstrous site', in J. Margolis and T. Rockmore, *The Heidegger Case: On philosophy and politics*. Philadelphia, Pa.: Temple University Press.

Schürmann, R. (1993) 'Technicity, topology, tragedy: Heidegger on "That Which Saves" in the global reach', in A.M. Meltzer, J. Weinberger and M. R. Zinman, *Technology in the Western Political Tradition*. Ithaca, N.Y.: Cornell University Press.

Schürmann, R. (1994) 'A brutal awakening to the tragic condition of being: on Heidegger's *Beitrage zur Philosophie*', in K. Harries and C. Jamme (eds), *Martin Heidegger Art, Politics, and Technology*. New York: Holmes & Meier.

Schürmann, R. (2003) *Broken Hegemonies*. Bloomington, Ind.: Indiana University Press.

Sloterdijk, P. (2009) 'Rules for the human zoo: a response to the letter on humanism', *Environment and Planning D: Society and Space*, 27(1).

Smith, N. (2010) *Uneven Development: Nature, capital, and the production of space*. London: Verso.

Vaneigem, Raoul. (2001) *The Revolution of Everyday Life*, trans. D. Nicholson-Smith. London: Rebel Press.

Whole Earth Catalog (1968–1986) *Whole Earth Catalog*, ed. P. Warshall and S. Brand. Menlo Park, Calif.: Whole Earth Press.

PART IV

THE ANARCHIST MOMENT

11

THE ANARCHIST MOMENT

Andrej Grubačić

What is anarchism? Let me offer a preliminary answer to this question in the form of an anecdote. I became an anarchist when I was 13 years old. I blame this entirely on my grandmothers – both of them. One of them was anxious, terrified even, of my becoming an idealist. Her strategy was to give me books – Feuerbach, among others – designed to prevent me from going to 'the other side'. These were big books; in them, I barely understood anything. I remember asking her, a lifelong communist revolutionary, 'What do you think? Do you still believe in communism?' This conversation took place in state-socialist Yugoslavia, which was falling apart at the time. Her answer was immediate and I will always remember it. She said, 'Yes, I will be a communist for the rest of my life. But my generation found a wrong path to communism. The responsibility of your generation is to find a different path.' Around the same time my other grandmother – also a communist revolutionary – gave me a book by Alexander Ivanovich Herzen, a man who would become my hero. It was his memoir, *My Past and Thoughts* (1982). Here I encountered an anecdote about Mikhail Bakunin, a Russian anarchist with a wandering spirit who was, for many years, chained to a wall in Siberia. He somehow escaped, swam across the freezing Volga, went to the United States and, after a truly incredible journey, finally ended up in London. Herzen was waiting for him. Bakunin's first words to him were, 'Do they have oysters here, or should I go back to Siberia?' I was completely in love, with Bakunin and with all other romantic exiles of the nineteenth century.

Not too long after my literary meeting with Herzen and Bakunin, I joined the Belgrade Libertarian Group, a left wing of the Marxist Praxis experiment in socialist Yugoslavia. Anarchism, as I learned it from my comrades, was about taking democracy seriously and organizing prefiguratively. That means building the facts of the future in the present; not after the revolution but in the shell of the existing social order. It was a distinct socialist tradition but also an ethics of practice, one which insisted that our means needed to be consonant with our ends; that as much as this is possible, we needed to embody the society we wish to create; that we could not and cannot create freedom through authoritarian means. This seems to me still to be a good definition of anarchism.

Interestingly, I never read about anarchism in my school books. I had to endure what was called Marxist education. Marxism was a mandatory high-school class and in it there was absolutely no mention of anarchism. Our knowledge of the left, and of the history of the left, was that old and parochial eurocentric narrative: it all began with steam and guillotine, with the curious meeting of the French Revolution and the Industrial Revolution. The anti-systemic sensibility of utopian socialists like Saint-Simon and Fourier was improved upon by Karl Marx and his allies in the First International. After the death of the great master, the history of the left is a long and yet stunted narrative of the Second International, socialists and social-democratic groups and, of course, Lenin and Tito. For a long time I thought this absence of anarchism was a Yugoslav peculiarity, something that was particular to the Yugoslav-Marxist experience.

My relationship with Marxism was becoming increasingly romantic at the same time as I was becoming romantically involved with a Marxist revolutionary from Germany. Though she was a very serious woman, I soon discovered that the absence of any serious knowledge about anarchism was not limited to Yugoslav socialists. My girlfriend, a political theorist, had never heard of Gustav Landauer, of Martin Buber, or Erich Muhsam or Rudolf Rocker. For her, anarchism was a youthful synthesis of Bakunin, the Sex Pistols and the German Autonomen movement. I was taken aback. On one occasion, I remember waiting for her at what was then her workplace, the Institute for Critical Research in Frankfurt. I waited, reading an interview with Jurgen Habermas that somebody had left on the table. It was a description of his theory of discursive rationality as a new universal model of communication. At some point in the interview he answered a question about whether his theories and ideas could be of any help and assistance to socialist forces in the third world, and if third-world struggles were of any use for his theory and his critique of advanced capitalism. Habermas, to the best of my recollection, answered no to both questions, saying: 'I know this is a limited Eurocentric view.'

That was an interesting surprise. Here we have a universal theory of communication that begins by excluding four-fifths of the world population from participation! If this is a universalism, I remember thinking, it is of an imperial variety. And later on at the institute (I am obliged to admit we were there stealing furniture), I remember having formulated for the first time the thought that one of the vital differences between the anarchist and Marxist traditions was that the former was a project of the South, while the latter was a project of European Modernity.

Boaventura de Sousa Santos (2004) proposed to use this concept, the South, in order to signify three things. First, it is both an actual place and symbol of imperial construction. Second, it is the form of human suffering caused by capitalist modernity, a form of silencing aimed at local knowledges and languages, eccentric, and peripheral traditions. Finally, for Sousa Santos, the South functions as a metaphor, as a privileged site for excavation of the hidden modernity needed to reinvent emancipatory energies and subjectivities.

Armed with this hypothesis, I went back to the Balkans. I started studying Balkan history from a different perspective, as a hidden historical experience outside, or on the periphery of, capitalist modernity. In the course of my research, a different picture of the region emerged. With it came a different history of radicalism: the Balkans as a world of synthesis, with many local groups melding ideas of anarchism and with local practices. Take, for instance, Serbian socialist Svetozar Marković. According to Marković, who lived in the late nineteenth century, local conditions will determine the nature of the new society that the working class will establish in each country. The problem of bread, he wrote, is a problem of direct democracy. It is hard not to see the similarity between Marković's eclectic, ethical socialism – which he defined not as a new economic system, but a new way of life – and proposals arriving from contemporary peasant movements gathered around Via Campesina. In a dialogue with both anarchism and Marxism, he sought a balkanized socialism based upon communal institutions and instincts rather than upon inexorable historical laws. He argued for socialist movements that are not only anticolonial with respect to the West and the East, but also revolutionary with respect to the Balkan past. His balkanized socialism was ethical and visionary, eclectic and humane, and on all accounts unacceptable to later state socialist critics who dismissed him as a 'utopian socialist'. His aim, he wrote in 1874, was both internal social reorganization on the basis of sovereignty, and communal self-government and federation in the Balkan Peninsula. In his federalist plans lies what may perhaps be his greatest contribution: his feverish attempt to subdue the separate nationalisms of the Balkan peoples in favour of all-inclusive and directly democratic federalism. This anti-authoritarian eclecticism, a revolutionary tradition that possesses the ability to connect local and global, subaltern and modern, and a precious feature of Balkan societies, is what I advocate under the name of the balkanization of politics.

While some western and Yugoslav historians suggest, almost in unison, that it is this eclecticism that 'led him to theoretical mazes', I maintain that it was precisely his balkanized socialism that led him out of theoretical determinism and violent abstractions of Marxian theory. He valued Marx as the most profound critic of the social and economic development of the industrialized west, but he held Chernyshevsky and Bakunin in the same esteem. His entire revolutionary career embodied a search for a method of translation between Western and Russian socialism, in the light of their possible application to Serbian reality. It was the earliest statement of what we called in Yugoslavia 'separate roads to socialism', or one of the first postcolonial statements of what Arturo Escobar and Gibson-Graham call 'politics of place'. Svetozar Marković died at the age of 28. His death was a result of years spent in exile and in the prisons of the Serbian state. One of his last acts before his death was to help found the first school for women in Serbia. He was buried on March 16, 1875, in the presence of thousands of peasants, some of whom shouted at the police, assigned to maintain order, to remove their hats in the presence of the saint. In 1878, three years after his death, 500 people gathered in the city of Kragujevac, singing the *Marseillaise*, shouting,

> Long live the Republic!
> Long live the Commune!
> Long live communal autonomy!

and chanting a Serbian Carmagnole:

> Against God and the ruler,
> Against the priest and the altar,
> Against the Crown and the scepter,
> And the merchant usurer,
> For the worker, for the peasant,
> We fight the good fight.

How is it possible to say, as almost all Balkan historians do, that the nineteenth century in the Balkans is a century of nationalism? On the contrary, what we see is an amazing interplay of ideas and traditions, a radical synthesis of anarchist ideas and emancipatory strands of what used to be known as the pan-Slavic movement. It was only much later that this radical synthesis was obliterated through its incorporation into Marxist and nationalist histories. After discovering this hidden, suppressed tradition, I started seeing the same pattern everywhere. After reading scholars like Maia Ramnath, James Scott, Lucien van der Walt and especially Benedict Anderson and Ilhan Khuri-Makdis, I discovered what I shall call here the first anarchist moment. The period between 1870 and 1917, or the so-called first wave of globalization, was the time when, in terms of world systems analysis, semi-peripheral regions of the world economy were in the process of (deeper) incorporation into the capitalist world-economy. Khuri-Makdis, from whose splendid book (2010) I shall borrow this description of the anarchist moment, describes a contested process in which sites of globalization, like ports, railways and tobacco factories, were transformed into sites of labour struggle as well as into sites of encounter. Workers from all over the world would meet there to exchange ideas and militant practices, forming instances of synthesis akin to those I discovered in the forgotten past of the Balkans.

This was, by all accounts, a most remarkable period, and yet anyone would have trouble finding much mention of it in Marxist histories, in which, for the most part, the late nineteenth century serves as a background for the unfolding history of the real left. It is unsurprising, that they should miss a period and a type of militancy that lacks traditional Marxist categories and concepts. What we find instead is a multiplicity of radicalisms and a global convergence of subversive ideas revolving around anarchism. Benedict Anderson, in his book on anarchism and anti-colonial imagination, suggested that:

> While Karl Marx was writing in the British Library, Errico Malatesta was organizing in Buenos Aires. The anarchist movement of the 19th century period, in the first stage of globalization, was open to what in those days liberals and Marxists were not: the equal and active participation of people that most Europeans of the day considered inferior. Hostile against imperialism, it had non-theoretical pragmatists against a-historical nations, argued passionately against the concept of small nations, and those sympathetic to the strategy of anti-colonial nations. The anarchist movement lived off the trans-oceanic vibrations of the era and formed the center of a vast, rhizomatic network that spread from Russia to Cuba and was the real heart of revolutionary movements of the day. It was a gravitational force between militant, anti-colonial struggles on opposite sides of the Atlantic.
>
> (Anderson, 2005, p. 2)

In the same vein, Ilhan Khuri-Makdis writes that:

> in the parts of the world under semi-imperial, imperial, and colonial rule, anarchists ideas often merge with anti-colonial struggles. Those various networks were entangled in a way that would no longer be possible with the subsequent hardening of communism and nationalism, which made this radical, eclectic bricolage impossible or much more difficult.
>
> (Khuri-Makdis, 2010, p. 19)

This first anarchist moment was marked by anti-imperialist and anti-colonial struggles, and by nationalist, pan-nationalist and regionalist movements, such as the pan-Balkanists, pan-Africanists, pan-Asianists and many others. Anarchism intersected with all of these movements. Errico Malatesta, as is well known, fought in 1882 in Egypt against the British. Stepniak, another of my personal heroes, fought in Bosnia in 1878. After joining Malatesta in Italy, where they liberated villages and formed autonomous provinces, Stepniak went back to Russia to assassinate the Russian minister of the police. With this successful mission accomplished he went to London, where this remarkable fellow was killed in a train accident.

In coming back to the relationship between anarchism and anti-colonialism, we would do well to spend some time reading the most influential anarchist paper of the time, *Le Revolte*, edited by Jean Grave. In 1907 the journal published a letter that chronicles the experiences of a group of anarchist sailors, mostly French, who wondered how is it possible that the French think of themselves as a superior civilization after all the suffering they have inflicted on the people of Algiers. Another anarchist named Zuli, living as an exile in Tunisia, agreed, saying that there is nothing more repugnant than the miserable reality of European colonialism. This anarchist moment was a time of mass-migration, and the anarchist movement was a movement that migrated. As a result, anarchists and anarchist ideas were to be found everywhere. Libertarian militants created a tremendous network of communication. *Le Revolte* was not the only journal whose readership spanned continents. Libertarian periodicals were published in Belgrade, Beirut, Cairo, Alexandria, Buenos Aires, Paris and even Patterson, New Jersey – which was a far more exciting place then than it is today. Malatesta, who together with Francisco Ferrer and Elise Reclus was a favourite figure of the time, was read aloud by Cuban cigar-rollers, translated into Ottoman Turkish and discussed in Brazil.

To go back to radical-socialist Serbia for a moment, on June 1 of 1871, Svetozar Marković started the first socialist newspaper in the Balkans. The name of this publication was *Radenik* (The Worker). The name was chosen to signal the internationalist cause of their radical-socialist group, their unwavering hostility to the project of Greater Serbia, and their support for the Paris Commune, which had an enormous influence on Marković. This was a recurrent theme in the newspaper, together with translation of both anarchist and Marxist literature. The reception of the journal was truly remarkable. It had a circulation of 1500, an incredible figure in the city where an average newspaper printed no more than 500 or so copies of each issue. The church and state were quick to react. The government declared the newspaper and all student associations illegal. The students of the 'Ecole Superieure', Seminary, Military Academy, and Gymnasia countered the dictatorial acts of the state by founding secret reading and discussion societies known as 'komune', or communes, which met at night in the suburbs of Belgrade and served as centres for the teaching of crafts and the dissemination of knowledge and anarchist propaganda.

Now the question, of course, is what made anarchism become a global movement and a vehicle for translation of such diverse struggles? I agree with David Wieck:

> Long before anybody had used the term postmodernism, anarchism has always been anti-ideological. Anarchists have always insisted on the priority of life and action to theory and system. Subjection to theory implies in practice subjection to an authority, which interprets the theory authoritatively. And this objection would fatally undermine the intention of creating a society without central political authority. That's why anarchist writings are not authoritative or definitive, in the sense that Marx's writings have been regarded by his followers.
>
> (Wieck, 1996, p. 377)

Anarchism, not an ideology but a tradition, was extremely flexible, allowing for selective adaptations from a very broad repertoire of anti-authoritarian ideas. Another distinctive anarchist quality was the particular nature of its propaganda. Instead of focusing exclusively and narrowly on the urban industrial working class as a presumed agent of revolutionary change, anarchist propaganda was aimed at peasants, intellectuals, migrant and stable unskilled workers, artisans and artists. This facilitated the creation of a genuinely popular movement. Errico Malatesta and many other unnamed anarchists in Italy and in Spain participated in peasant revolts, in occupation of peasant lands and destruction of land records.

Anarchist propaganda entailed, according to Khuri-Makdis, an incredible ability, a brilliance, even, in using new, popular media and new public spaces, such as libraries, reading rooms, taverns and even theatres, such as those where they were 'performing persecution' of Francisco Ferrer and many other anarchist martyrs. Ferrer was killed by the Spanish state in 1909. Incredibly, a play about his untimely death premiered in Beirut in the same year, 1909, and then circulated in Buenos Aires and Paris. The so-called Ferrer affair was one of the main moments, one of the key episodes in the global popular, radical culture of the nineteenth century and early twentieth century.

Another space susceptible to anarchist propaganda was the so-called mutual aid society. This was, arguably, the most popular immigrant institution. It could be found everywhere, from South America to East Asia. It was a fairly non-revolutionary organization, a mutual savings fund, which existed in order to help workers in need or to help them build agricultural cooperatives. Anarchists were, however, brilliant in radicalizing these spaces. It is no wonder that Peter Kropotkin's famous book on mutual aid was listed under the most popular radical readings in the Global South. There is a lesson here for contemporary anarchist movements, which would do well to rediscover relationships with local institutions, such as immigrant societies, or local union halls.

Propaganda was not limited to political texts; anarchists believed in the magic of letters and the emancipatory effect of literature. In clubs and taverns of the anarchist century, workers read Moliere, Dumas and Anatole France. Yiddish anarchist papers in London's East End were publishing literary masterpieces. In my country, Macedonia, people would assemble in free reading rooms and libraries to discuss Beethoven's Ninth Symphony. In Spain, anarchists created an informal system of education where workers read La Revista Blanca, a journal written in accessible, simple language – often read aloud, as were many magazines that spoke to a population in which many were still illiterate. Here too, there is a lesson for anarchist movements, especially those ensconced in places of higher learning and sophisticated discourse. If our politics is to be effective, our language needs to be simple and understandable, as well as beautiful. In Cuba, theatre was used for the purposes of education, especially for the education of women. Aside from this 'informal sector', anarchists produced a whole system of formal education, as well as pedagogical networks and internationals, such as the Libertarian League for Education. Francisco Ferrer's Modern School was one of the most celebrated educational institutions, one followed by networks of popular universities established by the anarchists in Paris in 1898, imitated in Beirut and also in Alexandria. Then too, there is Tolstoy's school, Jasnaja Poljana. Academics do not like to remember that Tolstoy was an anarchist, but this was a very popular school back in its day, hugely influential, and a most fascinating approach to learning. Anarchists believed that the real social transformation, the real work of revolution, begins not in the factory but in the classroom, in a liberated school. A century or so later, anarchist interest in education, and interest in anarchist education, was revived by Herbert Read, Paul Goodman, Alex Comfort, Murray Bookchin and other 'new anarchists' in England and United States.

Anarchist ideas had a deep resonance in the periphery. Many of the people from the colonized world arrived in Europe in order to learn how to make explosives. There was an Indian group in the 1900s, referred to by British authorities as 'Gentlemanly Terrorists', who, according to the British, combined an interest in anarchist literature with indigenous forms of religious practice and physical training. An even more interesting Indian movement was that of Ghadar, who constituted a hybrid radical network of militant peasants and exiled militants grounded in the Bengali tradition of Kropotkinism, who were in regular contact with both Irish and Egyptian revolutionaries and Russian populists. These militants would meet in the global cities of their time, in Geneva, Paris, London, New York, Istanbul and Alexandria. It was in Paris where Li Shizeng met Elis Reclus. After embracing anarchist political ideas, he formed the World Society, one of the most important institutions in the history of East Asian anarchism. Another important site was San Francisco, where Japanese anarchist exiles concocted some of their wildest and most memorable actions.

It is important to emphasize that the period between 1870 and 1917 was the first anarchist moment. Eric Hobsbawm, a wonderful historian with an unfortunate ideological bias against anarchism, admits that before 1917, 'the revolutionary movement' was predominantly 'anarcho-syndicalist'.

Between Marx's death and Lenin's sudden rise to power in 1917, orthodox Marxism was in the minority as far as leftist opposition to capitalism and imperialism was concerned, successful mainly in the more advanced industrial and Protestant states of Western and Central Europe, and generally pacific in its political positions.

(Hobsbawm, 1993, pp. 72–3)

Militants of the periphery read Karl Marx. There was an Armenian translation of *The Communist Manifesto*. Bakunin famously translated *Das Kapital* into Russian. However, judging from the available sources, Marx was not considered to be terribly important for the political culture of the anarchist moment.

This would change after 1917, when Marxism became a dominant strategic perspective for the antisystemic movements. This is the beginning of the Marxist century, but the shift did not happen immediately. Both social and national movements in the nineteenth and twentieth centuries went through a parallel series of great debates over strategy, which encompassed debates that raged on between those whose perspectives were 'state-oriented', and those who pushed instead for an emphasis on revolution as a process that does not involve taking the power of the state. For the social movement, this was the debate between the eurocentric Marxist left and the anarchists; for the national movement, it was between political and cultural nationalists. Unfortunately, the ideas of socialism and social revolution became interchangeable with the idea of the modern nation as an institutional axis of the social revolution. The state obtained its central role in the ideological universe of Liberalism, but also, and often in a more emphatic manner, in the ideological universe of historical materialism. Marxism is a profoundly modernist project, in which the utopian dimension is covered by a veil of scientific determinism, and emancipatory practice remains anchored in the ideology of productivism, scientism and progress as infinite economic expansion.

Anarchists were horrified by this approach. For Bakunin and Kropotkin, such a program of state 'socialism', or centralized state-capitalism, centralizes all power into the hands of the state and objectively entails for the working class a 'barracks' regime, 'where regimented working men and women will sleep, wake, work and live to the beat of a drum.' (Bakunin, 1971, p. 289). They argued, instead, for federalism and regionalism, and for the regeneration of social and political life from below on the basis of regions. Peter Kropotkin wrote in 1920 that:

Imperial Russia is dead and will never be revived. The future of the various provinces which composed the Empire will be directed towards a large federation. The natural territories of the different sections of this federation are in no way distinct from those with which we are familiar in the history of Russia, of its ethnography and economic life. All the attempts to bring together the constituent parts of the Russian Empire, such as Finland, the Baltic provinces, Lithuania, Ukraine, Georgia, Armenia, Siberia and others' under a central authority are doomed to certain failure. The future of what was the Russian Empire is directed towards a federalism of independent units.

(quoted in Berneri, 1942, p. 15)

Kropotkin, Reclus and many others recognized region as the basis for the total reconstruction of social and political life. It is the region, not the nation, which is the motor force of human development, suppressed, attacked and eroded by the centralized nation-state and by capitalist industry. They opted for an alternative organization of socialist society, neither capitalist nor bureaucratic-socialistic. Rather, it envisaged a society based on voluntary cooperation among men and women, working and living in small self-governing communities. A century later, the economist Leopold Kohr published *The Breakdown of Nations*, arguing, once again, that most of the world's problems arise from the existence of the nation-state. He said, 'we have to free ourselves from national ideologies in order to act locally and think regionally. Both will enable us to become citizens of the whole world, not of nations nor of trans-national super-states' (1975, p. 32).

Anarchist voices were erased, sometimes killed and ultimately defeated in the historical struggle. State-defined and party-defined movements, those that came to be known as the Old Left, triumphed after the Russian Revolution in 1917. With immense cruelty, the twentieth century has shown that taking the power of the state is not enough, and that the statist-evolutionist concept of progress, defined as an eschatological end of history, is a dangerous illusion. In discovering a history of what I have here called the anarchist moment, it is clear that that the image of anarchist history and tradition needs to be altered fundamentally. Anarchist history is written by militants and theorists hostile to anarchism. For this reason, anarchist history, in the standard narrative, becomes the flat-footed, anti-intellectual cousin of historical materialism. According to the standard account, anarchism was announced by Godwin, invented by Proudhon and popularized by Bakunin and Kropotkin. It is time to set the record straight. Anarchism was not invented by anyone. It was not born with a long beard, nor was it – counter to the popular image – invented by people with long beards. Those theorists who helped fashion anarchism as a political movement did not think that they were inventing anything new. They were talking about self-organization, mutual aid and direct democracy – concepts as old as humanity, expressions of radical and insurgent common sense. A relatively unfinished representation, anarchism displayed great availability for cross-cultural fertilization and translation.

In terms of the geography of contestation, as a political practice, anarchism flourished in the Global South, and in the southern countries of the North, where it had its fullest concretization in 1930s Republican Spain. As the most marginalized tradition of European modernity, as a project of the South, anarchism served as a bridge to other, non-Western philosophies and to other practices of social interpretation and social transformation, and as a vehicle and instrument of translation of struggles. This was, and this is, the greatest strength of anarchism not only in the first anarchist moment but also today, in the midst of the present revival of anarchist practices. Anarchist or anarchist-inspired movements are growing everywhere; anarchist principles – autonomy, voluntary association, self-organization, mutual aid, direct democracy – have become the basis for organizing within the globalization movement and beyond. As both Barbara Epstein and David Graeber (2002) have pointed out, anarchism, at least in Europe and the Americas, has by now largely taken the place Marxism once occupied in the social movements of the 1960s. As a core revolutionary ideology, it is the source of ideas and inspiration, and even those who do not consider themselves anarchists feel they have to define themselves in relation to it.

Could this perhaps be the second anarchist moment? It depends. It seems Boaventua de Sousa Santos is correct when he calls for an:

epistemological reconstruction [that] must start from the idea that hegemonic left thinking and the hegemonic critical tradition, in addition to being North-centric, are colonialist, imperialist, racist, and sexist as well. To overcome this epistemological condition and thereby decolonize left thinking and practice it is imperative to go South and learn from the South, but not from the imperial South (which reproduces in the South the logic of the North taken as universal), rather from the anti-imperial South (the metaphor for the systematic and unjust human suffering caused by global capitalism and the resistance against it).

(Santos, 2004, p. 172)

He rejects general theory, and provocatively asserts that:

we have no need of a general theory, but still need a general theory on the impossibility of a general theory. In other words, we need a negative universalism: a general agreement on the fact that no individual, no single theory or no single practice has the infallible recipe to conceive of another possible world and to bring it about.

(Santos, 2004, p. 180)

As an alternative, Sousa Santos proposes something that resembles the anarchist consensus decision-making process:

To my mind, the alternative to a general theory is the work of translation. Translation is the procedure that allows for mutual intelligibility among the experiences of the world without jeopardizing their identity and autonomy, without, in other words, reducing them to homogeneous entities. The point is to create, in every movement or NGO, in every practice or strategy, in every discourse or knowledge, a 'contact zone' that may render it porous and hence permeable to other movements, practices, strategies, discourses, and knowledges. The exercise of translation aims to identify and reinforce what is common in the diversity of counter-hegemonic drive.

(Santos, 2004, p. 181)

It seems that this is precisely what anarchism was in the late nineteenth century, during its first moment: a genuinely popular, global, anticolonial movement that was able to translate between struggles. Hence it is crucial today, in our effort to reinvent social emancipation, to distance ourselves from the theoretical traditions that led us to the dead-end in which we have now found ourselves. We need to go to the South, conceived as a metaphor, a site for excavation of the hidden modernity needed to reinvent emancipatory energies and subjectivities. Anarchism, as a suppressed tradition of Western modernity, is singularly qualified to guide us in the construction of a noncapitalist, noncolonialist intercultural dialogue. It could help us reinvent a commitment to authentic emancipation, a commitment that unfolds itself as insurgent common sense.

One of the more interesting and eclectic Marxist thinkers, Immanuel Wallerstein, suggests that we are living in a transformational time space that he calls *kairos*, the right moment, in which:

> Freewill prevails. It is exactly for this reason it is impossible to foresee the outcome of the transformation—and social transformation must be thought more in terms of utopistics: we are approaching the end of the system—the long moment which we have already entered and thus we need to think about the possible leaps we might make, the utopias that are now at least conceivable.
>
> (Wallerstein, 2004, p. 197)

I hope that he is right, and that we indeed have such an opportunity. If he is right, the task of current revolutionaries is to transform the present anarchist revival into an anarchist moment, and then to turn it into anarchist *kairos*.

I return now to my grandmothers and to my Yugoslavia. Anarchism is not an intellectual tradition that can be encapsulated in an academic essay, regardless of how beautiful, theoretical and intelligent it might be. Anarchism is something much more. It is a lived tradition. Since I left the tutelage of my grandmothers I have been arrested for anarchism, fired from three universities because of anarchism, and finally exiled from Yugoslavia, my Yugoslavia, a country that I loved, because of anarchism. I do not regret for an instant that decision that I made when I was 13 years old, the decision to become an anarchist and enter into a tradition of mad stubbornness, of mad love for humanity and of absolute loyalty to the ideas of freedom, friendship and solidarity.

REFERENCES

Anderson, B. (2005) *Under Three Flags: Anarchism and the anti-colonial imagination*. London and New York: Verso.

Bakunin, M. (1971) 'Letter to la Liberte', in *Bakunin on Anarchy: Selected works by the activist-founder of world anarchism*, ed. Sam Dolgof. London: George Allen & Unwin.

Berneri, C. (1942) *Peter Kropotkin: His federalist ideas*. London: Freedom Press.

Graeber, D. (2002) 'New anarchists', *New Left Review* 13 (Jan–Feb).

Herzen, Alexander Ivanovich (1982) *My Past and Thoughts*, ed. Dwight Mcdonald, Berkeley, Calif.: University of California Press.

Hobsbawm, E. (1993) *Revolutionaries*. London: Abacus.

Khuri-Makdis, I. (2010) *The Eastern Mediterranean and the Making of Global Radicalism, 1860–1914.* Berkeley, Calif.: University of California Press.

Kohr, Leopold (1975) *The Breakdown of Nations.* London: Routledge.

Santos, B. (2004) 'Critique of lazy reason,' in Immanuel Wallerstein (ed.), *The Modern World System in the Long Duree.* Boulder, Colo.: Paradigm.

Wallerstein, I. (2004) *The Uncertainties of Knowledge.* Philadelphia, Pa.: Temple University Press.

Wieck, D. (1996) 'The habit of direct action', in Howard J. Ehrlich (ed.), *Reinventing Anarchy, Again.* Oakland, Calif.: AK Press.

12

PALESTINE, STATE POLITICS AND THE ANARCHIST IMPASSE

Judith Butler

We are perhaps most familiar with the claim of citizenship as it emerges at the established border of the nation-state, a petition for entry and for recognition by an existing state power and within the terms of its legal regime. The norms of citizenship may be contested by that petition if and when the demographics of the state are changing, have changed, or will surely change by virtue of admitting new populations. We see that very clearly as the United Kingdom and Europe, and the European Union, all dispute the politics of new immigration from North Africa, Turkey and the Middle East. As we doubtless know, there is a strong link between controlling immigration from those regions and waging war against those regions, between limiting immigration only to those with sufficient income and expanding markets precisely in those regions. In both cases, we witness different forms of managing global demographics and expanding markets, which means that the analysis of the relation between racism and capitalism has to be thought anew.

The United States has been particularly adept at vilifying and destroying populations and toxifying the land of precisely those regions in the Middle East and the Gulf where it seeks to expand its markets and its strategic power. And although I cannot in one chapter address the relation between war and new markets, let me at least suggest for the moment that the border is another name for the means through which markets are expanded, and that apart from explicit forms of military expansionism, we certainly have to understand the opening and monopolizing of new markets as one way to set the border outside the border. For examples of military expansionism's power to draw borders outside of borders, we need look no further than contemporary extraterritorial military courts and prisons, flagrantly exemplified still by Guantanamo. On the one hand, these are outside the border; but on the other hand, they are ways of redrawing the border and setting the border in a new way. Those who insist on a strong distinction between market and military expansionism provide the alibi for borders to be redrawn. The claim that 'this is not a new border' becomes the discursive moment of disavowal through which the new border is drawn and exercises its power.

As the title suggests, this chapter aims to think about forms of activism at or against the border of the state of Israel, but here we must pause in order not to take for granted what is being said. The state of Israel has a border, but that border has a history, and it is a border that is constantly shifting and expanding in new ways that are not always registered by the available political maps of the region. The UN Partition plan of 1947 gave 55 per cent of the land to Jews who, at the time, owned only 6 per cent of the land. By 1948, when Israel declared statehood and more than 750,000 Palestinians were dispossessed of their land, the state laid claim to 78 per cent of historic Palestine, a catastrophic move which was given legal codification in the land distribution laws in 1953. Since then, it has expanded to lay claim to approximately 90 per cent of that land through various means: land confiscation, the annexation of East Jerusalem, the invocation of emergency laws in the West Bank, the expansion of settlements in the West Bank, the building of the wall (500 miles of it) and the daily changing of checkpoint locations within the occupied territories all become strategic ways of establishing the border (or the police power of the border) in arbitrary and obstructive ways.

So something we might call 'the state of Israel' does not have a static and unmoving map of its own borders, but is itself characterized by a flexible and recurrent expansionism, aided by illegal occupation, illegal settlements, legal violence and military control. This is surely one reason why the bid for Palestinian statehood at this moment, and under these conditions, is at best controversial within Palestine itself. For some, the bid for statehood ratifies, rather than reverses, the occupation and would require the ceding of both sovereignty and self-determination to continuing Israeli military and economic powers. Another concern is that the West Bank will sever itself from the political and legal claims of all Palestinians who were dispossessed of land and citizenship, invalidating the one-state solution, the right of return and the legitimacy of the Palestinian Liberation Organization.

One of the most trenchant criticisms of the statehood thesis was voiced by Joseph Massad in *Al Jazeera*. He argued that the present bid for statehood effaces the historic claims of the Palestinian people to their vanishing land:

> The question ... is not whether the UN should recognise the right of the Palestinian people to a state in accordance with the 1947 UN Partition Plan, which would grant them 45 per cent of historic Palestine, nor of a Palestinian state within the June 5, 1967 borders along the Green Line, which would grant them 22 per cent of historic Palestine. A UN recognition ultimately means the negation of the rights of the majority of the Palestinian people in Israel, in the diaspora, in East Jerusalem and even in Gaza, and the recognition of the rights of some West Bank Palestinians to a Bantustan on a fraction of West Bank territory amounting to less than 10 per cent of historic Palestine. Israel will be celebrating either outcome.
>
> (Massad, 2011)

Indeed, Nu-man Kanafani, among many others, writes on the website of the Middle East Research and Information Project (MERIP) that the statehood project is a contract that would abdicate self-determination, furthering the status of the Palestinian Authority (and 'Fayyadism') as a compromised extension of Israeli security forces and subjugating its own economy to contracts that cede Israeli control over roads and construction. This brings up a crucial question: how do we think of the practices and politics of self-determination outside or against the presumption that statehood is the ultimate form for political self-determination?

The Palestinian struggle for self-determination may or may not be a struggle for full citizenship within any existing state, present or future, even though one part of the national Palestinian struggle demands that Palestinian Israelis be accorded rights to housing, employment, land and mobility equal to Jewish Israelis. But apart from that explicitly legal bid for citizenship within the jurisdiction of the state of Israel, the struggle takes another form. And so, along with the question of how we think of self-determination such that statehood is not its ultimate expression or realization, we have to think about in what way, if any, the language of citizenship can be used to talk about the political struggles of the stateless.

This chapter is exploratory; it proposes no strict, all-encompassing solution. Instead, it considers two non-state centred forms of activism, Israeli anarchism and Palestinian modes of struggle that hold open the distinction between self-determination and statehood. It might be thought that some actual or potential alliances could emerge precisely here, and this analysis will suggest that they do, and do not, and for some interesting reasons. To start, let us review in some basic ways the anarchist position within Israel, or against Israel, or rather, the anarchist position that seeks to hold open the distinction between its own politics and the politics of the state.

In my view, it is clear that Anarchists Against the Wall, originally called Anarchists Against the Fence and Jews Against Ghettos, have represented a radical resistance to the Occupation. They continue to show up, and put their bodies on the line, in various villages along the path of the separation wall. There is no question that the weekly demonstrations at Bi'lin, where many have suffered physical injury and death, the important triumph at Budrus, where intervention was aimed at steering the wall away from olive trees, the persistent rallying of support in Sheik Jarrah for those threatened with the confiscation of their homes and those whose homes have already been transferred to Jewish Israelis, the important engagement with Ta'ayush during the second intifada, when medical supplies were illegally brought into the West Bank, have been but a few of many insistent and important political actions against an illegal occupation. They are undertaken mainly by Israeli citizens, mainly but not exclusively Jewish, and they constitute acts of civil disobedience and anti-authoritarian politics on the part of citizens who seek to resist state policies, and on occasion resist Zionism and the state itself. They are clearly acts of citizenship at the same time as they disaffiliate with state politics. Are they non-state actors, or are they seeking in some way to do and undo their state-based citizenship in ways that are at once responsible (that is, ways that demonstrate one of the only morally right ways to live out Israeli citizenship) and a part of a political resistance (a way of deconstructing that citizenship through forms of civil disobedience without legally renouncing it or electing for emigration)?

To a certain extent, these are actions that are intended not only to support Palestinians, but also to work within the stated terms of Palestinian resistance movements, which often means deferring to those goals and entering into political action at the wall or within the occupied territories only when explicitly invited to do so in certain clearly delineated ways. Although anarchist in name and action, those Israeli activists are in an important sense defined by their legal citizenship even as they oppose the state.

This is one reason why the alliance between Israeli anarchists and Palestinians is not exactly smooth. It makes sense, for instance, that anarchism would not be the name for the struggle undertaken by Palestinians living under the occupation or in Gaza, where the Israeli siege continues the occupation after the withdrawal of its settler population. After all, the Israeli state exercises complete control over its borders, deciding what goods move in and out, vetting human rights and non-governmental organization workers and undertaking bombardments, often against civilian populations, that destroy both lives and the infrastructural conditions of life. This continues to be the case even at the Rafah gate which links Gaza and Egypt.

Anarchism, when defined explicitly as anti-authoritarian or as anti-statist, assumes the existence of a state against which it rallies, even though it also practises and instates forms of sociability that are unrestricted by the terms of the state. In some forms, as we know, anarchism has now focused on global corporate monopolies, and this focus has to a certain extent displaced the centrality of state as the primary site of opposition. Hence we have seen the possibility for anarchism to shift its object of opposition to broader technological and corporate forms of exploitation, especially as they produce extreme differentials of wealth and expose vast populations to conditions of precariousness and economic destitution. But if the object of resistance is either the state or networks of corporate exploitation and monopoly, what about enduring forms of colonial state power?

It doubtless makes a difference how we interpret an occupation when we oppose that occupation. In other words, can anarchism conceptualize its resistance to the occupation as an opposition to settler colonialism? After all, forms of land confiscation and territorial expansion work in tandem with the denial of the right to political self-determination to a population who are also denied employment, mobility, freedom of expression, electoral rights, rights against imprisonment for political viewpoints, rights against harassment, rights to life itself, and against harassment, invasion and bombardment. Indeed, more than the denial of this list of rights – and it is important to formulate them as such – is the way that both occupation and expulsion foreclose on the right and the power of self-determination. Resistance to such denial and foreclosure is only possible by a full resistance to continuing forms of colonial subjugation. Indeed, the occupation and the settlements need to be understood as a continuation of the project of settler colonialism that has defined political Zionism from the start, if such resistance is to be possible at all.

No doubt there are anti-Zionist anarchists in Israel – there surely are, and their work and contributions should be gratefully received. But a further suggestion emerges here: that the lexicon for understanding the problem of Palestinian oppression may well differ in Palestine and in Israel. This bears consequences for, first, thinking about why anarchism is not the name for Palestinian resistance, even though it sometimes shares anti-statist forms of political organizing; and second, asking what possible alliances, if any, exist between forms of Palestinian political resistance that take distance from the statehood project, and Israeli anarchists who, in a different way, also take distance from that statehood project. It is, of course, odd to say this when the anarchists have been among the most successful of Israeli leftists to forge those alliances, a point not lost among Palestinians, who remark on the courage and radicalism of those anarchists, and who have, for specific aims, entered into temporary alliance with them. But it is precisely because anarchism has been among the most successful efforts that the point can be pressed further, since the chasm between Israeli resistance to the occupation and the Palestinian struggle for self-determination still remains large.

As I read the thorough and thoughtful book *Anarchy Alive!* by Uri Gordon (2007), the question arose whether the version of Israeli anarchism he defends in his final chapter is one that opposes the state but never quite escapes the nation. Are there forms of community produced through anarchist resistance to the state that remain dependent on that state for their mode of resistance, or are they formed, as it were, to the side of the state, without being negatively determined in relation to the state? In a way, this is the age-old question of whether a dialectical relation holds between anarchy and state power, or whether anarchy can and does produce an ethos and mode of sociability that escapes that dialectical determination, constituting a third term, effectively exceeding the dialectical opposition that forms its condition. And yet in this particular case we can ask, does the argument for anarchism as an ethos of sociability depend upon citizenship? After all, citizens can and do perform civil disobedience, but to speak of the civil disobedience of the non-citizen does not make sense. The non-citizen who is struggling either for citizenship or for some other mode of political self-determination (and let us keep those aims distinct for the moment), is struggling against a form of domination and disenfranchisement in order to achieve a legible and effective mode of political self-determination. To engage in civil disobedience, or to engage in actions that seek to jam the machinery of the state, is to risk jail and imprisonment as a citizen; and under extreme conditions, that citizenship can be revoked by the state, to be sure. Indeed, we are presently witnessing the expansion of the legal definition of treason in Israel to encompass all acts of resistance, including the public documentation of civilian casualties in Gaza, as potentially treasonous.

Without for a moment underestimating the kinds of risks that Israeli citizens take, it is important to call attention to the *institution* of citizenship: that is, how citizenship is systematically instituted and deinstituted. Citizenship in the established state of Israel has always been regulated in order to maintain Jewish demographic advantage, and the expansion of settler communities within Palestine has been a way of establishing Jewish Israeli political rights to the land and extending the sovereignty of the state of Israel. Most clearly, the occupation constitutes a mode of militarized power that limits and undercuts Palestinian self-determination. It is colonial power that acts when Israel retains for itself the sovereign right to approve or disapprove of the results of Palestinian elections, the right to invade at will, to expand its settlement populations within those lands and to maintain full military control over the borders of the Palestinian territories, which become sites for ritual harassment, intimidation and injury. So from within the borders of Israel, and for Israeli Jews in particular, the state appears as authoritarian (which is why Gordon's subtitle proclaims anti-authoritarianism) and people fight against its militarism and its policies. But to frame the struggle only within those terms is to accept not only the perspective of citizenship, but its privileges as well. And this, it would seem, is not really adequate insofar as it is the institution of state citizenship – and the management of its deinstitution – that links the occupation to settler colonialism and links settler colonialism to Zionism and the presumption, ever more fiercely amplified by Israeli law, that Israel is a Jewish state based on principles of Jewish sovereignty, where even Palestinians who wish to retain their citizenship must publicly declare fidelity to those principles.

Of course, it has come down to us that the kibbutzim are an exception to all of this, and that some of them were enclaves for anarchists, communists and anti-Zionists. Hannah Arendt reserved words of praise for them even as she criticized the Israeli state, and in her early years generally followed Martin Buber's justifications for a cultural Zionism that did not seek to be realized through a state structure. Uri Gordon's chapter on 'Homeland: anarchy and joint struggle in Palestine/Israel' begins in this same spirit, with a quotation from Emma Goldman in 1938, where she remarks that:

> the fact that there are many non-Zionist communes in Palestine goes to prove that the Jewish workers who have helped the persecuted and hounded Jews have done so not because they are Zionists, but [so] that they might be left in peace in Palestine to take root and live their own lives.
> (quoted in Gordon, 2008, p. 139)

On the one hand, it is historically true that some Jews came to Palestine not because they were Zionists, but because they wanted the chance to work the land or to live in communal structures and to experiment with socialist ideals. And indeed, prior to 1948, there were active debates among Jews in Palestine over the pros and cons of Zionism, debates that continued in diminished form after the vanquishing of the proposals for a binational federated authority in 1947, and then faded altogether from public discourse, surviving only in the margins after the 1967 war. And yet, it seems we have to ask about the link between contemporary anarchist communities and those that existed within the early kibbutz movement. At issue is whether or not the early kibbutz movement, even those parts of it that gave safe haven to European anarchists, was not engaged in land confiscation and the forcible dispossession of populations undertaken in the name of a larger national liberation movement – a liberation, as we know, achieved through dispossession and expulsion. And so the question is raised: for whom was this ever a liberation movement?

Let us turn briefly to the important scholarly work of Gabriel Piterberg, in particular his book *The Returns of Zionism* (2008). Indeed, it would be interesting to read this text together with Uri Gordon's book, published that same year, in order to understand the differences in perspective that concern us here. According to Piterberg's extensive research in this area, even the early kibbutz movement was determined by 'the conditions and desires of colonization' (Piterberg, 2008). Colonization programmes developed for Germans in Eastern Europe provided the basis for the work of Franz Oppenheimer, a German Jewish settlement expert. The point was to find and take over farms that could be sustained self-sufficiently, that is, without any reliance on external labour. In 1911, he developed a plan for colonization that could be implemented, as far as he was concerned, in either Palestine or Africa. Piterberg also points to the key contribution of Arthur Ruppin, known as the father of Jewish settlement, who established the Palestine Land Development Company in 1907. A believer in social Darwinism, Ruppin developed a rationale for Jewish settlements that sought to get rid of the 'semitic' elements of the Jewish race, by which he meant their Arab history and culture, for the purpose of transplanting a European Jewishness to Palestine where, through principles of self-sufficiency, its European character might effectively be preserved. The very first cooperative farms were based on these proposals of Oppenheimer and Ruppin. So the first and second Aliyahs to the region were fundamentally structured by these ideas, and only with the third Aliyah, which took place in 1918-23, did socialism enter into the framework.

Piterberg is joined by many scholars of this period in concluding that 'the kibbutz was first and foremost a colonizing tool for the formation of a settler project' (2008). He cites Gershon Shafir from the University of California at San Diego, whose work on comparative settler colonialism is key to this argument. Shafir writes:

> the national character of the kibbutz was its foundation and *raison d'être* and determined its composition, and in part its structure. The Kibbutz became the most homogenous body of Israeli society; it included almost exclusively Eastern European Jews, since it was unwilling to embrace Middle Eastern and North African Jews, and was constructed on the exclusion of Palestinian Arabs.
>
> (quoted in Piterberg, 2008, p. 87)

And, we might add: their labour. If some of these Eastern European members of the kibbutz were anarchists or Marxists, did their presence contravene these fundamental tenets of nationalism and colonization, or were these accommodated, if not contained, by the kibbutzim movement? For those contemporary anarchists who seek to recall the anarchists of the kibbutz movement as important political predecessors for their own activism, it makes sense to ask whether or not those forms of nationalist local community more aptly prefigure the right-wing settler movements. The effort to find predecessors for contemporary Israeli anarchism among the socialist and anarchist members of the earlier kibbutz movement is confounded by the fact that this was a movement with clearly national and colonizing aims. So another tack is needed if anarchist aims are to prove not only separable from colonizing trends, but actively opposed to colonialism. For this to be the case, Israeli anarchism would have to break from the nationalist ethos at the same time that it reckons with the moral and political predicament of state citizenship.

At issue is whether there can be an anti-statist anarchism that does not mobilize the prerogatives of citizenship at the same time that it reproduces a certain nationalism. If the point is to claim that 'this is the way to be an Israeli', then 'being an Israeli' remains the uncontested ground of the position, and this allows nationality to be the frame for political action. On the one hand, it is impossible and even irresponsible to deny the nationality; on the other hand, it is surely a complicity with nationalism to embrace it as the defining framework for political action. Gordon points out that Bakunin distinguished between forms of nationalism produced by the state, and other forms of sociability or modes of belonging that belong to what he and others have called 'natural communities'. Of course, there are all kinds of reasons to be suspicious of natural communities – this can hardly be contested. But is there a significant distinction between a nationalism produced and sustained by the state (sustaining the state as well) and forms of communitarian belonging that form in opposition to the state or seek to establish themselves to the side of its operations?

Gordon himself remarks that 'the issue of nationalism in the national liberation struggles of stateless peoples received far less attention from anarchists' in the past (2008). It would seem, then, that the ideal of a local or global community is important to anarchist mobilizations not only as a way of countering state-centred forms of nationalism, but also as a way of countering forms of atomistic individualism required and reproduced by capitalism. But to the extent that such forms of communitarian belonging depend on a solidarity among Israelis who commit civil disobedience, or indeed put their bodies on the line and at risk as they oppose Israeli militarization, they can unwittingly become forms of solidarity among Israeli leftists who are actually bonded together by their internal opposition to the state. This can then operate as a mode of communitarianism that is certainly not the same as binationalism or the active deconstruction of nationalism.

Of course, there are modes of solidarity among local Palestinians and Israeli leftists that have clearly and effectively formed in Budrus and Bi'lin, and in several other villages, and those are often invoked as instances of a radical potential for cohabitation and coexistence. The same has surely been said about figures such as Juliano Mer Khamis, the former director of the Freedom Theatre in Jenin, assassinated in April 2011, who described himself as 100 per cent Jewish and 100 per cent Palestinian. Many have pointed to the important work of Andalus, the Hebrew-Arabic publishing operation that brought Arabic literature to the Israeli public. Some also, understandably, point to the existence of bilingual schools such as Neve Shalom/Wahul al-Salam and villages as signs of hope or as living instances of cohabitation that undo the claims of nationalism and defy the explicit aims of the state. Others look to Seeds of Peace or bereavement groups like the Bereaved Families Forum which gather Israelis and Palestinians (those who are allowed to travel and who speak English, and so a very small minority) into 'dialogue'.

I want to suggest that no matter how moving and important some of these coexistence projects may be, they remain sporadic and isolated as long as their work fails to address the concrete legal, military and economic means by which the state maintains discrimination against Palestinian Israelis and the denial both of political rights to Palestinian self-determination under the occupation and the rights of Palestinian refugees forcibly dispossessed in 1948 and in the following years. Indeed, such modes of dialogue can function as deflection from the fundamental structures of oppression unless those structures are addressed explicitly within those institutions. And yet most of these dialogues require the suppression of any reference to power, to subjugation, to colonialism, and mandate a nearly exclusive focus on the interpersonal.

If the structure of occupation remains the same, if Israeli citizenship is not democratized for all of its inhabitants, and if the rights of refugees continue to be dishonoured, then such carefully structured instances of cohabitation become transient moments, eclipsed time and again by these overwhelming structural realities. They do not build an alternative future or an alternative conception of citizenship. And if we call for cohabitation or even 'peace' – a term that has become identified with indefinite subjugation since Oslo – without addressing these enduring structural inequalities of settler colonialism, then we run the risk of trying to instate a form of coexistence that, by definition, is unsustainable, and whose transitory and exceptional qualities confirm rather than contest the functioning of violent political power. When Palestinian activists claim that there can be no peace without justice, no coexistence without the end of occupation, they make clear that notions of peace and cohabitation as ethical ideals can be realized only on the condition of political equality and justice. When they are delinked from the opposition to colonial subjugation, then they deflect from the political and economic realities of occupation, and in that way support their operation, naturalizing the effect of their inevitability.

This is more often than not the issue that divides people on the issues of boycott, divestment and sanctions (BDS), since there are those who believe that the cultural and intellectual domains should be safeguarded as the site where Israelis and Palestinians might freely exchange views, come to appreciate each other's perspectives, and engage in civil discourse. The effort to separate the zones of cultural and intellectual life from the continuing project of colonial subjugation is defended as the 'civil society' alternative, and the idea, the hope, is that ties can be forged at the cultural level that can eventually affect the broader political realm. The problem, of course, is that such a conjecture assumes that there is symmetry between Israeli and Palestinian positions, or asks each of them to act as if there is symmetry, when it does not exist. It very often seeks recourse to the discourse of 'persons' or 'individuals', drawing attention to this or that person's good credentials, or the possibility of 'mutual understanding', that sets aside the concrete forms of power that differentiate those in dialogue. In this sense, it institutes and ratifies a structure of disavowal, an especially problematic move when the continuation of the occupation depends, in part, on a systematic disavowal on the part of Israel of what is happening on the other side of, or at, the wall itself.

One reason that symmetry does not exist is that no major university or cultural institution in Israel is willing to speak out against the occupation. This means that whenever an artist or intellectual from outside of Israel comes to such an institution, they effectively make the claim, 'It does not matter if you fail to oppose the occupation, I will come and visit you and shore up your cultural legitimacy anyway'. Hence for some of us, to arrive on an Israeli campus is effectively to declare yourself against the boycott and to be used precisely for that purpose, which is one reason some of us do not go, and will not go.

In other words, the problem with this version of coexistence is that it assumes a diluted Kantianism that claims 'We are all people here and there is basic respect between us.' That strategy seeks to cast as an ethical relation between equals a situation in which the domination of one group over another is denied and deflected. So if we agree to that mode of dialogue and equality, then we effectively agree to put out of sight and out of mind the existing political reality of either second-class citizenship within the existing borders, or no citizenship at all, outside of those borders.

Against this point of view, it could be argued that only through local instances of living together or *Taayush* is binationalism brought into being through the practices of ordinary life. This view assumes it must be practised first in smaller communities, in local sites, in order finally to expand in ever-widening circles to build an alternative ethos. By 'binationalism' I do not mean to imply a two-state solution, since there are ways of affirming binationalism as part of either a one-state or two-state solution, and even ways of affirming binationalism as a deconstruction of nationalism altogether.

For anarchists, this alternative ethos could be part of a stateless society, or conceived as a practice of anti-statism, one in which certain communitarian ideals are realized through daily practices of cohabitation. To be sure, sometimes local changes do actually build over time and space and come to present an alternative ethos, an alternative form of sociability. But if such forms of sociability fail to contest an existing state structure, then they can become cultural alibis for the state itself. This happens when the Israeli state can point to examples of 'free and open exchange among people otherwise in conflict' as possible on its own terms, establishing itself as a liberal bastion, even a site for progressive forms of multiculturalism. If the occupation permits such moments of coexistence, then the occupation does not need to change and is not really so bad after all – in fact, we can now point to its humanity! Of course, the Anarchists Against the Wall are not only building new modes of sociability, often between Israelis and Palestinians, especially in Bi'lin, they are also quite literally opposing the state, intervening to halt or derail its militarized expansion. And this is a crucial activity, critical, radical, and exemplary in the way that it seeks to both build a new ethos and stop the wall, which is the state, as we know, as it destroys the livelihood of Palestinians, their villages and their lands, their access to water, to medical facilities and to family and work on the other side of the barrier.

But this form of alliance seems to come up against a limit precisely when the question emerges whether anarchists can or should support the Palestinian national struggle if that struggle is for a state of their own. I want to turn to this issue briefly before I return to the question of cohabitation, which is where my chapter belatedly takes a queer turn.

Uri Gordon formulates this paradox in Israeli anarchism when he writes, for instance, 'While anarchists surely can do something more specific in solidarity with Palestinians than just saying that "we need a revolution", any such action would appear hopelessly contaminated with a statist agenda' (2008). He discusses various alternatives: anarchists could, following Kropotkin, consider the state as a necessary strategic move but one which would have to be dissolved in the future. Or they could say that, given that Palestinians are already under state control, they might as well have their own state even though the state cannot legitimately represent their final aspirations. Or they could say, as Gordon himself seems to say, that anarchists can take action in support of the 'dignity and livelihood' of Palestinians 'without reference to the question of statehood' (Gordon, 2008, p. 156)

In some ways this is a perfect strategy, since it restricts the role of activists to supporting Palestinians without intervening in the question of whether or not a state should be built, or what mode of governance is most desirable. But is this really enough? Does this strategy stay restricted within the national frame, and fail to really find out how Palestinians are framing their struggle, and what it might be to support them? It is interesting to me that the ethical principles in defence of which anarchists would then struggle are restricted to dignity and livelihood, although elsewhere, especially in the contributions of Yossi Bartal,[1] it is clear that Israeli anarchists affirm Palestinian self-determination as well. Bartal makes clear that they do not come with an agenda that they seek to impart to Palestinians, that they do not arrive in a saviour role but only to assist an agenda that Palestinians themselves formulate. This self-limiting move within the anarchist agenda is crucial. But still, how important is self-determination, and is it in fact more primary than, and finally distinct from, the question of state structure, or even independent of the question whether or not to engage in a state formation project? This question underscores the difference between Palestinian resistance struggles that seek to exercise and establish self-determination, and those that immediately assume that the form or mode of expression for self-determination is the establishment of a state.

Gordon assumes that the paradox of Israeli anarchism and Palestinian political aspirations is that the former are *against* the state and the latter are *for* the state. He asks:

> how anarchists who support the Palestinian struggle reconcile [the desire of the majority of Palestinians for a state of their own] with their anti-statist principles? How can they support the creation of yet another state in the name of 'national liberation', which is the explicit or implicit agenda of almost all Palestinians?
>
> (Gordon, 2007, p. 12)

Here we may legitimately ask why it is that, at this juncture, Gordon and others within the Israeli left do not actively consult the long and complex Palestinian debates on statehood? This seems especially important to do if, first, Israelis want to be able to think about the regional conflict outside of their own national frame, and second, they seek to find sites of solidarity with the Palestinian struggle.

Surely, the state-building practices of the Fayyad government have been cause for debate and even schism within the Palestinian population. Some Palestinians argue, for instance, for a one-state solution, like Omar Barghouti and the late Edward Said, affirming the idea of a secular state for the region that does not discriminate on the basis of religious or ethnic belonging. Others, like Hanan Ashrawi, and sometimes Azmi Beshara, argue for a two-state solution, fearing a division of Palestine into Bantustans that would replicate the worst dimension of South African apartheid. Beshara, a Palestinian Israeli who was a member of the Knesset and who was sent into exile in the aftermath of the last military war against Lebanon, holds a view that is more complex. And yet, before his political exile, he not only argued for a radically egalitarian revolution within the so-called Israeli democracy, but also suggested that the struggle against colonization must be temporally distinct from any struggle for state formation. His view is clearly not the same as Arafat's promotion of a state-centred project in the early 1970s, and it is clearly different from the state-building efforts now undertaken by Abu Mazen and the Fayyad leadership in the Palestinian Authority.

Indeed, a quite important dissertation has been written by Tariq Mukhimer, entitled *State Building Process: The Case of Palestine* (2005), tracing the reluctance of Palestinians to accept state structures in the 1920s and 1930s insofar as such structures were taken as colonial impositions and as the central means by which to consolidate colonial control. This same sentiment was clearly voiced ironically by Azmi Beshara in a television interview in Israel in June 2009, one which visibly scandalized the leftist Israelis seated on either side of him: 'It is true there has never been a separate Palestinian State. Like all Arab states this is a colonial invention. There is only an Arab nation, which Palestine was part of.' (It is interesting to contrast this with the claim made by Francis Boyle, the US lawyer assisting the Palestinian statehood bid in the United Nations, who argues that the Palestinians already have a state and that it only has to be recognized as such.) Perhaps Beshara's most relevant point here, however, is that the struggle against colonization (which is the meaning of the struggle against occupation) has to precede any question of state formation and must be kept distinct from it. Samera Esmeir (2012) builds on this thesis to argue that the means of struggling against colonization must remain distinct from the political goal of achieving a state.

Marwan Barghouti, the jailed senior member of Fatah, underscores the importance of rights. Yet we cannot help but note that the form of resistance he invokes relies upon a discourse of rights that are not exclusively tied to the legal apparatus of the state and are not, in fact, necessarily inscribed in any existing legal code. Something similar happens in Azmi Beshara's language when speaking about Palestinians with limited rights of citizenship within Israel. He remarks:

> Arabs are much more aware of their rights, not only to eat and have a home and teach their children, but also their right to express their political views and not get shot for that, as citizens of the state of Israel, not only as Palestinians. Some say that Arabs in Israel are hopelessly marginalized both in Israel and in the Arab nation. We think that Palestinians who are living with the contradiction of being Arabs and Israeli citizens at the same time should turn it into an accelerator of development. This contradiction should become the source of the dialectic that pushes the Arab consciousness towards the most sophisticated consciousness, the most sophisticated understanding of national identity and of citizenship at the same time. A synthesis of Arab nationality and democracy would be the greatest gift we can give the Arab world.
>
> (quoted in Toensing, 2000)

Prescient words, indeed. For Beshara, there is a strong sense that the struggle for self-determination is one with no clear terminus and no pre-established goal. He claims additionally:

> I would like to see a long-term struggle that realizes that there is no just peace in the near future.
>
> But for that you must have determined leadership, consistent, not hasty, which does not waste the sacrifices of its people in a short time – which means a change in the mode of struggle. Such a struggle would leave the Palestinian question open for a long time – a struggle that people can live with in their daily life, a struggle with the economy, a struggle with the society. That's what I would like to see.
>
> (quoted in Toensing, 2000)

Clearly distinguishing self-determination from state-formation, he calls instead for 'a democratic channel to express self-determination. Occupation is violent. Occupation deprives the Palestinian people not only of self-determination, but the elementary right to plan their lives every day, the most banal details.'

Of course, we might wonder how best to read the nationalism to which Beshara refers when he claims that the only nationalism Palestinians have is an Arab one (especially in light of the proclamation by recent US politicians that the Palestinians are not 'a people' but belong more generally to the regional Arab population). This nationalism crosses existing territorial boundaries; it is not produced or exemplified by a single state, whether existing or potential. The nation expresses tradition, community and shared forms of aspiration, including counter-statist trends and the important links between Palestinians and other Arab peoples. The nationalism that supports the nation-state is not the same as the nationalism that brings together those who are stateless, or who are maintained in subordination or in forced exile. And so we might ask whether what is called nationalism in this instance is a form of citizenship that precedes and exceeds state formation.

Perhaps most important here, however, is the claim to a set of rights that a people may assert even when those rights are not granted by any positive law, and precisely when the positive law in existence seeks to deprive those people of those rights. We may suggest here that the right to self-determination, the right to plan one's life, the right to live free of fear of being imprisoned or killed or sent into exile for one's political viewpoints, the right to mobility, and even the right to find a mode of governance that would be what Beshara calls a 'democratic channel to express self-determination', are rights that are asserted by Palestinians prior to any reference to a legal regime. In fact, in Beshara's discourse (which can be found scattered in various public statements) the exercise of a right is part of an open-ended struggle without a perceivable end. Is there any other way for the stateless to exercise rights than through a struggle that endeavours collectively to bring into being the very rights that it exercises? Such rights are not grounded in personhood, nor are they derived from natural laws; indeed, they are not grounded in any form other than the one by which they are invoked and exercised – their common exercise is their ground. Of course, there are those who seek recourse to international law or human rights doctrine – Omar Bhargouti's case for BDS is among the most important and influential of these. He claims that the movement for BDS is the largest non-violent Palestinian form of resistance, a way of insisting upon compliance with international and human rights laws that existing nation-states and international authorities flagrantly and tactically fail to enforce.

Reacting to the accusations of treason against Azmi Beshara and his subsequent exile in Jordan, Ali Abunimah, known for his concept of 'one country' – sharply distinguished from one state – and editor of *The Electronic Intifada*, made clear his differences from the prevailing state-building policy of the current Palestinian Authority:

> In practice this means that the Palestinian solidarity movement needs to fashion a new message that breaks with the failed fantasy of hermetic separation in nationalist states. It means we have to focus on fighting Israeli racism and colonialism in all its forms against those under occupation, against those inside, and against those in exile .... In practice we need to start building a vision of life after Israeli apartheid, an inclusive life in which Israelis and Palestinians can live in equality sharing the whole country. If Sinn Fein's Gerry Adams and hardline Northern Ireland Unionist leader Ian Paisley can sit down to form a government together, as they are, and if Nelson Mandela and apartheid's National Party could do the same, nothing is beyond the realm of possibility in Palestine if we imagine it and work for it.
>
> (Abunimah, 2007)

These forms of struggle are very often local and provisional, and they rely on forms of nongovernmental action that disrupt the course of routinized military intimidation. Rema Hammami, a sociologist at Bir Zeit University, articulates modes of resistance at the checkpoint among Palestinians that are relatively spontaneous and without hierarchical form, as when people from the community converge at the checkpoints, forming networks of peddlers, workers, and even Israeli witnesses to checkpoint harassment. Hammami underscores that such networks can affect a change in consciousness. Interestingly, in her research on the formation of informal checkpoint communities, she cites Asef Bayat's *Street Politics: Poor people's movements in Iran* (1998), which refers to the 'quiet encroachment of the ordinary', the effect of slow, daily practices on the part of the 'the urban poor [who] were able to slowly take over and remake areas of Tehran to meet their needs' (Bayat, 1998).

These modes of relatively spontaneous and networked action

are something other than deliberative democracy or even collective forms of direct action, and they are not dialogic encounters shorn of any reference to broader political conditions. In Hammami's view, these modes of networked action are the result of 'the everyday tactics of survival that were mostly individual, spontaneous and without clear leadership or ideology. But when protracted and taken together they created a kind of molecular change to urban space despite the overwhelming power of the state' (Hammami, 2010). She continues, 'by initiating gradual molecular change, the poor in the long run progressively modify the pre-existing composition of forces and hence become the matrix of new changes' (Hammami, 2010). Her research on informal networks formed at the Qalandiya checkpoint between Ramallah and Jerusalem led her to conclude that:

> there is an ideological framework sustaining individual and collective actions – national survival. But what primarily motivates checkpoint workers is necessity – the quest for dignity in the face of the destruction of their regular livelihoods. Thus through daily tactics of survival they crept into the spaces of opportunity that existed between the whims and violence of the military and the various needs of the community. They could not overthrow the checkpoint but they could 'poach' it back from being a space of pure brutality and oppression to one in which their own dispossession could be redressed ... and inequality undone.
>
> (Hammami, 2010)

Where does this leave us? There is, of course, the impressive movement of radicals in Israel, the former work of Black Laundry, the contemporary work of Who Profits?, the Queer Anarchists Against the Wall, the various disruptions and fabulous counter-demonstrations to gay pride – the Ninth Queeruption Festival – in its hypernationalist versions, and the strong criticism of pinkwashing, that is, the policy by which the Israeli government seeks to 'sell' its human rights records on lesbians and gays as a way of deflecting from the military suppression of Palestinian lives; the feminists at the checkpoints, the radical draft resistors, and those who maintain an active memorialization of the hundreds of villages destroyed in 1948 through organizations like Zochrot. It seems that, as important as it is to have what is called an 'internal' critique of the state of Israel, it is equally important to ask about the political constitution of what counts as 'internal' and what counts as 'external'. Which border establishes that distinction, and how was that border drawn? What do we make of settlements? Are they inside or outside? And Palestinian Israelis – are they inside, or outside, or both? We cannot understand forcible expression and the right to return for Palestinians, or the occupation, or the internal subordination of Palestinian Israelis, without understanding how the line between internal and external is drawn again and again, and without protesting against the land confiscation that is enacted through that constantly expanding border.

Thus, it makes sense to formulate a queer Israeli politics at the border, as many have already done, but also to develop a framework that makes central the important work of queer Palestinians, of Al Qaws, of Aswat, and of Palestinian Queers for BDS. They are insisting that one cannot struggle for sexual freedom or alliance without opposing the occupation and without support for BDS, which itself includes support for the right of return and the equal rights of Palestinian Israelis. One point of this struggle is to insist that the struggle for gender and sexual freedom cannot be achieved within the framework of occupation, and that struggles to overcome subordination must be linked.

It is true that self-determination becomes an absolute priority under the condition of occupation for Palestinians, but this is no reason to turn away from that struggle as if it belongs to someone else. After all, the struggle for self-determination also consists in making a global appeal for support; and thus the terms of solidarity have been made clear. The rights of Palestinians to determine the course of their mobilization is the very instance of the principle of self-determination which all allies have to affirm. This cannot be done in ways that affirm the structural asymmetry between Israeli citizens and Palestinians either in Israel, under occupation, or in a condition of indefinite expulsion; through civil society methods that refuse the call of BDS; in ways that fail to contest the national frame furnished by the nation-state as the restrictive theatre for radical action; or in ways that refuse to separate antistate activism from anticolonial politics. Neither the civil society method nor the demand to work exclusively within the borders of the militarized nation-state will furnish the perspectives we need for new and effective forms of solidarity and sociability. Luckily, there are many signs of non-state-centred struggles to assert dignity and freedom within ordinary life emerging on both sides of the border, at the border, in the dismantling of the border, ways of actively supporting self-determination that do not determine its terms. That is the risk and the demand of the fragile ground of alliance.

NOTE

1 These comments were made in conversation with the author.

REFERENCES

Abunimah, A. (2007) 'What the persecution of Azmi Bishara means for Palestine', *The Electronic Intifada*, April 16. http://electronicintifada.net/content/what-persecution-azmi-bishara-means-palestine/6862 (accessed September 4, 2012).

Bayat, A. (1998) *Street Politics: Poor people's movements in Iran*. Cairo: AUC Press.

Esmeir, Samera (2012) Personal communication.

Gordon, U. (2007) 'Israeli anarchism: statist dilemmas and the dynamics of joint struggle', *Anarchist Studies*, 15(1).

Gordon, U. (2008) *Anarchy Alive! Anti-authoritarian politics from practice to theory*. London and Ann Arbor, Mich.: Pluto Press.

Hammami, R. (2010) 'Qalandiya: Jerusalem's Tora Bora and the frontiers of global inequality', *Jerusalem Quarterly* (Spring), 41.

Kanafani, N. (2011) 'As if there is no occupation: the limits of Palestinian authority strategy', Middle East Research and Information Project (MERIP) Online, September 22. www.merip.org/mero/mero092211(accessed September 4, 2012).

Massad, J. (2011) 'State of recognition', *Al Jazeera Online*. www.aljazeera.com/indepth/opinion/2011/09/20119158427939481.html (accessed September 4, 2012).

Mukhimer, Tariq (2005) *State Building Process: The case of Palestine*, unpublished Ph.D. dissertation, Humboldt University, Berlin.

Piterberg, G. (2008) *The Returns of Zionism: Myths, politics and scholarship in Israel*. London and New York; Verso.

Toensing, C. (2000) 'A double responsibility, MER beyond Oslo', *The New Uprising*, 30.

13

SPREAD ANARCHY, LIVE COMMUNISM

The accused of Tarnac

There is a confrontation underlying this world. There is no need to be in Misrata today to perceive it. The streets of New York, for instance, reveal the extent to which this confrontation has been refined, for here we find all the sophisticated apparatuses needed to contain what is always threatening. Here is the mute violence that crushes down what still lives under the blocks of concrete and fake smiles. When we talk of 'apparatuses', we don't only invoke the New York Police Department (NYPD) and the Federal Bureau of Investigation (FBI), surveillance cameras and body scanners, guns and denunciation, anti-theft locks and cell phones. Rather, in the layout of a town like New York – the pinnacle of the global petit-organic-hipster-bourgeoisie – we mean whatever captures intensities and vitalities in order to chew them up, digest them, and shit out value. But if capitalism triumphs every day, it is not merely because it crushes, exploits and represses, but also because it is desirable. This must be kept in mind when building a revolutionary movement.

There is a war going on—a permanent, global civil war. Two things prevent us from understanding it or even from perceiving it. First, the denial of the very fact of confrontation is still a part of this confrontation. And second, despite all the new prose of the various geopolitical specialists, the meaning of this war is not understood. Everything said about the asymmetrical shape of the so-called 'new wars' only adds to the confusion. The ongoing war we speak of does not have the Napoleonic magnificence of regular wars between two great armies of men, or between two antagonistic classes. Because if there is an asymmetry in the confrontation it is less between the forces present than over the very definition of the war itself. That is why we cannot talk about a social war: for if social war is a war that is led against us, it cannot symmetrically describe the war that we wage from our side and vice versa. We have to rethink the words themselves in order to forge new concepts as weapons.

We call hostility that which governs almost completely the relationships between beings, relationships of pure estrangement, pure incompatibility between bodies. It may take the shape of benevolence or malevolence, but it is always a distance. I beat you down because I am a cop and you are a shit. I invite you to the restaurant because I want to fuck you. I leave you the bill because I don't know how to tell you how much I hate you. I don't stop smiling. This is hostility.

We need to act toward this sphere of hostility with the same non-relationships that it imposes within itself: to reduce it, to take aim at it and annihilate it. In other words, Empire is not a subject that is in front of me but a milieu that is hostile to me. It cannot be a question of being victorious over it, only of annihilating it. All that we learn to know singularly escapes from the sphere of the non-relationship. All that gives rise to a circulation of affects escapes the sphere of hostility. It is what friendship is about. It is what enmity is about. That is why we don't try to crush any enemies; rather, we try to confront them. 'My enemy is my own question taking shape', said a horrible jurist. In this confrontation, it is less existence that is at stake than potentiality. All means are not equally useful in the confrontation between these two political positions. To say it differently, a political enemy is not to be crushed, it must be overcome. Distinguishing the sphere of hostility from that of friendship and enmity leads to a certain ethic of war.

For the anarchists, the paradox of the current historical situation can be formulated thus: everything proves them right, and nowhere do they manage to intervene in a decisive way, which means the obstacle does not come from the situation or from the repression but from the very inside of the anarchist position. For more than a century, the figure of the anarchist indicates the most extreme point of Western civilization. The anarchist is the point where the most hard-lined affirmation of all the Western fictions – the individual, freedom, free will, justice, the death of God – coincides with the most declamatory negation. The anarchist is the Western negation of the West.

Schürmann (1982) rightly characterized our time as a deeply anarchic one, a time where all the principles of the unification of phenomena collapsed. Anarchy describes our epochal situation. From there, calling oneself an anarchist is to say nothing. It means either, when directed against a dominant order (as is the case in Greece), a way to expose to everyone the inner split and malaise of civilization, or a posture.

All the tired chatter of the particular anarchist literature today is held to this: how is it possible to violently affirm our existence without ever affirming any singular ethical content? Those who said 'There are no nihilists, only impotence', were not mistaken. To claim yourself to be a nihilist is only claiming your impotence. Isolation is a cause for an impotence more dreadful than that caused by repression. Those who don't let themselves be isolated do not let themselves be reduced to impotence. Malatesta understood that well in his time.

All the doctrines of government are anarchist doctrines. They do not trouble themselves with any principle. They do not presuppose order; they produce order. This world is not unified *a priori* by some fantasy of truth, by some universal norm or principle that would be posed or imposed. This world is unified *a posteriori*, pragmatically, locally. Everywhere is organized the material, symbolic, logistical and repressive condition of an 'as if'. Everywhere, in every locality, everything goes 'as if' life obeyed this principle, this norm compatible with other localities. It is how empire covers globally the anarchy of our time. We manage, we manage phenomenality.

This is what testifies to the insurrectional movements of the last years in the Maghreb, in Europe or in Asia. And that is precisely why they are meant to always disappoint anarchists.

The contemporary figure of a man without qualities that we call the Bloom is struck by what we must call an ethical impotence. It cannot live one particular thing without worrying about missing everything else. It never is here without its own being-here being doubled by the anxiety of not being everywhere else too. That is why it is so dependent on ubiquitous technological apparatuses: the cell phones, internet and global transportation. Without this prosthesis, he would collapse on the spot. New York, as the absolute metropolis, condenses this experience where the price of not missing anything is to not live anything. Anarchism is the spontaneous political consciousness of the Bloom. The ambition to deny everything is what legitimates people to never fully deny something and thus to start to affirm something singular.

The desperate conservatism that presently spreads in the political sphere only expresses our inability to seize the ethical underpinnings implicit in Western civilization. We need to settle up with the muted, unnoticed totality of what underlies all our actions, words, feelings and representations. But the scale of the task is such that, for an isolated individual, any stupid affirmation of any neoconservatism is always more reassuring in the end. The current fallback toward the most dogmatic ideological forms of anarchism or communism, towards the fetishism of a radical political identity, comes from the same fear of throwing yourself into the unknown of such an adventure.

It is necessary to do away with the reigning confusion. One of the main flaws of the revolutionary movement is that it remains imprisoned in false oppositions; or worse, that it forces us to think in the shackles of these very false alternatives. Activism or wait and see? The great evening or the process? Vanguard or mass movement? They are called false not because they will not express actual differences. Quite the contrary, it is because they transform all the decisive questions into binary and unsatisfying polarized alternatives. This said, the debate around the necessity to create our own little oasis or to wait for the insurrection to come before creating troubles within the radical milieu, was firstly a theological question. We could wait for the coming of the Messiah, staying at the very position God gave him, or we could pretend to fasten the second coming. There is another way, of a different nature. There is a Messianic time that is the abolition of the time that passes: the rupture of the continuum of history, the end of waiting. That also means there are sparks mixed with the blackness of reality. It means there exists something Messianic: the kingdom is not merely to come but already, by fragments, here among us.

What we say is that it is not more urgent to act than it is urgent to wait. Because we want to get organized, we have time. We don't think there is any outside to capital, but we don't think that reality is capitalist. Communism is a practice that starts from those sparks, from those forms-of-life.

We said 'all power to the communes', but a commune is never something given. It is not what is here, but what takes place. A commune is not two people who meet or ten people buying a farm. A commune is two people who meet to become three, to become four, to become a thousand. The only question for the commune is its own potentiality, its constant becoming. It is a practical question. To become a war machine or collapse into a milieu? To end up alone or begin to love each other? The commune does not describe what we organize but how we organize ourselves, which is always at the same time a material question. A commune is only as it becomes. There is no preliminary to communism. Those who believe otherwise, by dint of pursuing their goal, manage only to lose themselves in the accumulation of means.

Communism is not a different way to distribute wealth, to organize production or to manage society. Communism is an ethical disposition, a disposition that lets itself be affected, at the contact of being, through what is common to us. Communism is as much the beyond and the below of capitalist misery. What we put behind this vocable 'communism' is radically opposed to all those who use and used it to lead it to dislocation. War also passes through words. How many times in activist circles have we had this dead-end discussion? What are we fighting against? You just have to raise the issue and everyone will go for their own petty fantasy that, in the last resort, subsumed all the others. 'What we need to confront is patriarchy.' 'No, it's racism.' 'No, it's capitalism.' 'No, it's exploitation, and alienation is only a moment of it.' 'No, it's alienation, and exploitation is only a moment of it.' The finest theologians even managed to build a small activist trinity that articulates a triple oppression. At the same time one and three: sexism, racism and capitalism. All the good will of the world failed to produce the decisive answer to this question. That failure sums up the impotence to which our false conception condemns us.

When we are looking for an enemy we start by projecting ourselves on an abstract scene, wherein the world has disappeared. Let us ask ourselves the same question, but starting from the neighbourhood where we live, from the company where we work, from the professional sector we are familiar with. Then the answer is clear; then the front lines can be distinctly seen, and who is on what side can easily be determined. This is because the question of the confrontation, the properly political question, only makes sense in a given world, in a substantial world. For those who are nowhere, cybernetic philosophers or metropolitan hipsters, the political question never makes sense. It refuses itself to them and leaves them walking backward into abstraction. And that is the price to pay for so much superficiality. As compensation, they will prefer to juggle with some great folkloric significance, to give themselves some post-Maoist or post-situationist thrills. Or, perhaps they will accommodate their nothingness with the last glosses of the ultra-left logorrhoea.

To all the metaphysical principles overhanging reality, Schürmann opposed 'faithfulness to the phenomena'. That is also what we need to oppose to the political impotence. For, besides a few heroic moments, it is over the ordinary and the daily that the anarchist discourse breaks itself. There we experience the same disjunction between the political and the sensible that is the disastrous background of classical politics. The powerful things that we live leave us mute. And what we experience in terms of silent but manifest failures, these we have no words for. Only the anarchist gesture sometimes comes to save its profound inconsistency, and yet during this gesture we only obey an order corresponding to our anarchist identity. That we have from time to time to obey our identity in order to realize our discursive existence – this reveals our poverty in worlds, a poverty that one is not even distracted from by belonging to a milieu. Identity politics captures us in the negation of all the implicit, all the invisible, all the unheard, which composes the frame of the world.

We have called this the ethical element. It is the same underlying principle behind Wittgenstein's forms of life. It is on the basis of everyday life, of the ordinary, that this war against the world must be conceived. From Oaxaca to Keratea, from the Val di Susa to Sidi Bouzid, from Exarchia to Kabylie, the great battles of our time emanate from a local consistency. A street vendor who will self-immolate in front of the local administration after being slapped in public by a policewoman expresses the implicit and adiscursive affirmation of a form-of-life. This gesture of negation contains a clear affirmation that this life does not deserve to be lived. At root it was the power of this affirmation that took over Tunisia. Genoa would never have become the summit of the counter-summits without the rebellious Genovese proletarians.

To say that the war against Empire arises from everyday life, from the ordinary, that it emanates from the ethical element, is to propose a new concept of war stripped of all its military content. In any case, it is comical to see that for the last ten years the strategy of all the Western armies, as well as the Chinese army, is to approximate a concept which, because of their forms-of-life, escapes them. It is enough to see a special forces soldier speak of battles of hearts and minds to understand that they have already lost. It is an asymmetrical war not because of the forces present but because the insurgents and counter-insurrectionists are not waging the same war. This is why the notion of social war is inadequate. It gives rise to the fatal illusion of symmetry in the conflict with society, that the battle takes place over the same representation of reality. If there actually is an asymmetric war between people and governments, it is because what sets us apart is an asymmetry in the very definition of war. We welcome, in passing, the nomination of General Petraeus to the head of the Central Intelligence Agency (CIA). It no doubt ushers in an exciting decade in the United States.

It has been four years since the publication of *The Coming Insurrection* (Invisible Committee, 2009). It was, at that time, crazy but also rational to pose insurrection as the world's horizon. We could say that the present period has confirmed this analysis. A social movement, like that of the pensioners in France, adopted as its slogan 'Blockade everything'. An entire country, like Greece, saw the insurrection coming (though it was ultimately aborted), over the course of a month. Not to mention Tunisia, Egypt or Libya – where the determination, often unspoken, to destroy structures of power remains exemplary. To be sure, there are still too few heads of state sunning themselves in Saudi Arabia – away from the countries they once presumed to lead – but something is definitely accelerating.

We have only to look around in order to see that the content of this book is realizing itself. Yet, at the same time, it withers. Its limits are becoming apparent. The real movement provides the only admissible critique of a text's historical impact. The field of tactics is always the domain of the counter-revolution. And so we understand: when we are forced onto the field of tactics, when we are only a little step ahead, when we chase after events as they happen, then we can no longer act in a revolutionary way. At the present moment, in order to escape being forced onto the field of tactics, we must overcome the question of the insurrection. That is to say, we must take this horizon as given and begin to think and act on that basis. We must take the insurrectionary situation as our starting point – even now, even here, when it is the counter-insurrection that dominates reality.

In this regard, we locate two crucial questions that pose themselves to the revolutionary movement. The first is the exit from the framework of government. Since its origin in Greece, politics has carried within itself a metaphysics of order. It begins from the premise that people must be governed, either democratically by themselves or hierarchically by others. The same anthropology underlies the notion of the individualist anarchist – who wants to express their own passions fully, or to govern themself – and that of the pessimist – for whom people are hungry beasts, who will devour their neighbours if only they can free themselves from the binding power of government. Various political positions thus organize themselves, ultimately, according to the answers they propose to this question: the question of the government of human beings and their passions. All are rooted in a readily discernible notion of human nature.

But in fact, the question of government only poses itself in a void. We must produce enough of a void around individuals, or even in them – or within society, a space sufficiently devoid of content – in order to wonder how we will arrange those disparate, disconnected elements of the self as much as of the society. If we have a politics to advance, it is one that begins from an opposite hypothesis. There is no void. Everything is already inhabited. We are, each of us, points of intersection: of quantities of affect, of families, of histories, of realities that fundamentally exceed us. The point is not to constitute a void in which we finally begin to recover everything that eludes us, but rather that we already have the means to organize, to play, to form links and bonds. There is an open battle between, on the one hand, this fear, at once senile and childish, that we can only live on the condition of being governed, and on the other hand, an inhabited politics that dismisses the question of government altogether.

Whether from the Tunisian situation, from attempts to block economic flows in France, or from the coming insurrection latent in Greece, we learn that we cannot separate the tearing down of power from the material establishment of other forms of organization. Everywhere, when power falters, the same chasm opens beneath our feet. How is it to be done? We have to figure it out materially, but also technically: how can we effect a shocking exit from the existing order, a complete reversal of social relations, a new way of being in the world? We say that this paradox is not a paradox at all.

All power to the communes! This means: tear down power, globally, locally – wherever it captures, manages and controls us. It means: organize by and for ourselves, first of all in the neighbourhood, the city and the region. Food, transportation, healthcare, energy – in each case we need to find the level at which we can act without recreating the power that we only just deposed. The commune is a not a form, but rather a way of posing problems that dissolves them. And so the revolutionary imperative reduces itself to this simple formula: to become ungovernable and to remain that way.

It is from this horizon, for example, that we can understand the failure of the recent movement of pensioners in France. By blocking the infrastructure that regulates the country – rather than begging the government for demands, for reforms, or for anything – the movement implicitly recognized that it is the physical organization of society that constitutes its real power. By blocking the circulation of commodities rather than occupying the factories, the movement took leave of the classical workers' perspective, which understood the strike as a prelude to the occupation of sites of production, and understood the occupation of sites of production as the prelude to their takeover by the working class. The people who made the blockade were not only those who worked in the places that were blocked, but also a motley crew of teachers, students and trade unionists; of workers from other sectors; of troublemakers of every kind. The blockade was not the prelude to an economic reappropriation but to a political act: in each flow, the sabotage takes aim at the social machine as a whole.

Nevertheless, this movement was defeated. Whether this was because of the intervention by unions or because of the architectural flows of networks that allow their rapid reorganization in the case of interruption, the gas supply in France – which the movement spontaneously chose to target – could not be blocked permanently. We could go on and on about the weaknesses of the movement. What is certain is that it did not have sufficient knowledge of what it tried to block.

This example suffices to illustrate how we must henceforth understand the materiality of domination. We must 'investigate', we must research: we must search out, and above all share and propagate, all of the necessary information about the functioning of the capitalist machine. How is it fed by energy, information, arms and food? What we need to understand is: in a situation where everything is suspended, in a state of exception, what do we turn off, what do we transform and what do we want to maintain? Refusing to pose these questions today would oblige us to return to the normal situation tomorrow, if only to survive.

We can predict that such an investigation, having reached a certain degree of reality, would not fail to produce a scandal as big as the threat that it poses to the good functioning of everything. Contrarily to the amusing fraud of Wikileaks, it is the sharing and diffusion of accessible information to everyone, which would allow them to feed off or consequently paralyze a region or a country. In a world of lies, the lie can never be defeated by its contrary, it can only be defeated by a world of truth.

We don't want a programme. We must constitute a science of apparatuses that reveals the structures and weaknesses of the organization of a world, and at the same time indicates practicable paths outside of the current hell. We need fictions, a horizon of the world, which will allow us to hang on, which will give us breath. When the moment comes, we must be ready.

To conclude, if we have come here to talk, it is only because we have been persuaded of this: we must be done with radicalism and its meagre comforts – now. The intellectual, the academic, both remain mesmerized by the contradictions that banish thought to the clouds. By never beginning from the situation, from their own situation, intellectuals distance themselves from the world so much that, finally, it is their intelligence itself that abandons them. If hipsters succeed in perceiving the world with precision and subtlety, it is only to aestheticize the sensible ever further, that is to say, to keep it at a distance, to contemplate their lives and their beautiful souls and thereby to promote their own impotence – their particular autism, which expresses itself in a valorization of the tiniest aspects of life. Meanwhile, the activist, in refusing to think, in adopting the ethic of middle managers, runs grinning into every single wall before him before finally collapsing into cynicism. If taking part is the only option in war, the lines that are offered to us visibly are not the ones that we should follow. We have to displace them and we have to move ourselves in between them.

Whether it is the Marxist theologian or the anarchist anti-intellectual, the identitarian moralist or the playfully transgressive hipster, all of this is an apparatus. We have said enough about what we want to do to with apparatuses. Each of these figures – the hipster, the academic and the political activist – expresses as much a singular attachment to a power as a common amputation. And here we see the fundamental divisions on which Western civilization has been built: that is, the separation between the gesture, the thought and life. If we wondered what tiqqun could mean, it could mean, for instance, here not letting ourselves be comfortable in those very splits, through those very amputations, but rather starting from those very attachments – thinking, acting and living – asking how could this, instead of being maintained separated in figures (the hipster, the academic, the activist), how could all of this be the plane of consistency that would actually enable us to draw lines more interesting than the lines between those figures?

If the life of militant radicals in Western societies shows the dissatisfaction proper to a revolutionary existence without a revolution, the recent uprisings in the Maghreb attest to an insufficiency of revolutions without revolutionaries: that is, the necessity of building the party. When we speak of building the party, we do not mean as organization, but as a plane of circulation, of common intelligence, of strategic thinking, just as much as local consistencies. There is a threat that weighs on all attacks starting from singular worlds, and it is that they remain incomprehensible by lack of translation. The party must be that agent of faithful translation of local phenomena, a force of mutual knowledge, of experiences underway. And it must be global.

What is at stake is how we are able to flee and keep our weapons. What is at stake is how we can extract ourselves from the milieux in which we are stuck, whether it is a university or the anarchist scene itself. Many have wondered about the very situation we face now, claiming 'there is no situation here'. We respond: there is no 'no situation'. It does not exist. From where we are we must run into the first world we encounter, to follow the first line of power that we get to. Everything follows from this.

REFERENCES

Invisible Committee (2009) *The Coming Insurrection*. Los Angeles, Calif.: Semiotext(e).

Schürmann, Reiner (1982) *Le principe d'anarchie. Heidegger et la question de l'agir*. Paris: Seuil.

POSTFACE: OCCUPATION AND REVOLUTION

Jacob Blumenfeld

I

> The coming occupations will have no end in sight, and no means to resolve them. When that happens, we will finally be ready to abandon them.

When we wrote that in December 2008 in New York City, after occupying the New School for Social Research, we were treated as youthful idealists, nihilist anarchists, even fascist thugs. What are your demands? they asked. But what are you for? they wondered. Occupy everything? they shrieked.

Alas. Our premonitions have come to pass.

It was only a matter of time. When the crisis first hit in the fall of 2008, its effects were diffuse, with individuals all over the country feeling it simultaneously but not collectively. Students, who have the time to both act and think free from the imperative to work, naturally reacted first. With an insurrection in Greece brewing, and a legitimation crisis of the American economy at hand, occupations without demands spread from New York to California, with thousands involved. Demands are irrelevant when no one can hear you, and so the only real demand was to occupy itself. Immature maybe, but not stupid. With foreclosures growing exponentially, and unemployment skyrocketing as well, occupying your own space and means of living is the most obvious of actions. In the most unpolitical of Western democracies we must first create a space for politics to emerge.

But students on their own are nothing. Especially left radical ones.

Always half way in and half way out of work, students can

235

only express frustration over what is to come, not what has been. Hence, the theoretical advantage of the current wave of occupations, which takes its starting point as not the looted future, but rather the broken present. From here, we no longer needs to 'convince' others what 'might' happen; rather, the present itself is cracking underneath everyone's feet. And only those living in skyscrapers can avoid the initial fractures.

Occupy Wall Street and its subsequent multiplications followed the trajectory of American social struggle which began in the labour riots after the Civil War and continued with punctuated equilibrium up unto the most recent flare-ups in the anti-globalization protests of the early second millennium. What is this trajectory? Simply put, at the beginning of the refounded republic of the United States, the working population demanded shorter hours and better pay, with independent representation and collective bargaining rights. These specific demands, which sometimes merged and sometimes conflicted with demands for women's suffrage and civil rights, were backed up with massive waves of violence: strikes, sit-downs, street battles, riots, looting, arson. While demanding specific guarantees for life by words, people demanded nothing from the destroyed factories and trains by deeds. The normal American citizen, the 99 per cent, from Reconstruction to the Second World War, was baptized in blood and blessed with material gains. Citizen engagement in politics receded to the background of enjoying fresh commodities. With a relative peace gained for white working men, the sphere of political engagement opened to the other 99 per cent, the black population. The slowly building postwar struggle for civil rights exploded in the 1960s, with not only demands for equal treatment and respect, but also demands for inclusion in the material gains that the white working population had temporarily secured. These political and social demands voiced in Washington and Selma were only the small foreground to the colossal mute rage in the background which, when heard, shattered the merchandise-filled windows of Newark, Detroit, Los Angeles, Oakland, Chicago, and almost every other inner-city neighbourhood in the United States. The self-destruction of their own neighbourhoods was the sign of people having 'nothing left to lose,' a political position which cannot but win.

As the movement for equality and civil rights crested, the youth and anti-war movements of the mid-1960s and early 1970s gained in strength. Taking the physical message of the race riots to heart – that there is no victory without struggle – the young radicals mixed early labour tactics with civil rights strategies, which blended into an ideology that asserted their *right* to own the fruits of American society. Everything was up for grabs, and everything shall be ours. The specificity of political movements in this period was in the nature of its general demands: freedom, equality, peace, everything.

But the struggle for a total demand broke in the mid-1970s, when the crisis of the US economy led to a renewed class assault on those who make the country run. This assault is ongoing. No longer could anything be *given* to those who demanded, no longer must business and government be beholden to its employees and citizens. This new relation between governing and governed, between owners and labourers, was called *austerity*. From this point on, the gains of the last century slowly receded. Real wages stagnating while prices increased, income inequality exploding while unemployment rose, unimaginable wealth produced while unbelievably few own it – the American dream bought on bad credit, paid with a high interest rate, only softened by a coupon to the movie theatre. What can we demand when there is nothing left to give?

'Not' having a demand is not a lack of anything, but a contradictory assertion of our power and our weakness. We are too weak to even try to get something from those who dominate working life, and simultaneously strong enough to try to accomplish the direct appropriation of our soul, time, and activity apart from representation. A demandless struggle reveals the totality of the enemy we fight and the unity of those who fight it. Such a struggle 'lays claim to no particular right because the wrong it suffers is not a particular wrong but wrong in general' (Marx, 1975, p. 256). This 'general wrong' is the impersonal structure of exploitation at the heart of our economic system – the forced selling of our time and life activity to someone else in return for a wage – which can never be overcome by any particular change, only by a total one.

Yet the demandless struggle is not 'radical' because it has no demands, just as the struggle for better wages is not 'reformist' because it does. More important than the demands waged against power are the demanding responsibilities that the situation itself calls forth. What is specific about the current moment is the explicit recognition by people themselves in public, together, out loud, indefinitely, of their own condition in the conditions of others. In other words, people are materially recognizing themselves while mutually recognizing each other. The forms of these encounters, while spectacular, are nothing compared with their contents. The questions of work, money, community, family, sex, colour, time, class, education, health, media, representation, punishment and faith are no longer individual questions. To think through any is to think through all, and to really think through all requires an occupation without end. Occupations without end are infinite and free, not because they are everywhere and last forever, but because there is nothing outside determining them but themselves. The overcoming of the occupations is the practical realization of such freedom, a task that can only be accomplished historically.

Take heed: there is a rationality at work here, a reason of social inferences which is made even more clear by the current lack of adequate concepts to understand it. The major premise of the 99 per cent perfectly synthesizes the universal emptiness of the modern American, expressing fully their entire being without reference to one determinate quality. The truth of the occupations is not only in their substance, but in the subjects as well. The minor premise of occupation locates the subjects of the syllogism in a particular place and a particular time. Tied together through material relations of interdependency, we are compelled by logic to conclude that not even revolution is impossible.

The new era is profoundly revolutionary, and knows it. On every level of modern society, nobody can and nobody wants to continue as before. Nobody can peacefully manage the course of things from the top any longer, because it has been discovered that the first fruits of the crisis of the economy are not only ripe, but they have, in fact, begun to rot. At base, nobody wants to submit to what is going on, and the demand for life has now become a revolutionary programme. The secret of all the 'wild' and 'incomprehensible' negations that are mocking the old order is the determination to make our own history.

Occupy Wall Street is the first major American response to the economic crisis of 2008. But the economic crisis of 2008 is the first major result to the failed response to the crisis of the 1970s. In effect, the delayed class war of the last three decades, in which Americans with good faith gave businesses and government a generation to fix the problem, has emerged with a vengeance. The time for waiting is over. The age of austerity has hit its limit. Occupying everything without demands is only the first baby step in the gigantic shoes of the new American proletariat.

II

In May 2011, arguing for an 'anarchist turn' in the United States was something of a scandal. A year later, it is already banal. This radical shift can be explained with reference to one verb: Occupy.

Inspired by the massive democratic protests in North Africa as well as the anti-austerity movements in Greece and Spain, the Occupy movement unleashed the floodgates of rage, discontent and imagination that had been building in the United States since the economic crisis began in 2008. During the autumn of 2011, hundreds of Occupy camps across the United States and the world brought individuals together to practise forms of direct democracy through general assemblies, consensus and direct action.

Erupting faster than academics, the media or political parties could understand it, Occupy Wall Street proved once again that substantive social change only occurs when people take it upon themselves to act collectively without the sanction of official political channels. From the beginning, the movement was anarchist-inspired, not only explicitly by those particular anarchists who started to organize Occupy Wall Street in New York, but implicitly through the ethical relations and tactical choices that defined the movement overall. The emphasis on horizontal decision making, matched with the rejection of demands and the widespread occupation of public spaces, produced a powerful antidote to the feeling of political helplessness engendered by the two-party system. Powerless to counter the effects of an economic crisis that levelled the so-called 'middle' class, both parties were finally revealed for what they are: managers of an economic system that cannot be allowed to fail, no matter how devastating the social consequences. The Occupy movement materially announced the rejection of such politics, and it was the theory and practice of anarchism that filled the epistemic vacuum.

Finally, it seemed as though something had broken the spell of apathy and denial that dominated the US left since 9/11. Almost exactly a decade after the attacks on the World Trade Center, the mole of the alter-globalization movement reared its head again, but this time not as a movement of anarchists and leftists organizing on behalf of others at large summits once or twice a year. Rather, the injunction to occupy everything, everywhere, without demands was made by people on behalf of themselves and their own miserable conditions. Recognizing each other's situation and articulating that in public through general assemblies without demanding anything was the most shocking aspect of it all. Every pundit on the left and right showered ridicule on this movement at one point, hoping to shame the occupiers into formulating just one demand they could understand. Only the fake newspaper, *The Onion*, seems to have understood the hesitation to make any demands, when its headline from October 12, 2011 stated: 'Nation waiting for protesters to clearly articulate demands before ignoring them.'

The anarchist turn in political life is clear, but its meaning is still far from certain. Has there been a corresponding shift in political thinking? While there has been an overflow of sympathetic academics theorizing about the movement, the theory produced by the struggle itself has been disappointing. This is not because there are no good ideas being expressed, but because the ideas themselves remain abstract in the Hegelian sense: that is, separate from a dynamic view of the their own conditions of emergence. Hence, it still remains a political task to synthesize and render explicit the coherence of self-activity that emerged throughout the camps, squares, occupations and revolts of the period from 2008 onwards. We should refrain from offering only cheerleading narratives or participatory sociologies, but instead attempt a synoptic grasp of the whole. The plurality of the movements can at first seem to reject such big thoughts, but it is the very universality of the crisis that unifies the various occupations across all their local particularities, giving the struggle itself its global resonance.

Every struggle produces not only its own subjects, but also the theory in which those subjects articulate themselves to each other and the world. This theory is first of all material, expressing itself through the forms of action that occur at certain places and certain times. Every strike is a syllogism, and every occupation is also an argument. In 2011, more was done to rethink revolutionary politics than for a decade. But understanding the theory that was produced through the struggle does not occur immediately. The temporal lag between action and its understanding cannot be overcome through social media, academic surveys or more action. Such a gap is necessary in order to give time to let the limits and restraints of the movement come into view. It is such limits that I want to describe now, limits that are not based on bad strategy or tactics, but limits that come from the era in which we live and the kinds of movement that emerge within it.

Although new social conditions have produced new social struggles, the revolutionary horizons that people aspire towards in such struggles have stayed frozen. The general, unarticulated vision of revolution that remains in the background is usually some mix of postmodern liberalism and antiquated socialism. Revolution, on this account, happens through forming a positive unity out of all the classes of society – the oppressed and the exploited, the precarious and stable, the employed and the unemployed. Together, affirming their social identity in the face of political neglect, the hidden power of the people emerges through collectively taking over and self-managing their work, schools and cities in a strategy that is called 'dual power'. The people will gradually grow big enough to delegitimize political authority, eventually being able to wrest power away from those managing and controlling their lives, so as to redistribute wealth and form a new society of self-managed, self-organized democracy.

What separates this account from the classic narrative of the working class uniting and affirming its revolutionary role in society by expropriating the expropriators? Nothing really, except that now instead of the working class, it is the 'people' or the 99 per cent, and instead of the bourgeoisie, it is a mix of greedy corporations and rich politicians, the 1 per cent. The ahistorical, revolutionary essence of the 'people' will grow through great acts of unity, and all that is left to discuss is how to best develop processes for collective decision making. What this account leaves out of the picture is the very core of why people are struggling today at all: it is not simply the forms of decision making that are wrong, it is the very content of their lives that is being destroyed.

None of the massive struggles of 2011 seemed at all close to gaining some power for a unified people; rather they were all unities of fragmented individuals who had nothing in common with each other except their objective submission to the force of the market and their subjective experience in the struggle itself. The participants of the struggles of the squares in Spain, Greece and the United States sought to maintain the experience of squares above any one demand, for it was only in the squares that some temporary common humanity was forged. This unity, however, was not enough to overthrow any of the logics of austerity being imposed everywhere. Even in Egypt, where the cross-class unity of the people overthrew the regime, they have not been able to change the economic conditions. Now that was not their main goal, but it was expressed by numerous segments of the movement, and it still resonates.

Such phenomena are the limits of this cycle of struggles, a limit which forces itself upon people in struggle, and demands either a revolutionary way forward, or not. The problem is that this revolutionary response is itself unknown in its particulars until it is accomplished. Every cycle of struggles is also part of the history of political economy, and from this history, revolutionary dreams are born and killed. The theorist's task is to write the history of these dreams, mapping them onto the shifting grounds of capitalism. This also means pointing out what the current historical conjuncture makes possible. The current production of revolution as seen under the conditions in which we live is determined by a moment in the development of capitalism where the very success of accumulation is based on the complete evacuation of the power of any working class. This dynamic is completely different from the period preceding it, in which the growth of capital was tied to the strengthening cohesion and incorporation of the working class into both consumer society and the state.

There have been different horizons, ones in which offensive struggles of the working class predominated. From 1890s to 1970s, victory for these struggles meant strengthening the power of the proletariat, building unions, increasing wages and bettering working conditions. All these factors helped to build what is called a 'workers' identity,' an empty signifier that effectively bound together competing sections of the working class and their various ideologies. The goals of this era of struggles were expressed in reformist and revolutionary ways; both of these ways, however, were united in thinking of victory as the domination of proletariat over bourgeoisie, through force, dictatorship, voting, self-organized councils or unions; all thought a non-communist transition was necessary, no matter whether it was organized or spontaneous. Losses and retreats did not deflect from this general aim.

We can say with certainty that the shape of class struggles today, at least since the 1970s, has a different horizon, one in which defensive struggles predominate. Victory today means softening the loss of a job, getting better layoff packages, improving working conditions so that you don't die from overexhaustion. No victory strengthens the class of labour against capital, it merely fractures it individually. Individual victories, in other words, weaken general conditions. Today, the struggle to defend your condition tends to be identical to the struggle against your condition. For instance, in India, Algeria, Bangladesh, wage demands transform into the destructions of means of production; in the United States, anti-union struggles arise with no alternative to put in their place; in France, struggles emerge not for employment but for layoff payments; in the riots of Greece, the United Kingdom, France and Italy, struggles without any demands at all proliferate, at least without any demands that would have been recognizable to militants of another era; in California, England and Quebec, students struggle not for better education but against their role as students in a world which has no future for them.

Little by little, what emerges in these struggles is a calling into question, through the struggle, of the role assigned to subjects by capital. All the unified identities of struggle (the unemployed, the worker, the community, the militant, the student) hinder the development of the struggle itself; in other words, for the struggle to continue even in the most modest way, it must overcome the identities which are its very basis. Today's struggles have different contents from previous ones: from 1968, 1977 or the anti-globalization movement. Social struggles today go face to face with global capital, and the demands do not even begin to challenge people's situation. Rather, struggles themselves point to the limit of demanding anything at all, even while people cannot help but go on making demands. At this point, when the content of struggles exceeds and overflows its form of demands, ruptures inside of struggles themselves emerge. These internal tensions and conflicts over violence, police, democracy, assemblies, property, gender relations and nationality are the struggles within the struggles that should not be ignored, swept under the rug of some false 'unity of the movement' or class. These breaking points are the key to understanding what can develop from within an impossible situation.

For instance, there is a whole set of practices that previously emerged at the limits of struggle which we could call 'direct action'. These were both the most radical and reformist expression of social struggle in the 1990s and early 2000s. They directly challenged the basis of some supposedly revolutionary proletarian identity outside of capital, by calling for and acting as the immediate negation of capitalism in the streets, anywhere and everywhere. This abstract call emerged from the abstract identity of militants, who could not identify with any of the previous mediations of workers' identity, because that identity was emptied of all content except of capital. This militant role had a definite place and function within the anti-globalization movement, which paradoxically provided a home for this homeless figure, an identity for this identity-less actor. Acting individualistically based on moral conviction alone, the militant was a symptom of the overabundance of useless and precarious proletarians in the West, a phenomenon which created scores of revolutionaries without a revolution.

Yet today, when the crisis has generalized impoverishment and made explicit the fact that no proletarian identity can provide sanctuary from the blind domination of capital, all the direct action practices of the militant have been put to use. Pensioners blocking the economy in France, Greek families stealing electricity and refusing to pay taxes en masse, apathetic Americans occupying public spaces and fighting cops across the country – the only property of the militant, direct action, has been expropriated by the rest of the class, and hence, the militant role itself is called into question as a separate sphere of activity. What this shows is that no unified identity – whether worker, anarchist, immigrant or democrat – needs to be forged for a proliferation of such practices to weave themselves throughout struggles. These struggles are generalizing not ideologies, but practices. Class struggle has not disappeared at all; on the contrary, it takes place more and more, yet under different conditions from before. Class unity is not what binds these people or struggles together; 'being part of the working class' is the negative basis which all these struggles seek to get rid of.

What brought people together to occupy the squares in 2011 was the destruction of their lives by austerity and other attacks on their material well-being, but it has been expressed in a political language of 'democracy' which was able to unify fragmented individuals across classes. The democracy called for, however, has little to do with the democratic calls of the anti-globalization era, where 'another world is possible' was heard side by side with 'democracy now'. Today, there is no alternative world possible within this one, and the word 'democracy' is simply the empty placeholder for the shared experience of powerlessness to determine one's life. This shared feeling, also felt all across the Occupy camps in the United States, speaks to a real shift in what brings people together in struggles today. Brought together by the material content of their lives, people instead fight over the forms in which their lives are managed. This limit is pushed against when confrontations heat up within the squares themselves over how the struggle should proceed. At these limits, when democracy is critiqued democratically, when the 99 per cent do not include the homeless but do include the police, when vague ideas of citizenship and nonviolence are seen to be the values of groups of people who are brought together by neither, at these limits, the struggle within the struggle occurs, and the horizon against which these limits are pushed is brought into the foreground.

Occupations today are the first act of revolution, for they shatter the separation which capitalism enforces between individual lives and social conditions. But occupations themselves become the obstacle to overcome when they are taken as the one prefigurative form of the future society within the shell of the old. On the contrary, no one form is revolutionary outside of its context; not until is has proved itself capable of confronting the sources which have thrown people together in struggle will any tactic be deemed in hindsight to have been the 'correct' one. Revolution is not simply people coming together to self-manage their own exploitation, but people coming together to abolish their own conditions of exploitation. Occupations are the material announcement of this revolutionary horizon, but not yet its accomplishment.

May 2012

REFERENCE

Marx, Karl (1975) 'A contribution to the critique of Hegel's *Philosophy of Right: Introduction*', in *Early Writings,* trans. R. Livingstone and G. Benton, London: Penguin/New Left Review.

INDEX

1 per cent, 241
9/11, 28, 237
99 per cent, 236, 238, 241, 244

A
Abensour, 3
abstract/concrete, 164
abundance, 39, 40
Abunimah, A., 220
action, 29, 35, 38, 39, 43, 85, 93, 94,
    128, 133, 138, 159, 165, 168–9,
    175, 179, 192, 219, 238, 241–2
    collective, 125, 167
    in concert, 35, 39
    direct, 219, 241
    emancipatory, 159
    nonviolent, 76
    political, 204, 210
    radical, 220
activist trinity, 228
Actually Existing Socialism, 149
Adorno, T., 95
Aeschylus, 101
affection, 51, 59, 65–6, 71, 89,
affiliation, 109
agonism, 35
Al Jazeera, 205
alcoholic, 130
Alexandria, 45, 192, 195
Algiers, 154, 192
alienation, 92, 135, 226
alterity, 75, 149
amity, 42
anarchism, 2, 4, 11–13, 20–1,
    23–6, 28, 60, 80, 86–7, 101,
    106–9, 112–13, 117–21, 126,
    129–31, 132–41, 158, 161, 168,
    172–3, 177–8, 187–9, 191–2,
    194, 196–9, 204–6, 209–10,
    213–14, 224–5, 237

classical, 25
concept of, 1
ethos of, 1
as ethos of sociability, 208
meaning of, 1
anarchist, 122
anarchist turn, 2, 25–6, 29, 40,
    236, 238
Anarchists Against the Wall, 206,
    215, 221
    Queer..., 221
anarcho-capitalism, 20
anarcho-communism, 121
anarcho-feminism, 111–22
anarcho-syndicalism, 121
Andalus, 213
Anderson, Benedict, 191
anecdote, 189
animality, 38–9
anomie, 84
anthropocene, 180–2
anthropology, 2, 44, 122, 228
anti-authoritarian kindergartens, 127
anti-fascism, 11, 127
anti-racism, 127
anti-statism, 215
Antigone, 101
antiquity, 44, 47
anxiety, 89
apartheid, 217, 220
apathy, 75, 237
apocalypse, 165, 167
aporia, 94
apparatus, 224, 226, 232, 233
    metaphysical, 85
Arab Spring, 28
Arafat, Y., 217
arche, 3, 81, 84–6, 90–6
Arendt, H., 2–3, 35–1, 43, 50, 52,
    103, 207

aristocracy, 44
Aristotle, 45, 59, 61, 65, 66, 69, 103
Armenia, 197
as if, 226
Ashwari, H., 217
attachment, 42, 175, 231
austerity, 237, 238, 239, 241, 244
authoritarianism, 23, 29
    anti-authoritarianism, 134, 207
authority, 1, 17, 24, 28, 86, 94, 152, 158, 169, 170, 172, 173, 192, 196, 203, 208, 215
    political, 239
autonomy, 12, 16, 18–20, 35, 37, 132, 136, 139, 197, 198
Awaye, A., 108

B
Badiou, A., 102
Bakunin, M., 2, 13–18, 20–3, 168, 187, 188, 195, 197, 210
Balkanization of politics, 190
Balkans, 189-193
Ball, J., 4
Bamyeah, M., 108
Barber, B., 62
Barghouti, O., 217, 218
barracks community, 102
barracks regime, 102, 196
Bartal, Y., 216
Bataille, 41, 66
Baudrillard, J., 62
Bauman, Z., 62, 68
beauty, 138, 139
Beck, G., 164
Becker, G., 63
becoming, 109, 159, 162
Beer, S., 179
Being, 92, 93, 94, 96, 176
Beirut, 192, 194, 195
Belgrade, 187, 192, 193
Belgrade Libertarian Group, 187
Bergson, H., 93
Beshera, A., 217
Betaville, 152-5

Bey, H., 150
beyond, the, 86, 93
Bi'lin, 206, 212, 215
binding/unbinding, 179
biography, 127
biopolitics, 26, 37, 39, 41
bios, 38
Black Laundry, 221
Bloch, E., 96
Bloch, M., 43
blockade, 230, 232
Bloom, 226
Blumenfeld, J., 1, 53
bodies, 16, 22, 23, 26, 35, 49, 166, 223
Boltanski, L., 177
Bookchin, M., 195
borders, 76, 208–9, 214, 221-2
Bosnia, 192
Bottici, C., 1, 53
Bourdieu, 127
bourgeoisie, 13, 21, 239, 240
    petit-organic-hipster-
      bourgeoisie, 222
Boyle, F., 217
Bray, T., 44
Brazil, 192
bricolage, 192
Buber, M., 84, 188, 207, 209
Budrus, 206, 212
Buenos Aires, 191, 192, 194
bureaucracy, 128, 133

C
caesura, 178
Cairo, 192
camaraderie, 59
capitalism, 20–2, 29, 36, 41, 47, 51, 61, 107, 130, 133, 135, 145, 159–60, 163–5, 169–70, 195, 198, 201, 210, 222, 226, 240-2
    birth of, 47
    centralized state-capitalism, 195
    critique of, 107, 120, 188
    early development of, 48,

Fordist, 29
post-Fordist, 26
care, 43, 51, 107, 138
maternal, 105
Castoriadis, 15
centripetal logic, 95
Chakrabarty, D., 180
chance, 169
charity, 36, 107
Charter of the Forest, 48–50
Charter of Liberties, 48–9
Chernyshevsky, 190
christening, 180
Christianity, 36, 76, 126
Cicero, 66
circulation, 165, 168, 229, 231
of affects, 223
citizenship, 104, 201–7, 210–12,
216–17, 242
institution of, 209
civil disobedience, 206, 208, 209,
212
class conflict, 39
coexistence, 38, 210, 211, 213
cogito, 177
cohabitation, 212
cohesion, 41, 44, 76–7, 179, 240
collaboration, 1, 5, 88
collective identification, 140
Colombia, 164
Comfort, A., 195
commensality, 36–7, 40–8, 50–3
commitment, 65, 72, 82, 91, 137
commodification, 22, 133
commodity fetishism, 22, 23
common good, 45, 106
common sense, 14, 197, 198
commons, 36, 47–52
commonality, 40, 42, 48
commonwealth, 50
commune, 109, 164–8, 225
versus the city, 165
communing, 36, 46–51, 52
communism, 24, 50, 51, 126, 129,
130, 131-141, 145, 187, 191,
213, 225–6

anti-communism, 130
platonic, 47
communitarian, 160, 212, 215
community, 36, 40, 42–5, 48, 50,
72, 75, 83–4, 102, 105, 108,
130, 160, 206, 209, 210, 217,
235, 241
companionship, 42, 59, 83
company, 42, 43, 181
competition, 39, 43, 50, 63, 72
conatus, 92
concealing/unconcealing, 175
confusion, 155, 225
consciousness, 13, 14, 40, 51, 82,
88–92, 95, 115, 128, 131, 132,
133, 134, 162, 218
class, 130
gender-, 138
intentional, 88
political, 224
self-, 132
consensus, 28, 72, 198, 237
consent, 90, 91
consumer, the, 62–4, 68, 70
consumer culture, 102
consumption, 21, 22, 41, 42, 48,
64, 68–9, 73, 77, 165
of meat, 42
contact zone, 199
contestation, 198
contract, 90
control society, 179
convivium, 42
cooperation, 5, 39, 41, 43, 47, 127,
133, 138, 164, 196
cosmopolitan, 21
cosmopolitanism, 22
counter-insurgency, 178
counterpoint, 213
creative chaos, 139
creativity, 132, 133, 136, 137, 154
crisis
ecological, 125
economic of 2008, 233–8
of Man, 179
management, 165

of modernity, 37
of nation states, 21
and natural world, 181
of the present, 166
Critical Theory, 2
cross-contamination of identities,
138–9
curandera, 127
cybernetics, 177, 179

D
Daiichi, F., 180
de Cleyne, V., 111–16
Debord, G., 22
debt, economy of, 67, 69
declassification, 70
deconstruction, 74-77, 86, 121–2,
138, 210, 213
deflection, 213
deforestation, 131
Della Porta, 140
democracy, 3, 60, 75, 187, 189,
216, 239, 241, 242
deliberative, 219
direct, 28, 197, 237
insurgent, 3
Israeli, 215
mass, 38
demographics, 203, 209
deregulation, 62
Derrida, J., 59, 67–78
desire, 135, 139
of majority, 214
sexual, 114
social, 120–1
destabilization, 149
determinism, 47, 190, 196
scientific, 195
deterritorialization, 163
deviant, 71
dialogue, 189, 199, 213, 214
Diamenti, I., 126
Diani, 140
Diodorus, 45
direct democracy, 29, 189, 197,
237

disavowal, 47, 204, 214
discipline, 18, 26, 45, 49, 103,
136–7
disenfranchisement, 208
disorder, 81, 86, 90, 92–3, 96
dispossession, 39, 50, 71, 208, 219
disturbance, 82, 89–90, 92–6
division, 70, 141
DJ Spooky, 152
dollar, the, 163
domination, 19, 35, 72, 87, 94,
102–7, 112, 115–16, 118–19,
121–2, 172, 212, 230, 240, 241
Dorlin, E., 122
dual power, 241
Dunbar, R., 105, 129
Dupuy, 179
Durkheim, E., 83

E
ecology, 132–8
economics, 2
education, 17, 18, 45, 136, 138,
145, 193–4, 235, 240
Marxist, 188
egalitarian, 40, 43, 46, 51, 70, 73,
111, 136, 137, 215
politics, 69
egalitarianism, 75, 165
ego, 13, 88, 91, 92, 132
egoism, 13, 20
Ehrlich, C., 117
emancipation, 12, 16, 36, 49, 71,
112, 115, 121, 135, 136, 138,
165, 198
emancipationism, 115–16
Emerson, R. W., 59
empire, 25–6, 109, 223–5, 227
empiricism, 161
encounter, sites of, 191
Encuentros, 128
Engels, 114, 162
enjoyment, 66, 68
enmity, 43, 51, 74–5, 223
enterprise, 63
entrepreneurship, 62–4, 74

epochal stamps, 176
Epstein, B., 198
equality, 16, 35, 41, 46, 60, 69, 70-74, 94, 132, 134, 135–9, 211, 212, 218, 234, 235
equilibrium, 164, 234
Escobar, A., 190
Esmeir, S., 218
essence
    of anarchism, 130
    of the feminine, 104
    of friendship, 60, 70
    of man, 12
    of the people, 239
essentialism, 105
ethics, 81, 93
    feminist, 104
    of practice, 187
    of sabotage, 168
ethnicity, 44
ethnocentrism, 162
etymology, 18, 42
evolution, 169
    of geography, 162
exclusion, 39, 44, 46, 76, 126
    of homosexuals, 75
existence, 16, 25, 35, 44–5, 63, 67, 75, 95, 103, 107, 117, 128, 223, 224, 227
    revolutionary, 231
experience, 42, 43–5, 242
    of time, 167
    social, 40, 48, 50, 87, 88, 127
exploitation, 12, 21, 116, 121, 126, 163, 166, 177, 205, 226, 235, 243
    of class, 113, 115, 119
expropriation
    authoritarian, 163
    of forests, 49
exteriority, Being as, 84
extravagant hypothesis, 94

F
face, 90–1
faith, 87

false oppositions, 227
Farrow, L., 101, 117–18
fascism, 11, 127, 145
Fatah, 218
fault, 174
faultline topology, 173–8
Federal Bureau of Investigations, 224
federalism, 17–18, 25, 28, 190, 195, 196
federation, 17, 28, 161, 189, 196
    anarchist, 134
fellowship, 41, 48, 50
feminism, 71, 101–2, 104–5, 108, 111–12, 115–22, 126–7, 129, 132–8, 139
    divide between cultural/ political, 131
    emancipationist, 113
    poststructuralist, 113
    radical, 117–20, 122
    second wave, 111–16
Ferrer Affair, 194
Ferrer, F., 192, 194–5
feudalism, 145
Feuerbach, 187
fidelity, 59, 207
field of tactics, 230
filiation 42, 176
finance, 63, 163
Finland, 197
Foucault, M., 14, 18, 26, 59, 60, 61, 62–4, 69–71, 77–8, 103
fourfold, 175
Fourier, 188
Frankfurt School, 2
Fraser, N., 177
fraternity, 36, 89–90, 101
fratricide, 101
free association, 17, 150, 154
freedom, 11–25, 27–9, 35–41, 49, 52, 76, 82, 92, 93, 128, 130, 132, 133, 134–8, 141, 145, 150, 161, 169, 180, 188, 199, 205, 211, 220, 223, 235, 236
    of equals, 11, 12–16, 18, 20–4, 27–9

of the individual, 20
limitative view of, 18–19
Marx's positive conception, 17
free market, 61
free trade, 61
free will, 84, 223
Food Not Bombs, 107
Forza Italia, 126
Friedman, M., 70–1
friend/enemy distinction, 74–5
political enemy, 223, 226
external/internal enemy, 1
friendship, 36, 40, 43, 45, 51,
59–61, 64–77, 199, 223
fusion, 83

G
G8 Summit, 28
galleon, 9–11
Gaza, 205, 207, 209
gender roles, 71, 114
general theory, 199
general wrong, 237
genetically modified organisms, 127
Geneva, 106, 195
Genoa, 29, 227
Gentlemanly Terrorists, 195
geography, 2, 159, 197
anarchist, 145–55, 158–64,
168–70
definition of, 158–9
radical, 159
social, 150, 160, 161, 164
Georgia, 197
German Autonoman Movement, 188
Gestell, 176–9
gift, 41, 67–9, 138
Giles, P., 147–8
give me five, 131
Global South, 196, 198, 199
global warming, 25
globalization, 1, 21, 22, 24–9, 127,
162, 164, 172, 190–1, 197, 234,
237, 241–2
Godwin, 197
Goldman, E., 111–16, 208

good will, 42
Goodman, P., 20, 194, 195
Google sketchup, 152
Gordon, U., 208–10, 212, 215–17
governance, 26
modes of, 26, 214, 217
systems of, 170
governmentality, 26
Graeber, 28, 172
Graham, G., 190
gratitude, 66, 67
Grave, J., 192
Grignon, 44
Gospels, The, 45

H
Habermas, J., 188
habeus corpus, 48
Hague, The, 2, 151
Hammami, R., 220
Hanton, W., 131
Hart & Negri, 25–6
Hartsock, N., 102, 104
Hegel, 14, 17, 96, 103, 162, 238
Heller, 111, 120–1
heroism, 39, 102
Herzen, A., 187, 197
heteronomy and autonomy, 19
historical materialism, 196-197
history, 2, 30, 44, 48, 60, 74, 162,
174
and anarchy, 178–9, 196
of the left, 188
of nonviolent struggle, 76
philosophy of, 4
of political economy, 239
time of, 91
Hobbes, T., 1, 25, 84, 104
Hobsbawm, E., 195–6
Holderlin, 176
holding, 105
homo oeconomicus, 63
Hodkinson, 44
homosexual, 59–60, 75, 77
hooks, b., 105
hope, 96, 132, 160

horizontality, 165, 173, 177–8
horizontal spatial imaginary, 172
hospitality, 75, 104
hostility, 102, 109, 225
human dependency, 106
human nature, 12, 116, 119, 120, 121, 228
human needs, analysis of, 106
human resources, 159, 167
humanism, 96
humanity, 13, 14, 25, 38, 39, 88, 90, 96, 101–2, 106, 107, 116, 162, 197, 199, 213, 239
Hythloday, 147

I
Icarus Project, 107
identity, 42, 52, 62, 87–8, 119, 129, 137, 165, 198
    anarchist, 227
    group, 44
    political, 139, 140, 225
    national, 216
    native, 131
    proletarian, 241
ideological miscellaneous, 138
ideology
    capitalist, 130
    national, 197
imaginal machine, 150
imaginary, 15, 18, 23, 26–7, 149, 172, 177, 181
    revolutionary, 50
    political, 52
    social, 23, 27, 149
imitation, 83
impossibility, 148, 149, 198
impotence, 226, 228, 233
inclusion, 39, 234
indigenous rights organization, 127
individualism, 13, 20, 72, 130, 139, 210
individualist, 20, 37, 120, 121, 228
Industrial Revolution, 188
inequality, 37, 46, 76, 92, 125, 219, 235

infinity, 93–4
infrastructure, 165, 166, 229
Institute for Critical Research, 188
insurrection, 230–1
interdependence, 14, 22, 26, 106, 114
International Federation of Anarchists (IFA), 111
International Monetary Forum, 61
International Workingmen's Association, 23
interruption, 166
investor, the, 63, 68
Invisible Committee, 109, 164, 166, 168, 228
irenism, 84
irony, 132, 148
irrationality, 65, 130
isolation, 14, 59, 224
Israel/Palestine, 203–22
    one-state solution, 217
Istanbul, 195

J
Jameson, F., 159
Janicaud, 3
Jarrah, S., 206
Jesi, F., 167–8
Jonas, H., 96
Jura Federation, 168
justice, 11, 16, 49, 50, 52, 84–5, 88, 89, 94–5, 126, 134, 140, 211, 223
    social, 134

K
Kafka, F., 154
kairos, 200
Kanafani, N., 205
Kant, I., 18, 59, 69–70, 177, 180, 181, 212
Kautsky, 46–7
Khuri-Makdis, I., 191, 192, 194
kibbutzim, 209–11
kinship, 42
knowledge, 18, 81, 85, 86–7, 88, 89, 127, 159, 189, 198

geographical, 158
scientific, 18
practical, 104
Kohr, L., 197
koinon, 103
Kornegger, P., 117–19
Kropotkin, 2, 46, 49, 106–7, 121, 158–9, 193, 195–7, 214
Kuhnian 'normal science', 125

L
labour, 38, 40–1, 43, 47, 50, 105, 145, 159, 190, 208, 209, 234
division of, 47
sexual, 115
Lance, M., 72
Landauer, G., 188
language, 13, 189, 193
of citizenship, 203
larval life, 179
Le Corbusier, 154
Le Revista Blanca, 194
Leighton, M., 117–18
Lenin, 188, 195
Leninism, 4
Levinas, I., 80–96
lexicon, 208
LGBT organizations, 127
liberal, 14, 18, 19, 30, 78, 115–16, 179, 191, 195, 213
neoliberal, 28, 62, 63, 64, 66, 69, 70, 71, 72, 74, 77, 127
liberalism, 195, 238
liberation, 18, 26, 92, 117, 130, 139, 164, 169, 170, 208
collective, 122
politics of, 121
self-liberation, 132
sexual, 113-114
women's, 71, 112–13, 116, 128, 135, 136
libertarian, 111, 117, 121, 126, 128, 158, 164, 192
liberties, 49–50
lifeworld, 50, 51
limits, 240–1

linearity, 92
Linebaugh, 48–51
literature, 9, 22, 25, 46, 126, 134, 193
anarchist, 194, 224
Arabic, 211
Greek, 101
Lithuania, 197
logos, 82, 94
London, 106, 161, 187, 192, 194, 195
love, 73, 114, 133, 136, 137, 139, 225

M
Macedonia, 194
Maghreb, 233
Magna Carta, 48–9
Malraux, 167
Mandela, N., 220
manifesto, 158
Manifesto of the Communist Party, 21
Maoism, 130
marginalization, 48, 112
Markovic, S., 189–90, 193
marriage, 113–15
Marx, K., 3, 12, 14–15, 21, 22–5, 27, 48–9, 62, 102, 131, 137, 160, 161, 164, 168–9, 188, 191–2, 194, 195, 235
and Engels, F., 13, 22, 21, 24
Marxism, 2, 11–12, 20–1, 23–4, 28, 60, 62, 128, 131, 158–61, 188–9, 195, 197
mass society, 35, 38, 39, 41, 102
Massad, J., 205
materiality, 104
maternal thinking, 105
maternity, 91
Mauss, 41
Mazen, A., 217
Mazzini, 17
means/ends, 23, 119, 173, 187
Melucci, A., 140
membership, 62

messianic, 75, 165, 225
meta, 81–2, 93
metaphysics, 4, 81, 85, 176, 228
    of freedom, 21
metapolitics, 3, 80–2, 93
metropolis, 165–6
microcosmos, 140
Middle Ages, 44
Middle East, 28, 201, 203, 209
Middle East Research and
    Information Project (MERIP),
    205
militant, 102, 163, 233, 243, 244
militarism, 102
Milton, J., 49
misrata, 224
misunderstanding, 119, 155
modernity, 21, 26, 36–9, 50, 176,
    179, 189, 197, 198
monism, 177
Montaigne, 59
mortality, 37
Muhsam, E., 188
Mujeres Libres, 116
Mukhimer, T., 217
multiculturalism, 215
Murray, 44
mutual aid, 48, 50, 106–7, 194,
    198
mutuality, 37, 51

N
narrative
    eurocentric, 188
    of modernity, 50
    synthetic, 131
nation-state, 17, 21, 24–6, 29, 165,
    196, 201, 217, 218, 220
national liberation movements,
    130, 208
nationalism, 17, 190, 191, 209,
    210–11, 217
    binationalism, 213
native cosmogonies, 128
natural communities, 212
nature/society dialectic, 164

necessity, 40, 52, 68, 73, 75,
    111–12, 225
    freedom and, 39
negative dialectics, 95
negative universalism, 199
Negri, 128
neighbourhood, 71, 229
neoliberalism, 27, 59, 61–4, 67–76,
    126, 172
networking, 28-29
New Babylon, 150–5
new global movements, 27–8
new social movements, 125–41
New Urbanism, 177
New York, 109, 150, 152, 170,
    195, 224, 226, 235, 239
New York Police Department, 224
Nieuwenhuys, C., 150–5
nihilism, 226
no nuke camp, 131
no-place, 148, 149, 155
nomadism, 156, 178
nomos, 18, 178
nonsense, 148–9
nonviolence, 244
Nord, L., 126
nothingness, 92
nourishment, 42, 48
nowhere, 40, 148, 228
nuclear energy, 127
nuclear explosion, 29
nuclear weapons, 25
null site, 89
nurturance, 102–9

O
observation, 161, 163
obsession, 81, 89–90, 92, 93
occupation, 194, 204, 206–9,
    213–22, 235, 238–40, 244–5
Occupy Wall Street, 236, 238, 239
oikonomos, 103
oikos, 103
one country, 220
ontology, 82, 86, 90, 92–6
Oppenheimer, F., 210–11

oppression, 16, 116, 172, 177, 211, 219, 226
  African American, 130
  gender, 121, 134
  Palestinian, 206
  self-oppression, 19
  women's, 112, 119, 121, 122, 137
optimism, 166
orderless, 179
ordinary, 41, 48, 52, 114, 215, 220, 229
originary double bind, 175
originary rootedness, 175
other, the, 66, 75, 76, 77, 81–91, 93–4
other-regarding, 66

P
Pahl, R., 61, 63
Palestine, 204–11, 217, 220
  bid for statehood, 204
Palestine Land Development Company, 211
Palestinian Authority, 205, 217, 220
Palestinian Liberation Organization, 204
pan-Slavic movement, 191
parallelogram of forces, 162
parenthood, 63
Paris, 111, 192, 194, 195
Paris Commune, 167
participation, 39, 40, 42, 46, 83, 133, 138
party, 233–4
  avant-garde, 23
patriarchy, 101, 118, 125, 226
Peasants Revolt of 1381, 4
Pedrini, B., 9–12, 29
Pereira, I., 122
periphery, 189, 195, 196
permanence, 40
Petraeus, General, 229–30
phantom, 148
Philo of Alexandria, 45
Picq, F., 121
pink triangle, 131

Piterberg, G., 210–11
place, 145, 147–8, 155, 173–7
Plan Obus, 154
Plato, 44–7, 83, 179
pleasure, 64, 66, 68, 70, 104, 132
polemic, 158, 166
polis, 102–3
political, the, 2, 35, 36–41, 48, 50, 81, 103, 104, 227
political philosophy, 2, 44, 48, 102, 103
political theology, 17
politics, 2–3, 27–9, 35–41, 43, 46–8, 50, 52, 59–60, 62, 69–73, 75, 80–2, 86, 93–5, 102–3
  anarchist, 164, 172
  anticolonial, 220
  classical, 227
  emancipatory, 170
  hierarchical, 28, 44, 70, 103, 104, 145, 173
  identity, 119, 227
  institutional, 125
  Israeli, 220
  of place, 190
  Queer Israeli, 222
  revolutionary, 50, 238
  self-determination, of, 203
  spectacularization of, 27
Poljana, J., 195
positivism, 162, 164
possession, 87
post-ideological representations, 139–40
post sovereignty, 25
postcolonial studies, 128
postmodern condition, 140
potentiality, 17, 37, 40, 121, 223, 225, 227
poverty, 16, 37, 107, 113, 227
power, 18, 24, 26, 94, 102, 105, 116, 119, 121, 133, 134, 170, 172, 177, 178, 179, 195, 201, 207, 211, 212, 228, 229, 235, 239–40
  critique of male power, 111, 112, 118

praxis, 2, 85, 126, 127, 129, 133, 135, 141, 158
presencing/absencing, 175
primal scene of separation, 158
principle, 81–6, 90, 93–4, 96
    anarchy, 175, 178–9, 181
private/public, 38, 43, 44, 51, 52, 59, 116
privatization, 62
process, 44, 72, 140
product placement, 164
production, 21, 25, 26, 47, 63, 68, 107, 138, 168, 169
    capitalist, 23
    economic, 47
    industrial, 47, 63, 180
    intellectual, 22
    mode of, 163, 164, 169
    political, 43
productivism, 196
progress, 164, 195, 196
proletariat, 23, 242, 236
    dictatorship of the, 23
propaganda, 168, 192–3
property, 14, 22, 44, 103, 106, 133, 140, 163, 241, 242
    common, 138
    private, 44–5, 61, 106, 135, 145, 147
prostitution, 113–14
Proudhon, P., 2, 24, 197
proximity, 80, 82–3, 85–95
psyche, 87–8
psychoanalysis, 15
public sphere, 35, 38–40, 48, 165
purple menace, 131
Putnam, R., 59, 61

Q
queer theory, 112
    and anarcho-feminism, 119–22
    as avant-gardism, 121

R
Radenik, 193
Ramnath, M., 191

Rancière, J., 60–1, 69–70, 74–6
rationality/spirituality, 120
Read, H., 195
realism, 160
Really Really Free Market, 107
Reclus, E., 158–70, 192, 194, 196
recognition, 15, 35, 44–5, 63, 67, 75, 95, 103, 107, 117, 128, 223, 224, 227, 237
regionalism, 196–7
Republic, The, 44, 83
representation, 83, 89, 90, 91, 235
respect, 51, 71, 72, 75, 108, 133, 134–6, 138, 139, 234
resistance, 51, 49–76, 88, 105, 112, 121, 137, 204, 206, 216, 218
    Palestinian, 214
reversals of history, 178
revolt, 9, 11, 17–18, 167–8
    peasant, 193
revolution, 23, 28, 38, 39, 102, 108, 117, 118, 131, 132, 135, 138, 162, 167, 168, 169, 187, 188, 194, 195, 231, 233, 236, 238–43
    counter-revolution, 228
    egalitarian, 215
revolutionary movement, 222, 225
rhetoric, 102
Rhineland, 49
rights, 16, 50–1, 207
    animal, 127, 131
    civil, 236
    of the forest, 49
    Palestinian, 218–22
Rimbaud, 167
Robinsonade, 13, 20–1
Rocker, R., 188
Rousseau, 18
Ruddick, S., 104–6
Ruppin, A., 211
Russia, 191, 192, 195, 196, 197

S
sacrifice, 42, 115
Said, E., 217

Saint-Simon, duc de, 188
San Francisco, 195
satire, 148
satisfaction, 68, 138
Schurmann, R., 2–3, 85–6, 96, 172–82, 223, 226
scientism, 196
Scott, J., 191
Seattle, 29
second class citizenship, 214
second intifada, 206
security, 3, 25, 108, 165, 203
Seeds of Peace, 213
self, the, 14, 18, 84, 87, 89, 91, 93–4, 180–1, 229
self(subject)/world, 181
    split between, 177
self-determination, 14, 18, 132, 133, 139, 202
    Palestinian, 203-222
self-organization, 136, 177, 179, 197
    autonomous, 116
    collective, 1
self-reliance, 165
self-sufficiency, 22, 134
Seneca, 45
Serbia, 189–90, 193
serious play, 148
servitude, 14, 19, 26
settler colonialism, 207, 209, 211, 213
Sex Pistols, 188
sexuality, 71, 105, 113, 115-116
Shafir, G., 211
Shelley, P. B., 4
Shizeng, Li, 195
Siberia, 187
signification, 15, 22, 89, 90
signifiers, 126
    empty, 240
signifyingness, 92
singularity, 75, 90
sisterhood, totalitarianism of, 111
Situationist International, 150
Skelton, C., 152
slavery, 15, 16, 49, 145

Sloterdijk, 176
Smith, N., 164, 169, 180
social, the, pluralist conception of, 83
social condition, 15, 37, 116, 238, 242
social darwinism, 211
social desire, 120–1
social movements, 1, 29, 125–7, 129, 140, 177, 197
social praxis, 141
social representation, 129
social reproduction, 159, 160, 167
social services, 62
socialism, 46–7, 149, 168, 189, 195, 209, 238
    antiquated, 238
    ethical, 189
    of Marx, 168
    state socialism, 195
    utopian, 21
sociality, 36, 41, 47, 87, 103, 104, 120–1
socialization, 15, 43, 47, 164
socio-erotic, 120
sociology, 2, 18, 44, 59
    aboriginal, 128
    reflexive, 127
Solanas, V., 130
solidarity, 36, 40, 43-47, 52, 71–2, 75–7, 106, 108, 109, 112, 117, 121, 132, 133–5, 139, 145, 164, 199, 210, 213, 215, 220
    political, 74
Sophocles, 101
soul, 76, 87
Soura Santos, B, 189, 198–9
source code, 149
South, the, 189
sovereignty, 3, 24, 25, 26, 49, 94, 96, 154, 168, 189, 202, 207
    Jewish, 207
Soviet Union, 23
space, 37, 42, 44, 52, 59, 75, 77, 96, 145–55, 159, 167–70, 173–4, 177–9, 199

public, 39
  and time, 65
  urban, 219
spaces of capital, 170
spatial fix, 160
spectacle, 22, 27-29
spectre, 152
speech, 13, 38, 93, 95, 96, 145, 169
Spencer, L., 61
staffeta, 127
Stalinism, 51
statehood, 204, 205-8, 216-17
statistics, 26, 35
Stepniak, S., 192
Stirner, M., 2, 12-13, 20
strife, 175, 178
struggle, 76, 88, 95, 115-19, 121-2, 127, 134, 136, 138, 164, 165, 169, 188, 192, 196
  Palestinian, 203-20, 235, 238-43
stupidity, 16
subaltern, 128, 133, 190
subject/object dyad, 181
subjective/objective, continuum of, 139
subjectivity, 36, 48, 80, 89, 90, 102, 103, 120, 135, 174
supermarket, 63
surplus value, theory of, 12
symbols, 167

T
Ta'ayush, 206
table, 36-8, 40-8, 50-3
Tahrir Square, 108
taming, 176
Tarde, 83
Tarnac, 165, 222
technicity, 174, 176
Telfer, E., 60, 65, 68-9
temporality, 90, 91
Ten Hours Act, 49
telos, 85, 95
territory, 132, 163

theology, 45, 46
  onto-theology, 90
  political theology, 17
theoretical reason, 24
thinging, 175
threshold of relation, 175
Tiqqun, 3, 102, 109, 231
Tito, Marshal J., 188
Togliatti, P., 9
Tokyo Electric Power Company, 181
Tolstoy, L., 195
topology, 174
topos, 147, 173
totalitarianism, 111
totality, 83, 84, 88, 92, 95-6, 112, 176
trace, 95-6
tradition, 145
  liberal, 179
  socialist, 187
tragic, 76
translation, 69, 190, 198, 199, 233-4
treason, 209, 220
trust, 60, 69-70, 130, 133
truth, 18, 23, 83, 176, 177, 178, 224, 230
Tunisia, 192, 230
Turkey, 203
turn, 81-2, 93
  anarchist, 2, 25, 40, 236
tyranny, 17, 93
  of society, 17-19, 22

U
Ukraine, 197
underneath, 82, 86, 93
uneven development, theory of, 164
unity, 44, 45, 175, 238, 239, 241, 242
universalism, 188, 199
unknown, 154, 225
United States, 20, 117, 187, 194, 201, 228, 233, 234, 236, 237, 239, 240, 242

University of California
at San Diego, 209
at Santa Cruz, 127
University of Nottingham, 126
UN Partition Plan of 1947, 204
urbanization, 163, 164, 180
utility, 66
utopia, 19, 21, 36, 44, 45–8, 52,
89, 132, 136, 145–50, 159, 165,
195, 199

V
Van der Walt, L., 191
Veblen, T., 62
verticality, 176–7
vertigo, 84
Via Comperina, 189
victory, 167, 236, 242
virtual, 65, 152
reality, 27
void, 231

W
Wall, the, 204, 206, 214
Wallerstein, I., 200
war, new kind of, 224–5

Ward., C. 4
Warhol, A., 131
West Bank, 204–6
Who Profits?, 221
Wigley, M., 150, 153
Wikileaks, 232
Wikipedia, 152
Winstanley, G., 49
Wobbly, 130
Woodcock, G., 4
*Women's Commission of the
Federation Anarchiste Francaise*,
111
World Bank, 61
worlding, 175–6, 182
World Social Forum, 128
World Society, 195

Y
Yugoslavia, 187, 190, 200

Z
Zapatistas, 128
Zionism, 206, 208, 209–10
zoe, 38
Zuli, 192

CONTRIBUTORS

Miguel Abensour, from the University of Paris, has been an editor of the Paris-based periodicals *Textures*, *Libre* and *Tumultes*. Since 1974 he has edited the 'Critique de la politique' series (Payot & Rivages editions) which notably introduced the Frankfurt School thinkers to France. He was for several years the director of the Collège International de Philosophie, and is professor emeritus at the University of Paris. In his books and his numerous articles, he strives to reconcile democracy, conceived as 'savage democracy' or 'insurgent democracy', with the idea of Utopia, whose history he has critically analysed in several books. He has published numerous articles on Emmanuel Levinas, Claude Lefort, Saint-Just, socialist Utopias (Pierre Leroux, William Morris), Blanqui and the various representatives of the Frankfurt School, in particular T. W. Adorno. His first book translated into English has just been released as *Democracy Against the State: Marx and the Machiavellian movement*.

The Accused of Tarnac: on November 11, 2008, French anti-terrorism police arrested around 20 people, mostly in Tarnac, a small village in the Corrèze region of central France. At first nine, and eventually ten, were accused of 'criminal association for the purposes of terrorist activity' in connection with the sabotage of train lines which had caused delays on the French railways. Very little evidence has been presented against them, but central to the prosecution was their alleged authorship of a book, *The Coming Insurrection*, and their supposed association with what the French government and media have termed an 'ultra-left' or 'anarcho-autonomous movement'.

Cinzia Arruzza is assistant professor of philosophy at the New School for Social Research, New York. She received her PhD in Rome from the University of Rome 'Tor Vergata' and subsequently studied at the universities of Freiburg (Switzerland) and Bonn (Germany). She has written on Plotinus and Plato as well as Marx and feminism. She is the author of two books, *Les Mésaventures de la théodicée: Plotin, Origène, Grégoire de Nysse* (2011) and *Le relazioni pericolose: Matrimoni e divorzi tra marxismo e femminismo* (2010).

Banu Bargu is an assistant professor of politics at the New School for Social Research, New York, where she teaches political theory. She received her PhD at Cornell University in 2008. Her main areas of interest are early modern, modern and contemporary political theory, with particular interest in theories of sovereignty and resistance, Marxist, post-Marxist and anarchist thought, and thinkers such as Machiavelli, Marx, Stirner, Schmitt and Althusser. Her articles have appeared or are scheduled to appear in journals such as *theory & event*, *Constellations* and *diacritics*, as well as various edited volumes: *Policing and Prisons in the Middle East: Formations of Coercion* (2010), *After Secular Law* (2011) and *'How Not to Be Governed': Readings and Interpretations from a Critical Anarchist Left* (2011). Her book *Biopolitics and the Death Fast* is forthcoming from Columbia University Press.

Jacob Blumenfeld is a PhD candidate in philosophy at the New School for Social Research, New York. He has taught at CUNY Staten Island, Laguardia Community College and the New School. He currently lives in Berlin, where he is writing his dissertation on the concept of property in Hegel, Stirner and Marx.

Chiara Bottici is an Italian philosopher and writer. Her grand-uncle was the anarchist poet Belgrado Pedrini. She taught at the University of Frankfurt before joining the Department of Philosophy of the New School for Social Research, New York. She is the author of *Men and States* (2004), *A Philosophy of Political Myth* (2007) and *Imaginal Politics* (forthcoming 2013). With Benoit Challand, she also authored *The Myth of the Clash of Civilizations* (Routledge, 2010) and *Imagining Europe: Myth, Memory, and Identity* (2013) and edited a collection of essays entitled *The Politics of Imagination* (Routledge, 2011).

Judith Butler is Maxine Elliot Professor in the Departments of Rhetoric and Comparative Literature, and the co-director of the Program of Critical Theory, at the University of California, Berkeley. She received her PhD in philosophy from Yale University in 1984 on the French reception of Hegel. She is the author of *Subjects of Desire: Hegelian reflections in twentiethcentury France* (1987), *Gender Trouble: Feminism and the subversion of identity* (1990), *Bodies That Matter: On the discursive limits of 'sex'* (1993), *The Psychic Life of Power: Theories of subjection* (1997), *Excitable Speech* (1997), *Antigone's Claim: Kinship between life and death* (2000), *Precarious Life: Powers of violence and mourning* (2004), *Undoing Gender*

(2004), *Who Sings the Nation-State? Language, politics, belonging* (with Gayatri Spivak, 2008), *Frames of War: When is life grievable?* (2009), and *Is Critique Secular?* (co-author, 2009). She is active in gender and sexual politics and human rights, anti-war politics, and Jewish Voice for Peace. She is also a recipient of the Andrew Mellon Award for Distinguished Academic Achievement in the Humanities.

Laura Corradi, who obtained her PhD from the University of California, Santa Cruz, is presently a researcher at the University of Calabria, Italy, and a professor in sociology of gender and sociology of health and illness for political science and social work students. She is the author of books about women working night shifts, AIDS prevention, and several articles on women's health, everyday life and activism. She is also the editor of the *Italian Country Report on Women's Health* for the European Women Health Network (2000–01) and co-author of the *Handbook for Women's Health*.

Simon Critchley teaches philosophy at the New School for Social Research, New York, at Tilburg University, and the European Graduate School. He is the author of many books including *The Faith of the Faithless* (2012), *Impossible Objects* (2011), *The Book of Dead Philosophers* (2008) and *Infinitely Demanding* (2007). A new book on *Hamlet* is forthcoming.

Stephen Duncombe is an associate professor at the Gallatin School and the Department of Media, Culture and Communication of New York University, where he teaches the history and politics of media. He is the author of *Dream: Re-imagining progressive politics in an age of fantasy* and the editor of the *Cultural Resistance Reader,* among other books, and is the creator of Open Utopia, an open-source, open-access, web-based edition of Thomas More's *Utopia*, found at http://theopenutopia.org. A life-long political activist, Duncombe is presently co-founder and co-director of the Center for Artistic Activism.

Andrej Grubačić is associate professor and department chair of the Anthropology and Social Change program at the California Institute of Integral Studies. He is an outspoken protagonist for 'new anarchism', co-author with Staughton Lynd of *Wobblies and Zapatistas* (PM Press, 2008) and author of *Don't Mourn, Balkanize!* (PM Press, 2010).

Todd May is a professor of philosophy at Clemson University, South Carolina. He teaches and writes in recent French thought, particularly poststructuralism. He is the author of *The Political Philosophy of Poststructuralist Anarchism*, and has written and spoken extensively on the relationship between poststructuralism and anarchism, as well as Foucault, Deleuze and Rancière. In addition to his academic work, he has been involved in liberation struggles from gay rights to anti-apartheid work to the Palestinian rights struggle. While living in Pittsburgh, Todd was the co-coordinator of campaigns against aid to the Contras and the anti-Gulf War (I) campaign. He also served as US national co-director of the Palestine Solidarity Committee and was a member of the Institute for Anarchist Studies board.

Alberto Toscano teaches in the Department of Sociology, Goldsmiths, University of London. He is the author of *Fanaticism: On the uses of an idea* (2010) and an editor of the journal *Historical Materialism*.

Mitchell Cowen Verter is a PhD candidate at the New School for Social Research, New York, working on a dissertation on anarchism, feminism and ecology. He is the editor of *Dreams of Freedom*, and the author of many papers on Levinas.

Stephanie Wakefield is a PhD candidate in earth and environmental science at the CUNY graduate center in New York, working on technologies of urban crisis management and green urbanism.